Ag. p. 45

RIVER NAVIGATION IN ENGLAND 1600—1750

RIVER NAVIGATION
IN ENGLAND
1600–1750

T. S. WILLAN

FRANK CASS & CO. LTD.
1964

This edition published by Frank Cass & Co. Ltd.
10 Woburn Walk, London W.C.1,
by arrangement with Oxford University Press

First published 1936
New impression 1964

Printed by Thomas Nelson (Printers) Ltd
London and Edinburgh

PREFACE

THIS book was first published in 1936. Since then some work has appeared on the navigation of individual rivers, but there has been no new study of the subject as a whole. This new work is conveniently summarised in Dr. W. H. Chaloner's Introduction to W. T. Jackman, *The Development of Transportation in Modern England* (Frank Cass, 1962). The books and articles published since 1936 have filled in the details of many of the river improvement schemes, but they have not, it seems to me, seriously altered or impaired the general picture given in this book. Indeed they have helped to confirm my view that river transport was much more important than earlier historians believed. Such transport formed an essential element in what Defoe called 'the Inland trade of England', and it is not really possible to understand the English economy of the period between 1600 and 1750 without taking account of that inland trade. Nor is it possible to understand the great changes which took place after 1750 without looking back to the earlier period in which those changes had their origin. In that sense this book may perhaps contribute to an understanding of those elusive forces which produced the Industrial Revolution.

In this reprint I have taken the opportunity to make a few minor factual corrections in the text.

T.S.W.

Manchester 1964

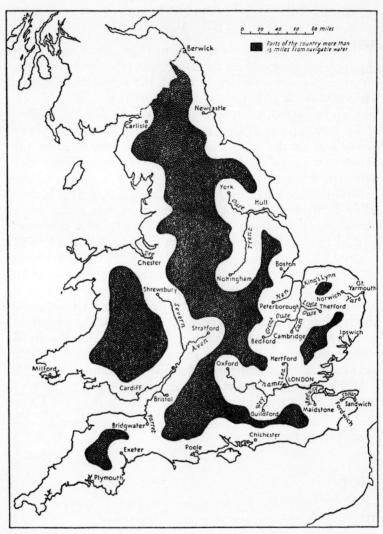

I. NAVIGABLE RIVERS, 1600–60

Only the navigable parts of rivers are shown.

CONTENTS

INTRODUCTION 1

I. THEORETICAL SCHEMES 6

II. PRACTICAL UNDERTAKINGS 16

    (i) COMMISSIONS OF SEWERS 16

    (ii) LETTERS PATENT 24

    (iii) PARLIAMENTARY ACTIVITY 28

III. THE UNDERTAKERS 52

IV. FINANCE 63

V. ENGINEERS AND ENGINEERING . . . 79

VI. THE MEANS OF CONVEYANCE . . . 96

    (i) THE BOATS 96

    (ii) THE BOATMEN 105

VII. THE COST OF CARRIAGE AND CARGOES . . 114

CONCLUSION 131

APPENDIXES 141

INDEX 157

MAPS

I. Navigable Rivers, 1600–60 vi

II. Navigable Rivers, 1660–1700 32

III. Navigable Rivers, 1724–7. (Defoe) 68

IV. River Acts, 1600–1750 90

V. Canal Schemes, 1600–1750 134

ABBREVIATIONS

The following abbreviations are used in the footnotes:

Cal. S.P.D. = *Calendar of State Papers, Domestic.*
D.N.B. = *Dictionary of National Biography.*
E.H.R. = *English Historical Review.*
Exch. K.R. = Exchequer, King's Remembrancer.
H.M.C. = *Historical Manuscripts' Commission.*
J. H. of C. = *Journals of the House of Commons.*
J. H. of L. = *Journals of the House of Lords.*
P.A. = Private Act.
V.C.H. = *Victoria County History.*

Rawlinson (Rawl.), Twyne-Langbaine and Tanner MSS., and the *Bromley Parliamentary Papers* are in the Bodleian Library, Oxford; Additional (Add.), Harleian (Harl.), Kings, Lansdowne, and Stowe MSS. are in the British Museum. The references to Pepys, *Diary*, are to the Everyman edition, and to Defoe, *Tour*, unless otherwise stated, to the reprint of the first edition edited by Mr. G. D. H. Cole (2 vols., Peter Davies, London, 1927). The titles of pamphlets are given in full in Appendix I.

INTRODUCTION

THE history of transportation in England is the history of an attempt to meet not only the increasing quantitative demands of a growing population, but also the qualitative requirements of an improving standard of life. During the period from 1600 to 1750 the population of England pursued a twofold course; it grew and it became more urban. About the death of Elizabeth it has been estimated at four millions, by the close of the century it had probably reached five and a half millions.[1] Fifty years later it stood at about six and a quarter millions.[2] With this growth went a concentration into urban areas that is not yet complete. Throughout the seventeenth century London absorbed an increasing proportion of the new population. With something less than a quarter of a million inhabitants in 1605, the city comprised 5·6 per cent. of the total population of England; ninety years later its population had more than doubled and then comprised 9·6 per cent. of the whole.[3] Such an increase was not confined to the metropolis. Provincial towns such as Birmingham[4] and Bristol[5] show a similar or greater relative increase. This concentration of population created a problem of supply that long-distance transport alone could satisfy. It would seem that the extension of the metropolitan marketing area had its counterpart in an extension of the importance of provincial towns as centres of collection and distribution. It was no mere accident that these centres, as, for example, Hull, King's Lynn, Great Yarmouth, Bristol, and Liverpool, should be river and seaports combined.

Thus transportation throughout this period had to meet the increased demands of a growing population for essential commodities like corn and wool. But it had to do more than this. It had to meet the demand for commodities the supply of which had previously been slight or non-existent. Men were requiring better, or at any rate different, things from those which had satisfied their ancestors. Almost universally

---

[1] Gras, *Corn Market*, p. 75.   [2] Clapham, *Economic History*, i. 53.
[3] Gras, *Corn Market*, p. 75.   [4] Nef, *Coal Industry*, i. 106, n. 2.
[5] Ibid., p. 107.

they were wanting coal in place of wood, and a line drawn from Bridlington to Lyme Regis cut off an eastern and a southern portion of England where the population was most dense and where no coal was mined. Glass for their windows, slates for their roofs, bricks for their walls, even clay for their pipes—for all these there was a demand which a purely local transport system could never meet. Of one aspect of that system little need be said; the stage wagons, the long trains of pack-horses, 'shuttles for ever moving across the warp and woof of English life',[1] belong to another story. It is true that transport by land and by water were interconnected. Pack-horses carried lead to Bawtry to be sent down the Idle and the Trent.[2] Pack-horses met the coal barges on the Tone and distributed their cargoes over the country-side.[3] Cheese was carried by land to Lechlade and so by water down the Thames or to the Trent and so down to Hull and by the east coast to London.[4] It is equally true that land carriage played a far greater role than that of conveying goods to, or distributing goods from, the heads of river navigations, but that role must be assumed rather than proved.

Here the subject is that other great branch of inland transport, carriage by water. For long it has been assumed that river navigation in England was something unimportant, something limited to the nebulous schemes of pamphleteers or the desultory attempts of adventurers. Macaulay set a fashion for ignoring this form of carriage which others have been quick to follow. Speaking of the state of England in 1685, he declared: 'There was very little internal communication by water. A few attempts had been made to deepen and embank the natural streams, but with slender success.'[5] More modern scholars, whose activities have lain in the field of economic rather than of political history, have been content to repeat this verdict. It has been said that, during this period, 'the attempt was barely made even to deepen a few rivers above the point at which they ceased to be navigable.'[6]

[1] Trevelyan, *History of England*, p. 280.   [2] *J. H. of C.* xii. 435.
[3] Fiennes, *Through England on a Side Saddle*, p. 205.
[4] Defoe, *Tour*, ii. 531.
[5] Macaulay, *History*, i. 325 (World's Classics edition).
[6] Renard and Weulersse, *Life and Work*, p. 66.

The late Professor Knowles, in fixing her attention upon the
Industrial Revolution and the extraordinary outburst of canal
building which marked its early course, assumed that Great
Britain had hitherto been dependent upon the turnpike
roads as her sole means of internal communication. 'It was
obvious', she wrote, 'that Great Britain with her growing
traffic and growing industry must improve her means of
transport beyond that of the turnpike roads.'[1] Even Mantoux, who recognized that there were improvements in
waterways, considered them 'in themselves of little importance'.[2] Others have done something to correct this view,[3]
but none has realized how fully the people of the seventeenth
and early eighteenth centuries felt rivers to be 'the cherish-
ing veines of the body of every Countrey, Kingdome, and
Nation'.[4]

Closely connected with river navigation was the coasting
trade. Hence in its original form this study included a
general survey of English coasting trade from 1600 to 1750,
but exigencies of space have demanded the omission of this
section. It is true that the neglect to consider river navigation as an important aspect of internal transport does not
find a full parallel in the case of the coasting trade. There,
indeed, the shipments of two staple commodities, corn[5] and
coal,[6] have received attention and acknowledgement of the
part they played in the economic life and development of
England. But these are only two species of goods out of
many, and it is still fair to say that the coasting trade, together
with the Port Books from which it can be studied, remains
largely a subject awaiting exploration. In this connexion
Dr. Clapham's words, which he applied to a later age, might
equally well refer to this period. 'The coasting trade', he
wrote, 'must not be thought of as a mean or secondary thing
because it was so little discussed at the time and has been so
very seldom described. It has always been a principal source

---

[1] Knowles, *Industrial and Commercial Revolutions*, p. 240.
[2] Mantoux, *Industrial Revolution*, p. 126.
[3] Nef, *Coal Industry*, i. 95–100, 258–9; Jackman, *Development of Transportation*,
i. 157–210; Wadsworth and Mann, *Cotton Trade*, pp. 212–13.
[4] Taylor, *Thame Isis*, p. 10.
[5] Gras, *Corn Market*, especially the Appendixes.
[6] Nef, *Coal Industry*, especially Part V and Appendixes.

of Britain's wealth, since few important places are far from tide-water.'[1] In the second sentence lies the key to this subject. England has always had more usable coast-line per square mile of territory than any other of the chief countries of Europe.[2] This was fully recognized in the seventeenth century, even if the methods by which it was proved were of doubtful accuracy. When Sir Robert Southwell gave his paper on Water Transport before the Royal Society in 1675, he suggested that by dividing the square miles of country by the length of the shore, the result would be the average distance from the shore, which in England was 24 and in France 86 miles.[3] Fifteen years later Petty propounded a similar thesis. He explained that the land and coast of Great Britain and Ireland would make a parallelogram 3,800 miles long and 24 broad, 'and consequently every part of England, Scotland, and Ireland, is one with another, but twelve miles from the Sea'.[4] Unfortunately his criterion for determining what was sea coast was rudimentary since he allowed 'for "coast" the distance at which any animall on the Shoare may bee seene to move from the Sea'.[5] But it is not the accuracy or inaccuracy of these statements that matters, it is the very fact that they were made, that men were realizing the importance of their coasting trade as a means of transport, and that they recognized the peculiar advantages they possessed from their extensive coast-line. It is clear that these advantages were utilized, when nearly forty years later Defoe could declare, 'our coasting trade is exceeding great, and employs a prodigious number of ships, as well from all the shores of England to London, as from one port to another'.[6]

Yet here it is not so much the importance of the coasting trade that must be emphasized as its connexion with river navigation. The physical connexion is indeed obvious. Coal

---

[1] Clapham, *Economic History*, ii. 528.

[2] In 1906 W. H. Wheeler, in giving evidence before the Canals and Waterways Commission, declared that England, south of the Firth of Forth, had 50 square miles of territory for every mile of coast; the figure for France was 134, Germany 384, and Belgium 263 square miles. *Canals and Waterways*, First Report, i, part ii. 187.   [3] Birch, *Royal Society*, iii. 208.

[4] Petty, *Works*, i. 293.   [5] *Petty Papers*, i. 226.

[6] Defoe, *Complete English Tradesman*, i. 259. Defoe's statement is borne out by the evidence in the Port Books.

that left the staithes at Newcastle was unloaded from barges at Cambridge or Abingdon;[1] cheese from Cheshire either passed down the Dee and the west coast, or the Trent, the Humber, and the east coast, to London;[2] butter from the Yorkshire dales reached the metropolis by the Ouse and the sea;[3] London goods for Beverley Fair went north by coasting vessel, by the Humber, the Hull, and Beverley Beck.[4] Even where this physical connexion did not exist, it must be emphasized that, paradoxical as it may sound, coasting trade and river carriage were both different aspects of the same system of inland navigation. These aspects may be separated for convenience of treatment, but basically they are indivisible. From the point of view of inland navigation the sea becomes merely a river round England, a river with peculiar dangers, peculiar conditions, and peculiar advantages. This fact, economically so obvious, geographically so absurd, has not entered into the judgements of those who dismiss so lightly the water transport of England in all but its overseas connexion. Yet any consideration of the importance of inland navigation, any attempt to show what area of the country was within a day's journey of navigable water, must take into account both the rivers and the sea. Only when this interconnexion is realized can inland navigation be placed in its correct perspective in the general development of English economic life.

[1] *J. H. of C.* xiii. 286, 313; Defoe, *Complete English Tradesman*, ii. 173.
[2] Defoe, *Tour*, ii. 531, 652.
[3] Ibid., p. 652; Maitland, *London*, p. 553.
[4] Best, *Rural Economy in Yorkshire*, p. 112.

I

THEORETICAL SCHEMES

RIVER navigation is as old as civilization itself. In England its origin is lost in the mists of the past just as its ultimate fate rests upon the forces of the future. It must not be assumed that river transport began in England in 1600 and ended in 1750. In the Middle Ages the rivers were used extensively for transport. York stood at the centre of a system of inland navigation by the Ouse, the Swale, the Ure, the Wharfe, and the Derwent, a system that has never been revived.[1] King's Lynn drew corn and other commodities from eight counties by water.[2] The Severn was then, as it remained for centuries, the waterway of the west.[3] The Thames had been used for transport 500 years before the death of Elizabeth.[4] These rivers, and many others, continued in use long after the middle of the eighteenth century, as they continue in use to-day. Yet, despite its artificial boundaries, there is a certain unity in the period from 1600 to 1750 which justifies its separate treatment. Before 1600 the attempts to improve river navigation were spasmodic and the evidence of their success or failure is largely lacking. After 1750 the history of river transport is indivisibly bound up with that of canals. But between these dates took place the greatest attempt to improve the rivers of England and to use them as means of communication that has been made in the country's history.

It is not too much to say that throughout this period river navigation was 'in the air'. Members of parliament and country gentlemen discussed in the lobby of the house or the parlour of a country inn the merits and demerits of water transport. In this atmosphere the pamphleteers were quick to show themselves, as always, the unacknowledged leader-writers of their times. Some, indeed, looked upon river

---

[1] Sellers, *York Mercers and Merchant Adventurers*, pp. i–ii; Sellers, 'York in the Sixteenth and Seventeenth Centuries', *E.H.R.* xii. 438; Drake, *Eboracum*, p. 199; *York Records*, p. 82.

[2] Gras, *Corn Market*, pp. 62–3.   [3] *Gloucester Records*, p. 52.

[4] *V. C. H. Berkshire*, i. 375; Thacker, *Thames, General History*, pp. 19–20, 27.

navigation as a mere incidental to their favourite scheme for the increase of foreign trade[1] or the general prosperity of the country,[2] others were concerned only in an individual river in which they had some interest,[3] but some went further and called for a general scheme of river improvement which alone could overcome the obstacles in the way of transport. Of these last named, one of the earliest and most interesting was John Taylor, waterman and innkeeper, poet and pamphleteer.[4] He sounded a clarion call to his countrymen to imitate the 'industrious Netherlanders' and remove the obstructions from their rivers, obstructions which he himself had seen and felt in his journeys of inspection up the Thames, the Severn, the Wye, and the Warwickshire and Wiltshire Avons.[5] He considered that 'there is not any one Town or City which hath a Navigable River at it, that is poore, nor scarce any that are rich, which want a River with the benefits of Boats'.[6] His advocacy was based on purely economic grounds:

> Thus men would be employed, and horse preserv'd
> And all the country at cheap rates be serv'd.[7]

His hatred was directed against the owners of mills and weirs, who were responsible for the 'miserable strange abuses'[8] of the rivers:

> Shall private persons for their gainfull use
> Ingrosse the water and the land abuse?[9]

Taylor's whole work can be summed up in his own words:

> I truely treate that men may note and see
> What blessings Navigable Rivers bee,
> And how that thousands are debarr'd those blessings
> By few mens avaritous hard oppressings.[10]

More than half a century after Taylor began writing, his advocacy of purely river navigation was continued by Yar-

---

[1] Roberts, *Treasure of Traffic*, pp. 44–5.
[2] Robinson, *Certain Proposals*, p. 9.
[3] Cooke, *Avona*. (Deals with the Wiltshire Avon.)
[4] b. 1580, d. 1653. See Humpherus, *Company of Watermen*, i. 263–7.
[5] Taylor, *A Discovery by Sea; Thame Isis; John Taylor's Last Voyage.*
[6] Taylor, *A Discovery by Sea*, p. 27.   [7] Taylor, *Thame Isis*, p. 27.
[8] Taylor, *Taylor's Last Voyage*, p. 7.   [9] Taylor, *Thame Isis*, p. 16.
[10] Taylor, *Taylor's Last Voyage*, p. 7.

ranton. But whereas Taylor told men what they should do,
Yarranton spent much of his time in telling them what he
had himself done, which included everything from making
the Warwickshire Avon navigable[1] to instituting a glass
bottle industry in Hereford.[2] He had surveyed many rivers
from the Chelmer and Mole[3] to the Thames[4] and Dee,[5] but
chiefly with a view to making them the instruments of his
own particular schemes for establishing river granaries at
the heads of navigation[6] or making mum at Stratford-on-
Avon.[7] Impracticable as these schemes might be, it is not
without significance that Yarranton considered river transport essential for the establishment of new industries.

Midway between Taylor and Yarranton stood Francis
Mathew, the most important seventeenth-century pamphleteer on river navigation. Like others, Mathew claimed
much for his subject. The improvement of rivers would
raise watermen for the king's service, would spare horses
for time of war, would cheapen carriage, raise revenue, and
generally improve trade.[8] But it is not in these all too common
eulogies that Mathew's importance lies; it is in two factors
which raise him above his contemporaries. In the first place,
Mathew was the only man who suggested that the work of
river improvement should be done by the State. 'Such great
and publick Works', he wrote, 'are not to be attempted by
private men, or any particular Corporations; But most fit
it were that the State it self should be the sole Undertaker,
performing all at its own proper charge.'[9] It was a solitary
cry raised against private enterprise, and it was in vain. The
State was too much occupied with fighting royalist insurrec-
tions[10] and with the more primary necessity of government,
keeping order, to attempt such refinements as state enterprise in the spheres of commerce and industry. In the second
place Mathew was the first man in England to consider any
systematic joining of rivers. Rivers, when they had been

---

[1] Yarranton, *England's Improvement*, i. 53.   [2] Ibid. i. 156.
[3] Ibid. ii. 59.   [4] Ibid. i. 188.   [5] Ibid. i. 191.
[6] Ibid. i. 116.   [7] Ibid. i. 120.
[8] Mathew, *Of the Opening of Rivers*, pp. 3–4; *Mediterranean Passage . . . from London to Bristol*, p. 1.
[9] Mathew, *Of the Opening of Rivers*, p. 2.
[10] *Of the Opening of Rivers* was published in 1655.

made navigable, were to be joined by a 'still River', 'with Sasses, alias Locks, or otherwise'.[1] Thus the Warwickshire Avon might be connected with the Welland[2] and the Little Ouse with the Waveney.[3] The real design of the latter plan was to unite 'in-land commerce upon Rivers between the North and East of England', by connecting Great Yarmouth and York by the Waveney, the Little Ouse, the Great Ouse, the Witham, the Foss Dyke, the Trent, and the Yorkshire Ouse.[4] By this method pit coal could be brought from Derbyshire and Nottinghamshire to a coal magazine at Boston.[5] In 1662 a Bill included provision for this passage from Great Yarmouth to York, but it never became law.[6]

The connexion of the Thames and the Severn by way of the Bristol Avon was another of Mathew's schemes,[7] but in this he was not original. This projected connexion was the most famous of the canal schemes of this period, all of which are worthy of some consideration, not only because they show the spirit of the times, but also because they have the distinction of anticipating the future. The idea of connecting the Thames and the Severn appears to have dated from Elizabeth,[8] but Thomas Proctor, in 1610, was the first pamphleteer to advocate it. He suggested bringing 'one river to or neare unto another, as Thames to or neare Severne, or Severne neare or to Thames', by which means the passage of coal from the Forest of Dean would be facilitated and 'a custome or rent may growe unto his Majesty'.[9] Twenty years later a Mr. Hill proposed to do the work, but nothing was done.[10] In 1641 Taylor put forward a scheme for connecting the Isis with the Stroudwater by way of the Churn, which would necessitate only a 4-mile cut.[11] Then came Mathew with an alternative method of making the Bristol Avon navigable to Malmesbury and connecting it

---

[1] Mathew, *Of the Opening of Rivers*, p. 5.   [2] Ibid.
[3] Mathew, *Mediterranean Passage . . . between . . . Lynn and Yarmouth*, p. 6.
[4] Ibid., p. 9.
[5] Ibid., pp. 10–11.
[6] *J. H. of C.* viii. 370; *Cal. S.P.D., 1661–2*, pp. 306–7.
[7] Mathew, *Of the Opening of Rivers*, pp. 7–9.
[8] Congreve, *A Scheme*, p. 13.
[9] Procter, *A Profitable Worke to this whole Kingdome*.
[10] *Cal. S.P.D., 1633–4*, p. 41; Thacker, *Thames, Locks and Weirs*, p. 32.
[11] Taylor, *Taylor's Last Voyage*, p. 13.

with the Isis at Lechlade or Cricklade.[1] Like Procter, Mathew had his eyes fixed chiefly on the Forest of Dean coal trade. He worked out a scheme whereby a fleet of 300 billanders, each carrying 30 London chaldrons of coal, was to operate on the Avon, 'every squadron by itself, having each his Admiral and Rear-Admiral, carrying their Flags of proper Colour'.[2] This coal was to be delivered in London at £1 0s. 2d. per London chaldron, but only in winter time[3] so that the Newcastle trade should not be damaged.[4]

Mathew, who employed Moxon to draw his maps,[5] petitioned in 1662 to have the sole right of undertaking this passage of which he claimed to be the inventor.[6] In that remarkable outburst of parliamentary activity after the Restoration, no fewer than four Bills were introduced for making a passage by water from London to Bristol,[7] but none became law. A final Bill was introduced into the Lords by the Earl of Bridgwater in 1668,[8] 'but some foolish Discourse at Coffee-houses laid asleep that design as being a thing impossible and impracticable'.[9] The design, though defeated, was not yet asleep. Yarranton's son surveyed the Cherwell and considered that it might be made navigable to Banbury at a cost of £10,000. The Stour from Shipston to the Warwick Avon might be made navigable at a cost of £4,000 and this would leave a connecting link of only 8 miles of land carriage over 'good, hilly, sound, dry land'.[10] Nothing came of these schemes, but the idea of joining the Thames and Severn continued to interest men[11] until its accomplishment in the age of canal building.[12]

The Thames–Severn was not the only scheme that sought to give London a canal connexion with other parts. In 1641

---

[1] Mathew, *Of the Opening of Rivers*, pp. 7–9.

[2] Ibid., p. 7. The London chaldron was about 26 cwt., Nef, *Coal Industry*, ii, App. C.

[3] Mathew, *Of the Opening of Rivers*, p. 10.

[4] Mathew, *Mediterranean Passage . . . from London to Bristol*, pp. 7–8.

[5] Yarranton, *England's Improvement*, i. 64; Boydell, *History of the Thames*, i. 44.

[6] *Cal. S.P.D., 1661–2*, p. 306.

[7] *J. H. of C.* viii. 370, 546, 571; *H.M.C. Heathcote*, p. 149.

[8] *J. H. of L.* xii. 222, 521.

[9] Yarranton, *England's Improvement*, i. 64–5.   [10] Ibid., p. 65.

[11] Atkyns, *Glostershire*, p. 34.

[12] Jackman, *Development of Transportation*, i. 374.

Edward Forde proposed to bring a navigable cut from Rickmansworth to St. Giles in the Fields. Forde had undertaken to bring a water supply to London and now proposed to make his watercourse navigable.[1] This would give employment, facilitate the carriage of chalk, manure, and meal, and preserve the highways.[2] His design was opposed by Sir Walter Roberts, who maintained that London had sufficient navigation by the Thames and that Forde had not really the £8,000 per annum in land that he had put forward as a security. Sir Walter favoured the widening and deepening of rivers in their natural courses rather than the making of canals.[3] This opposition was supported by the Corporation of the New River,[4] and although Forde did good work in improving London's water supply,[5] his connexion with navigation never got beyond a pamphlet project.[6]

After the Restoration there seems to have been an impracticable design for making London the centre of a system of inland waterways. Not only was the Thames–Severn project favoured in Parliament, but on March 21st, 1663,[7] a Bill was read in the Lords 'to make navigable or otherwise passable, divers Rivers, from Greenstead, Arundell, Petersfield, Darkin, and Farnham, in the Counties of Surrey, Sussex, and South'on to London, and from South'on to Winchester and Alsford'.[8] The Bill never got beyond the second reading.[9] Two years later an Act was passed 'to enable Henry, Lord Loughborough to make a River or Sewer navigable from or neere Bristowe Causey in the County of Surrey into the River of Thames'.[10] There seems to be no evidence that this Act was ever put into execution. In the same year, Sir Bernard De Gomme, Jonas Moore, and others were sent to survey and see if the Cam could not be brought

---

1 Forde, *A Design for bringing a Navigable River*, ed. 1720, pp. 3–4.
2 Ibid., pp. 4–6.
3 Sir W. Roberts, *An Answer to Mr. Forde's Book*, ed. 1720, pp. 16–23.
4 *H.M.C.* iv. 45.
5 *D.N.B.*; Pepys, *Diary*, i. 410–11.
6 *J. H. of L.* v. 153; *J. H. of C.* ii. 585.
7 Throughout this work the dates have been given with the day of the month in the Old Style, which was the English usage until 1752. The year has been taken from January 1st to December 31st.
8 *J. H. of L.* xi. 496.   9 Ibid., p. 497.
10 16/17 Car. II, P.A.; cf. *J. H. of C.* xiii. 586.

into the Thames, 'it being very desirable to bring rivers from counties Cambridge, Huntingdon and Norfolk to fall into the Thames'.[1] Ten years later 'a curious gentleman',[2] Sir Robert Southwell, proposed before the Royal Society that canals should be built to London at a cost of £300 per mile, in order to carry coals which lay within 100 miles of the capital. Southwell argued that London imported 300,000 chaldrons of coal per annum, which was worth 15s. per chaldron, but cost, in times of war, £2 5s.; thus in times of war London paid £450,000 per annum extra for its coal. As one year in three was a time of war, this cost averaged out at £150,000 per annum. This, capitalized at 15 years' purchase, equalled £2,250,000. A canal of 100 miles, at £300 per mile, would cost £30,000; to comprehend all accidents, ten times as much might be taken, making £300,000, and even this was only one-seventh of £2,250,000.[3] This reasoning was, of course, a tissue of fallacies. Coal was worth more than 15s. per chaldron, and its price was not raised to £2 5s. by war, one year in three. A single canal could not have tapped any field capable of producing any considerable quantity of coal within 100 miles of London. But, like other impracticable canal schemes, it served to show the interest men were taking in water transport in general and the river transport of coal in particular.

In the first half of the eighteenth century there was one canal scheme which differed in two respects from its predecessors. In the first place, it was proposed to connect the rivers of the west, the head of the Trent with the Severn. In the second place, it marked an advance in technical knowledge by the suggested use of reservoirs. This scheme, put forward by Congreve in 1717, proposed to connect the Trent and the Severn by the following method. The Sow and the Penk were to be made navigable to Penkridge, which was to be joined to Pendeford by a canal 8 miles long. From Pendeford to Tettenhall Regis there was to be a reservoir of 500 to 600 acres, and from Tettenhall Regis to Prestwood a 12-mile canal. From Prestwood to Stourbridge the course

---

[1] *Cal. S.P.D., 1665–6*, p. 57.
[2] Houghton, *Collection for the Improvement of Husbandry and Trade*, ed. 1727, ii. 287. [3] Birch, *Royal Society*, iii. 210.

was down the Stour and so into the Severn.[1] Congreve estimated that his scheme would save £100,000 per annum in land carriage, and if a tenth of the waste of Staffordshire, Derbyshire, and Leicestershire were enclosed it would be worth £10,000 per annum at 4s. per acre, 'which will make a Canal and keep poor Vicars'.[2] But Congreve lived half a century before his time and his scheme shared the fate of those of his predecessors.[3]

The greater part of these canal schemes shows two interconnected ideas, the union of the seas[4] and the creation of some sort of a network of inland waterways. Neither of these ideas was peculiar to English engineering thought, for they had both, in France, passed from theory to practice. It will always be a controversial point how far French practice influenced English theory in this direction during the seventeenth century. The French, while paying some attention to river navigation,[5] had gone further. The Canal de Briare, connecting the Loire at Briare with the Loing at Montargis, had been begun by Sully in 1605, interrupted in 1610, and finished by Richelieu in 1640, not indeed by the State, but by a company to whom it had been granted.[6] Nor was this an isolated undertaking. The canal from St. Omer to Calais was completed by Colbert as part of his scheme of internal reconstruction.[7] The still more famous Canal du Midi had been considered as far back as the reign of Francis I,[8] and the work, which was begun in 1665 and finished in 1681 at a cost of 20 million livres,[9] was the concrete expression of

---

[1] Congreve, *A Scheme*, p. 7.   [2] Ibid., p. 9.

[3] The Trent and the Severn were ultimately connected by the Grand Trunk and the Birmingham and Worcester Canals, Jackman, *Development of Transportation*, i. 376 (map).

[4] This is true also of the Forth–Clyde Canal which Defoe advocated (*Tour*, ii. 743) and of which he said there was much talk 'about the Time of the Union' (*Tour*, ed. 1742, iv. 5). This project dated from the reign of Charles II, 'who (perhaps by means of his residence in the Netherlands) appears to have acquired a just idea of the importance of inland navigation', Macpherson, *Annals of Commerce*, iii. 477–8.

[5] Coulon, *Les Rivières de France*, i. 241–2, 472; Boissonade, *Colbert*, pp. 9, 90.

[6] Pigeonneau, *Histoire du commerce de la France*, ii. 300–1, 390; Belidor, *Architecture hydraulique*, iv. 357.

[7] Sée, *L'Évolution commerciale et industrielle*, p. 92.

[8] Riquet, *Canal du Midi*, p. 4.

[9] Sée, *L'Évolution commerciale et industrielle*, p. 92.

countless schemes and projects.[1] This canal, too, formed that union of the seas which was so dear to the heart of the pamphleteers across the Channel. Though that union was only on the map, for in parts 'la navigation était presque nulle faute de profondeur',[2] the English felt that history could never produce the like.[3]

If it were true to say of France, 'les canaux étaient encore peu nombreux, à la fin du xviie siècle',[4] it was equally true to say of England that they were almost non-existent. Even Mathew's idea of a network of waterways had been anticipated by a hundred years in France. Adam de Crapponne, 'inspired by the bold ideas of Leonardo da Vinci,'[5] had not confined himself to an irrigation scheme, 'la dérivation des eaux de la Durance dans le Crau',[6] which was finished in 1558,[7] but had planned 'un réseau de canaux', of which the connexion of the Saône and the Loire and the Mediterranean with the Garonne were the chief links.[8] It is unlikely that Mathew or any other English pamphleteer had even heard of Crapponne, but French canal building itself can scarcely have gone unnoticed in England. Certainly the Dutch waterways were a constant source of comparison and approval. Though it might be felt that England was not capable of 'such waterings as the flat Netherlands',[9] where it was variously estimated that no part of the country was more than a quarter of a mile,[10] or alternatively more than a mile,[11] from navigable water, yet the English were constantly enjoined to imitate 'the industrious Netherlanders'.[12] They should

---

[1] Riquet, *Canal du Midi*, pp. 8–9. On the subsequent controversy over the responsibility for the canal, see Riquet, op. cit., and Andreossy, *Histoire du Canal du Midi*.

[2] Avenel, *Histoire économique de la propriété*, vii. 191.

[3] *H.M.C. Various*, ii. 281.

[4] Sée, *L'Évolution commerciale et industrielle*, p. 205.

[5] Renard and Weulersse, *Life and Work*, p. 139.

[6] Charleval, *Notice historique sur Adam de Crapponne*, p. 3.

[7] Ibid., p. 6.

[8] Ibid., pp. 6, 10; Pigeonneau, *Histoire du commerce de la France*, ii. 78; Sée, *Esquisse d'une histoire économique et sociale*, pp. 173–4.

[9] Mathew, *Of the Opening of Rivers*, p. 1. On the influence of Dutch waterways in favouring 'eine gewisse demokratische Struktur des Landes', see the suggestive paragraph in Huizinga, *Holländische Kultur*, p. 8.

[10] Birch, *Royal Society*, iii. 208.　　　　[11] Petty, *Works*, i. 256.

[12] Mathew, *Of the Opening of Rivers*, p. 1.

carry their goods to and from market in boats as the Dutch did.[1] They should build engine boats 'after the manner of those used in Holland and Flanders'.[2] It was 'but childish Rhetorick' to call water a free element when the Dutch used sasses and sluices to restrain it.[3] In commercial policy and economic ideas there was much 'conscious imitation of the Dutch':[4] Yarranton, in Holland, observing 'Laws, Customs, publick Banks, Cut Rivers, Havens, Sands, Policies in Government and Trade',[5] was typical of his age.

The Dutch, French, and Germans[6] might provide concrete examples for the English pamphleteers and engineers, but none of them was strong enough to influence the public mind in the direction of canal building. The English preferred to direct what energy they had for navigable waterways towards their rivers, and it was only when they had exhausted what appeared to be the possibilities of these that they turned to canals as the connecting links of a system the foundations of which they had already laid.

[1] Mathew, *Mediterranean Passage ... between ... Lynn and Yarmouth*, p. 7.
[2] 'Beverley Beck Navigation, 1699-1726', Lansdowne MSS. 896, f. 164.
[3] *News from the Fens*, p. 13.
[4] Clark, *Seventeenth Century*, p. 15.
[5] Yarranton, *England's Improvement*, i, Epistle.
[6] The Frederick William Canal, named after the Great Elector, was opened in 1669, Clark, *Seventeenth Century*, p. 50.

II
PRACTICAL UNDERTAKINGS
(i) COMMISSIONS OF SEWERS

UNTIL the seventeenth century the regulation of English rivers exhibited that combination of central and local control which is characteristic of our provincial administration. Though Acts of Parliament dealing with rivers were not unknown, the chief instrument of their administration was the Commission of Sewers. This was a royal commission with a local personnel consisting of the chief landowners of the district. The power of the commissioners was 'generally according to their Discretions, subject nevertheless to the Rule of Reason, and the Laws of the Land'.[1] They could compel proprietors to clean the part of the river adjoining their land, or levy a rate for such cleaning. But Commissioners of Sewers were not primarily concerned with navigation; their chief business was drainage and the prevention of floods. They could not 'make a new River, or try Inventions at the charge of the Country', though it had been held that they could make new cuts for drainage purposes.[2] The powers and functions of these commissioners, wide as they might be, were obviously inadequate where navigation was concerned. It is true that decrees ordering the removal of weirs or tree stumps from rivers might facilitate the passage of boats, but such decrees aroused a host of vested interests that were often strong enough to nullify them. The disputes that arose over the decrees of Commissioners of Sewers concerning the Medway, the Dee, and the Wye, at the very beginning of the seventeenth century, show that this form of supervision and regulation was inadequate.

In 1600 floods along the banks of the Medway led to disputes as to whether the damage was caused by weirs or iron works. The inhabitants of Wateringbury, Teston, and West and East Barming declared that their weirs acted as fences across the river, increased fish, and were not responsible for the floods, which they ascribed to the forges. The

[1] *Law of Sewers*, pp. 22-3.   [2] Ibid., p. 33.

owners of, and those interested in, the iron forges retaliated by ascribing all damage to the weirs, which were from 6 to 8 feet high and which caused such overflowing that they could not keep a fire even in their upstairs chambers, that they had to take their swine into their cottages and even upstairs 'emonge their wyves and children', and that their houses became damp, cold, and unhealthy. Added to this, was a controversy as to whether the river should be made navigable or not. The opponents of navigation maintained that the Medway had never been navigable under Act of Parliament, that the passage of boats decayed the bridges and the fishing, and that the watermen stole 'Hennes, Geese, Duckes, Piggs, Swannes, Eggs, Woode and all other such Commodytyes', besides causing strife by breaking down fences and trampling grass and causing decay of husbandry and the Subsidy Book by ruining land carriers. The supporters of navigation replied by affirming that the river belonged to the Crown and could be used as a highway, that land carriage spoilt the roads and ruined oxen, and that the removal of weirs did little harm to fish 'but onely maketh the fyshe subtiller'.

These defenders of navigation were supported by a Commission of Sewers which, in the early part of 1600, ordered the removal of the weirs. This decree was at once questioned by Sir John Scott, in defence of the weirs, and supported by Sir John Leveson, apparently the chief commissioner. On June 27th Scott wrote to Leveson asking the commissioners to reconsider their decision. Leveson refused. On July 14th the Lord Treasurer and the Lord Admiral wrote to the commissioners ordering them to stay their proceedings because of disputes with persons of quality. The commissioners immediately proceeded to fortify their position. They decided to take a new view of the river in time of flood, for low water was an advantage to the weir owners' case, and after that view reaffirmed the Jury's decision against the weirs, but agreed not to meddle with navigation. They wrote to the Lord Treasurer informing him that the work had been begun, three rivers falling into the narrow channel at Yalding had been cleaned, and consequently the floods would be greater if the weirs remained. They got into touch with the purveyor of timber for the Navy and showed him the advantages of the river for carrying timber. Finally they enlisted the support of the Lord Chamberlain, who ordered them to proceed. He was by no means a disinterested party, for a mill above Tonbridge not only damaged the inheritance of his ward, but also took away water from his own corn mill at Tonbridge. Equally important, the Lord Admiral was his brother-in-law and therefore susceptible to family interests. Thus, when on August 6th the Lord Treasurer wrote to the commissioners ordering both sides to appear before him, the Lord Chamberlain wrote telling them to proceed. He had talked with the Lord Admiral, who promised to desist, and with the Lord Treasurer, who promised 'better to apprehend and allowe the integritie of your proceedings'.

In face of this concerted action Sir John Scott was compelled to withdraw his opposition and leave the commissioners in the field. It might be said that here the Commissioners of Sewers triumphed, but it is clear from the mass of correspondence that their victory was at the price of surrendering any claim whatsoever to deal with the navigation of the river. They agreed to leave that to the law, the Lords of the Privy Council or the Officers of the Admiralty; their own duty they admitted to be merely to cleanse the river.[1]

Even this qualified victory was denied to the Commissioners of Sewers who dealt with the Dee. In July 1607 a commission was granted for the removal of obstructions in that river, both to prevent flooding and improve navigation.[2] Here the case was complicated by the fact that the chief obstruction was the causey which dammed up water to supply the famous Dee mills, upon which the life of Chester largely depended. The evidence given before the commissioners in December 1607 shows the different attitudes with which this obstruction was regarded. The county of Flint held that the river would be improved by a breach in the causey,[3] a view supported by Denbigh.[4] The County of Chester held

---

[1] The material for this account is in 'Medway Navigation, 1600', Add. MSS. 34218, ff. 37–57.
[2] 'Papers relating to the Dee', Harl. MSS. 2003, ff. 144–54.
[3] Ibid., f. 155.   [4] Ibid., f. 188.

that the causey and floodgates 'doe stopp and ympounde the water of the Ryver of Dee so as it hath not his full current into the sea', and thereby caused £100 per annum damage to lands by floods.[1] Very different was the view held by the citizens of Chester, who maintained that the corn mills had been built by Hugh Lupus, first Earl of Chester, after the Conquest,[2] and now served the king by grinding corn for Ireland in time of war;[3] that the fulling mills, although they stopped some part of the stream, enabled the shearmen to maintain their families and paid £11 per annum to the king;[4] that they themselves ground their corn, dressed their cloth, fished for their salmon, and got water for their houses, all by means of the river.[5] They maintained that the haven was as good as it was 400 years ago and anyway should not be improved as it stood open to Spain and Ireland;[6] that the flooding was only in winter and therefore an advantage to the land,[7] and if there were any annoyances from it, they had been endured for 500 or 600 years and were usual in grounds adjoining rivers;[8] finally they held that 'boates of small burthen maie have Free passage up and downe the River to and from the sea' at any tides, even if ships of greater burden had to lie 6 miles below the city.[9]

Not content with giving evidence and issuing a statement of their case, the Mayor and Aldermen of Chester proceeded to attack the commission itself. They declared that Sir Richard Trevor and others in Wales, 'either incyted with malice towardes the Cittie or possessed with a desyre of private lucre and gayne by the ruyne of others', had got the commission because they owned corn mills within 5 miles of Chester and would profit by the destruction of the Dee mills. They protested that Trevor had taken upon himself the custody of the commission, 'beinge a stranger, and havinge

---

[1] Ibid., f. 156.　　　　　　　　　　[2] Ibid. 2084, f. 106.
[3] Ibid., f. 107.　　　　　　　　　　[4] Ibid. 2003, f. 190, 2084, f. 107.
[5] Ibid. 2084, f. 107.　　　　　　　　[6] Ibid., f. 108.
[7] Ibid., f. 108 dorso. In this the City was not over-stating its case. In 1616 Dorothy Powell, who with her brother owned land worth £160 per annum, wrote to Arthur Paynter supporting the causey 'for yf the water should not come over the ground it would be farr worse then it is; and would be nothinge but a stife claye', ibid., f. 151.
[8] 'Dee Navigation, 1608', Add. MSS. 36767, f. 146.
[9] 'Papers relating to the Dee', Harl. MSS. 2003, f. 192.

noe landes within this countie', and therefore they begged
for a Supersedeas.[1]

This attack on the commission was in vain, for on January
14th, 1608, the commissioners issued their decree, together
with a summary of the evidence given before them, carefully
omitting that of the City of Chester which conflicted with
their case. They stated that lands were damaged to the value
of £300 per annum by flooding, occasioned by Eaton weir
above Chester and by the causey. They decreed that a third
of Eaton weir should be taken down and 10 yards of the
causey removed as far as the bottom of the river.[2]

The city appealed against this decree to the Privy Council,
who ordered another survey and the parties in dispute to
attend.[3] But on May 6th, 1608, the Privy Council requested
the Lord Chief Justice, the Lord Chief Justice of the
Common Pleas, and the Lord Chief Baron to hear the case.[4]
While the matter was still *sub judice*, the city put forward *A
Case presented to the Lords the Judges*, in which it altered its
tactics to asking whether the commissioners' authority could
extend to the causey at all.[5] Finally, on May 29th, 1609,
the judges gave their verdict that the causey had existed
time out of mind without enhancement and Commissions
of Sewers under 23 Henry VIII, c. 5, did not extend to
mills, causey, &c., erected before Edward I, unless enhanced.
Therefore the part of the causey should not be removed.[6]
On June 7th the Privy Council ordered the Commissioners
of Sewers not to put their decree into execution.[7] The Mayor
and Aldermen of Chester had won and celebrated their
victory by yet another of their interminable statements of
the whole case. In this they struck a truer note by ascribing
the badness of the haven to the loose sands brought by the
tides, but it was scarcely in a spirit of progress that they
declared, 'The passage of boats is not to be provided for in
all Rivers'.[8] They even doubted whether it would enrich
the city to improve the haven, for the very significant reason
that, 'The greatest trade of the Realme in effect is now

---

[1] 'Papers relating to the Dee', Harl. MSS. 2003, f. 227.
[2] Ibid. 2081, ff. 206, 221.   [3] Ibid. 2082, ff. 17, 29.
[4] Ibid., f. 39.   [5] Ibid. 2003, f. 166.
[6] Ibid. 2082, f. 37.   [7] Ibid. 2003, f. 175.   [8] Ibid., f. 164.

drawen to London; so that the trade of other Citties cannot exceed a certaine proportion'.[1]

This failure of a Commission of Sewers to fulfil the objects of its appointment was not always due to such direct supersession as at Chester. In 1622 the counties of Gloucester, Hereford, and Monmouth and the city of Hereford petitioned the Council for an order that a Commission of Sewers might proceed with its work. The commission had been appointed for removing nuisances on the Wye, which hindered navigation and fishing. Some of the weir owners had tried to get a Supersedeas, but the king had refused it. On the other hand, the Lord Keeper had ordered the commission not to meddle with weirs held by the king and in the possession of the Lord Privy Seal. The petitioners had tried to get a hearing before the Lord Keeper and the Lord Privy Seal, but they could not get a day fixed. As a result the proceedings of the Commission of Sewers were stayed 'and the whole benefitt thereof like to be frustrated'.[2] Though the petitioners were willing to pay the rent to the king of any of his weirs that were destroyed, it does not seem that the commission was ever put into execution.[3]

In face of these reverses, it must have been obvious that a Commission of Sewers was an inadequate method of dealing with rivers, at least as far as navigation was concerned. That inadequacy lay deep in the roots of property and ownership. To make a river navigable it was necessary to have access to it over the lands adjoining to it, to cut those lands in the process of widening the river or making new channels, to use the river itself and often the bank for a towing path. In all these processes the rights of private property were infringed. It is the basis of law in all civilized states that everything belongs to somebody or to the State itself. Rivers fall within the category of property and in the seventeenth century their legal position was clearly defined. There was, indeed, that almost inevitable discrepancy between the popular and the legal view. About the middle of the century certain supporters of a Bill for the navigation of the Wye

---

[1] Ibid., f. 162.
[2] 'Wye Navigation, 1622–62', Add. MSS. 11052, f. 80.
[3] Ibid., f. 80 dorso.

declared that it was not against 'equity and reason', because it was for the public good. They explained this conception by continuing, 'both equity and reason wills the good, and benefitt of the whole body, rather than any particular member'. Nor was the Bill against 'law and common right', for 'by both common and statute law, the Subiects have right of passage, with boates in, and uppon, all the great Rivers of the Kingdome, and have likewise right to hale, and drawe, uppon the banckes of the said Rivers'. Finally, they quoted 23 Henry VIII, c. 12, to prove their case.[1] But here they were maintaining a view that was legally untenable. The statute quoted referred to the Severn, a tidal river, and between the tidal and the non-tidal there was a fundamental distinction, not of hydrodynamics, but of law. According to *The Law of Sewers*, 'so far as the Sea flows and ebbs it is a Royal stream, and the Fishing belongs to the Crown'.[2] A tidal river, as far as the tide flowed, belonged to the Crown in the same sense as the highway, it was free and common to all. A non-tidal river belonged to the riparian owners and was private property as much as the land itself. A right of passage on such a river only existed if it had been granted by Act of Parliament, or agreed to by mutual consent, or established by long usage much after the fashion of a right of way on land.[3]

The conception of certain rivers being public and free to all went back to Magna Carta,[4] but the subsequent criterion, that a public river in the time of Edward I was for ever a public river, was capable of application only in the case of the greater rivers. In others, it was strong evidence of a public river if the passage had been continuously navigated and kept free from obstruction.[5] But the promoters of navigation in this period were little concerned with rivers that had been kept free from obstruction. Their main object was the creation of navigable passages, and in this work the infringement of rights of property was essential. For these undertakings, with their assessment of compensation and their

---

[1] 'Wye Navigation, 1622-62', Add. MSS. 11052, f. 82.
[2] *Law of Sewers*, p. 25.
[3] 'Derwent Navigation', Stowe MSS. 818, f. 86; Coulson and Forbes, *Law relating to Waters*, pp. 77-100; Appendix III.
[4] 'Derwent Navigation', Stowe MSS. 818, f. 86.   [5] Ibid., ff. 86-7.

monopolistic grants, the Commissions of Sewers were ill fitted. Their place was taken by bodies of men who derived their power either from Letters Patent or more frequently from Acts of Parliament. New bodies of commissioners were nominated to superintend each undertaking, and the rivers, or parts of rivers, over which they had authority were expressly excluded from the jurisdiction of the Commissioners of Sewers.[1]

The Commissions of Sewers continued to exercise their jurisdiction over rivers from which no Act of Parliament had taken away their powers. in 1663 a Commission of Sewers decreed that the Yare should be improved and made 22 yards wide,[2] in 1681 a Court of Sewers was cleansing the Thames and enforcing prescribed lock dues.[3] The navigation of the Lea was continually protected by Commissioners of Sewers throughout the seventeenth century. They ordered the river to be scoured and made navigable by the landowners on either side and levied a rate for that purpose in 1655.[4] Eleven years later, on complaint by the bargemen against the excessive rates levied by lock owners, they fixed the price for flashes, though their order was not obeyed.[5] They presented a dam built by the New River Company as a common nuisance[6] and, on the other hand, protected the supply of water for the Company's pipes.[7] Agreements between the City of Hertford and the owners of Ware Mills had to be enforced by an order of the commissioners.[8] They heard the case over Waltham lock in 1683 and ordered the lock, destroyed by bargemen, to be rebuilt and a toll paid.[9] But these activities became more and more exceptional as the more important rivers were gradually withdrawn from the jurisdiction of the Commissioners of Sewers by the increasing number of Acts of Parliament dealing with river navigation. Long before the end of the seventeenth century the interest had shifted to new groups of undertakers and new bodies of commissioners.

[1] 10 Will. III, c. 25, sec. 7 (Aire and Calder); 1 Anne S 2, c. 11, sec. 7 (Cam); 1 Anne, c. 14, sec. 8 (Derwent).
[2] *Records of Norwich*, ii. 395.   [3] *H.M.C. House of Lords*, N.S. i. 548.
[4] *Papers . . . relating to the Navigation on the River Lea*, pp. 4–5.
[5] Ibid., pp. 12–14.   [6] Ibid., p. 16.   [7] Ibid., p. 21.   [8] Ibid., p. 10.
[9] 'Suit concerning Waltham Lock', Add. MSS. 33576, f. 63.

(ii) LETTERS PATENT

If economic enterprises are to depend for their initiation upon Acts of Parliament, then regular meetings of Parliament are a *sine qua non* of a progressive economic life. In the first half of the seventeenth century those meetings were by no means regular, and had the promoters of river navigation been dependent upon them for the necessary powers for their enterprises, there would have been long periods of inactivity. But the promoters were not dependent upon Parliament, for the Crown's right of action in the economic sphere was still an essential part of its prerogative. Hence it is necessary to look to the Crown and its Letters Patent, rather than to Parliament and its Acts,[1] for the authorization of river improvements before the Commonwealth.

In granting these Patents the Crown was on less sure ground than in dealing with soap or glass or trade with the East, for river improvements involved interference with property that was not necessary in other monopolies. Lord Chancellor Macclesfield laid it down that the king could not grant a right of passage in private rivers,[2] and where there were several owners of several parts of a river no grant of the king could give the sole right of navigation.[3] It was precisely such a right that the Letters Patent did grant as the appropriate reward for the undertaker. On the other hand, the Patents merely authorized the undertaker to come to an agreement with the landowners concerned and, like the Acts, appointed commissioners to arbitrate in case of dispute.[4] In spite of this, the Crown was holding itself open to attack. While William Sandys was making the Warwickshire Avon navigable under Letters Patent he came into conflict with Sir William Russell, one of the commissioners and Sheriff of Worcestershire. In a petition to the Council Sandys declared that Russell not only refused to do anything, 'but in the face of the County had termed the service the betraying of the county, and had given out that petitioner went about to entitle his majesty to men's inheritances'.[5]

---

[1] There were two Acts from 1600 to 1650, 3 Jac. I, c. 20; 21 Jac. I, c. 32.
[2] 'Derwent Navigation', Stowe MSS. 818, f. 86.   [3] Ibid., f. 86 dorso.
[4] *Cal. S.P.D., 1635-6*, p. 280; Rymer, *Foedera*, xx. 6-7.
[5] *Cal. S.P.D., 1636-7*, p. 357.

How far such economic factors were responsible for the Civil War is still a matter for conjecture,[1] but within five years men were fighting for their inheritances as well as for their consciences.

The earliest of these seventeenth-century Patents was one from James to the Mayor and Aldermen of Bath, granted on July 16th, 1619. Bath had petitioned for the improvement of the navigation of the Avon to cheapen the carriage of goods from Bristol, which 'by reason of rockie and mountaynous waies' was very expensive. The Mayor and Corporation asked to have the benefit and profit of the carriage, which would cost only half that by land. By the Patent they were authorized to make the river navigable 'for boates of convenient burthen', and to cast down weirs and 'to erecte or make fludgates, sluces or other engins or devises', but for these the damage had to be compounded for first. They were given the right 'for ever hereafter from time to time to have and take the sole carying and conveying in such boates as they shall thinke moste meete of all men, women, passengers, goods, wares', for which they were to agree upon reasonable rates and enjoy the profits, 'without anie accompt or allowance therfore given to us'. Others were prohibited from carrying goods 'upon paine of the heavie indignation and displeasure of us' and of all such other penalties that could be inflicted for breach and contempt of a royal command. Any 'tumultous or other undue or unlawful courses' were to be suppressed with the assistance of the Sheriffs, the Justices of the Peace, and the Constables.[2] Despite this full grant it was almost a century before Bath began to improve its river.[3]

In other cases the Crown was less disinterested. On January 3rd, 1627, Arnold Spencer was granted a Patent 'to make other rivers, streams, and waters navigable and passable for boats, keeles, and other vessels to passe from place to place', having the sole right to use his own methods or engines for 11 years, paying £5 per annum to the Exchequer. He was to have all the profit for 80 years from rivers he made navigable during the 11 years, paying £5

---

[1] Nef, *Coal Industry*, ii. 283–4.
[2] S.P.D., Warrants, x, July 19th, 1619; *Cal. S.P.D., 1619–23*, p. 63.
[3] Latimer, *Annals of Bristol in the Seventeenth Century*, p. 71.

per annum for every river made navigable.[1] Later the grant was extended to 21 years.[2] Spencer had already made parts of the Great Ouse navigable before the grant of the Patent, for which he had been awarded a toll of 3*d*. a ton.[3] He received rights in the river in 1638,[4] but assigned them away to Samuel Jemmatt.[5] In the same year he received rights in the Essex Stour,[6] but these also he assigned away.[7]

Spencer's Patent did not prevent others from receiving grants for other rivers. In 1634 Thomas Skipwith was empowered to make the Soar navigable. The pretext for this grant was the fact that the 'County of Leicester, being a Champion Country and destitute of such Supplies for Fuel, as are abundant in other Places, is constrained to fetch their Coals into the most Parts thereof, at a distance of eighteen or twenty miles'. After the Earls of Huntingdon and Stamford had heard arguments for and against the suggested improvement, Skipwith was empowered to make the river navigable between Leicester and the Trent. He was first to make satisfaction for all damage done, but if he could not agree with the mill and land owners, then Justices of the Peace, or two of them, of the county or counties through which the river flowed, could fix the compensation. Skipwith was not granted a monopoly of carriage, but could take tolls, at rates fixed by himself, from others using the navigation. A tenth part of the clear profit was to go to the king.[8] Skipwith carried out the work for 5 or 6 miles from the Trent, but he was forced to leave off for want of money, and the navigation decayed.[9]

More important was the grant of the Warwickshire Avon to William Sandys in 1636.[10] Like Spencer, Sandys had

---

[1] *Abridgments of Specifications relating to Harbours, Docks, and Canals*, p. 3.
[2] Ibid., p. 5.   [3] S.P.D. Charles I, xxiv, f. 75.
[4] *H.M.C. Cowper*, ii. 196.   [5] *H.M.C. House of Lords*, N.S. i. 51.
[6] *H.M.C. Cowper*, ii. 196.   [7] *J. H. of C.* xiv. 474.
[8] Rymer, *Foedera*, xx. 597–600.
[9] Forbes and Ashford, *Waterways*, p. 71; Houghton, *Collection for the Improvement of Husbandry and Trade*, ed. 1727, i. 130. Houghton was mistaken in saying 'an Act was obtained' for this work (op. cit.). The first Act was in 1766 (Forbes and Ashford, op. cit.), though there was a petition for a Bill in 1737, *J. H. of C.* xxii. 785.
[10] There is no evidence in support of Bund's remark that Sandys's Patent was set aside as a monopoly, *Canals and Waterways*, First Report, i, pt. ii. 276.

already spent large sums before the grant[1] and, despite opposition, he completed the work at a cost variously estimated at £20,000[2] and £40,000.[3] Two years later John Malet received a commission under the Great Seal for making the Tone navigable and 'did at his very great Expence make the said River (in some sort) navigable from the said Towne of Bridgwater to certaine Mills called Ham Mills'.[4]

Finally, one Patent remains to be considered, which is of particular interest because of the trouble the Crown took to ensure that justice should be done. In 1635 an Order in Council declared that Henry Lambe had petitioned to be allowed to make the Lark navigable from Bury St. Edmunds to the Ouse and that commissioners, 'divers gentlemen of quality' of Suffolk, had found the work feasible. The work had been begun but had been checked by Sir Roger North and Thomas Steward because of alleged damage to Sir Roger's mill. The case was ordered to be tried in the Star Chamber.[5] But in February 1636 another Order in Council commanded a commission of ten to report on the benefit or damage of the work, which was not to extend to the river between Mildenhall and the Ouse.[6] Lambe agreed to make the Lark navigable from Mildenhall to Worlington,[7] and was ordered to set down the rates for water carriage, which he was not to exceed.[8] Meanwhile the commissioners were to examine the rates of land carriage between Worlington and Bury St. Edmunds, for 'unless the charge for water carriage will in some good proportion be less than the land carriage, the proposed river will not be a work for the benefit of the public'.[9] On September 9th, 1636, Lambe submitted his rates of 2s. 8d. per ton for carriage and 4s. a ton for goods to be delivered, whereas the rates by land were 4s. and 10s. respectively. He agreed to pay for land used as a towing path and for trees cut down and to preserve fords and erect bridges.[10] Eleven months later the commissioners reported, 'we have not found any that oppose the intended work'.

[1] Cal. S.P.D., 1635–6, p. 280; Rymer, Foedera, xx. 6.
[2] Bennet, Tewkesbury, p. 303.   [3] Cal. S.P.D., 1661–2, p. 628.
[4] 10 Will. III, c. 8, sec. 1.   [5] Cal. S.P.D., 1635, p. 524.
[6] Ibid., 1635–6, p. 209.   [7] Ibid., p. 255.
[8] Ibid., p. 434.   [9] Ibid., p. 435.   [10] Ibid., 1636–7, p. 119.

They recommended that treble damages should be paid for works that prejudiced mills, that Lambe should pay £40 per acre for meadow cut and £2 per acre per annum for land used as towing paths, and that the navigation from the Ouse to Mildenhall should be free for all.[1]

Lambe, not unnaturally, petitioned against these unreasonable conditions,[2] in which he had the support even of his former opponents, Sir Roger North and Thomas Steward.[3] An Order in Council of December 17th, 1637, commanded Lambe and 'such gentlemen who are the cause of the said hard conditions' to appear before the King in Council.[4] What followed this command is not clear, but on March 23rd, 1638, Lambe received licence to make the Lark navigable from Bury St. Edmunds to the Ouse, for which he was to have the benefit of all water carriage except that from Mildenhall to the Ouse. He was to pay the Crown a rent of £6 13s. 4d. per annum.[5] It must be admitted that here at least the Crown showed an admirable grasp of the situation and of the issues involved. Not only did it apply an excellent economic criterion in comparing the rates of land and water carriage, but it also attempted to ensure justice for all the parties concerned.

(iii) PARLIAMENTARY ACTIVITY

Acts of Parliament dealing with the improvement of river navigation were no new thing in the seventeenth century. They date back to a statute of 1424 which dealt with the Lea[6] and, in the sixteenth century, eight such Acts were passed for various rivers.[7] After the Restoration this parliamentary activity became almost continuous, though the bulk of it fell within three well-defined periods. During the Civil War and the Commonwealth only two Acts had been passed for river improvement,[8] and it was undoubtedly a reaction from this period of stagnation which accounted for the extraordinary activity of the years 1662 to 1665. During that time Acts were passed for the Stour and Salwarpe,[9] the Wye

1 *Cal. S.P.D., 1637*, p. 364.　　　　2 Ibid., *1637–8*, p. 26.
3 Ibid., p. 186.　　4 Ibid., p. 26.　　5 Ibid., p. 323.
6 Clifford, *Private Bill Legislation*, i. 468.
7 Jackman, *Development of Transportation*, i. 164.
8 Firth and Rait, *Acts and Ordinances*, ii. 514–16 (Wey Act). *J. H. of C.* vii. 577.
9 14 Car. II, P.A.　　　　　　　　　　　(Yorks. Ouse).

and Lug,[1] the Medway,[2] and the Wiltshire Avon,[3] besides an Act for bringing a navigable river from Bristowe Causey to the Thames[4] and one for making 'divers' rivers navigable,[5] under which the Itchen,[6] the Great Ouse,[7] the Mole,[8] and perhaps the Welland[9] were improved. Nor was this the full total of parliamentary activity, for Bills for the Derwent,[10] the Mersey and Weaver,[11] the Wey,[12] and various canal schemes[13] were initiated, but never became law.

The whole attitude of Parliament at this period is summed up in the words of a speech made by the Speaker of the Commons to the Lords on March 2nd, 1665:

> Cosmographers do agree that this Island is incomparably furnished with pleasant Rivers, like Veins in the Natural Body, which conveys the Blood into all the Parts, whereby the whole is nourished, and made useful; but the Poet tells us, he acts best, *qui miscuit utile dulci*. Therefore we have prepared some Bills for making small Rivers navigable; a Thing that in other Countries hath been more experienced, and hath been found very advantageous; it easeth the People of the great Charge of Land Carriages; preserves the Highways, which are daily worn out with Waggons carrying excessive Burdens; it breeds up a Nursery of Watermen, which, upon Occasion, will prove good Seamen; and with much Facility maintain Intercourse and Communion between Cities and Countries.[14]

The second outburst of parliamentary activity followed the Peace of Ryswick and lasted from 1697 to 1700. In those three years Acts were passed for the Colne,[15] the Tone,[16] the Yare,[17] the Aire and Calder,[18] the Trent,[19] the Lark,[20] the Bristol Avon,[21] and the Dee,[22] while Bills for the Wiltshire Avon,[23] the Derwent,[24] the Stroudwater,[25] and the Don[26] failed to pass. It is not surprising that, in discussing the

---

[1] Ibid. [2] 16/17 Car. II, P.A. [3] Ibid. [4] Ibid. [5] Ibid.
[6] *J. H. of C.* xvii. 493. [7] *H.M.C. House of Lords,* N.S. i. 48.
[8] *H.M.C.* vii. 179. [9] *J. H. of C.* xi. 388.
[10] Ibid. viii. 574. [11] Ibid., p. 444.
[12] Ibid. xiii. 391, 602; *J. H. of L.* xi. 605.
[13] *Supra,* pp. 10–11; there was even a Bill for 'divers rivers in the County of Cornwall', *J. H. of C.* viii. 572. [14] *J. H. of L.* xi. 675.
[15] 9 Will. III, c. 19. [16] 10 Will. III, c. 8.
[17] Ibid., c. 5. [18] Ibid., c. 25.
[19] Ibid., c. 26. [20] 11 Will. III, c. 22.
[21] Ibid., c. 23. [22] Ibid., c. 24.
[23] *J. H. of C.* xiii. 79. [24] Ibid. xi. 366.
[25] Ibid., p. 711. [26] Ibid. xii. 57, 61.

cheapness of water carriage in 1698, Houghton should have
written, "tis to be wish'd that we had more navigable rivers;
and those were lengthened and improved that we have, which
I hope I may live to see; because the Parliament seems well
disposed towards such things'.[1] Both these periods of activity
were reactions from war, civil or foreign, but the third bore
a different character.

River navigation, like almost every other form of economic
enterprise, became involved in the speculative outburst of
the South Sea schemes. From 1719 to 1721 Acts were
passed for the Derwent,[2] the Douglas,[3] the Great Ouse,[4]
the Idle,[5] the Kennet,[6] the Weaver,[7] the Mersey and Irwell,[8]
the Dane,[9] and the Eden.[10] It is noteworthy that only one
Bill, that for the Orwell, failed to pass.[11] On March 1st,
1720, a correspondent wrote from Westminster to Sir
Thomas Aston, 'I find the present Disposition of the house
of Commons is for passing all manner of bills for navigation'.[12]
Seymour Cholmondeley, who had gone up to London to
oppose the Weaver Bill, found his task almost insuperable.
On April 26th, 1720, he wrote, probably to Aston, 'that
combination of the projectors for 6 bills of this nature, had
worked up the temper of both houses to such a love of
Navigation, that I assure you, it is a mark of peculiar favour
to be suffer'd to speak against any bill with that title'.[13]
Cholmondeley managed to get the Bill defeated by a majority
of 4, but it was only by giving an assurance to introduce
another the next session.[14] The supporters of navigation
Acts were less unfortunate than others in the crash that
followed, but there was something of a reaction, and subsequent Acts were passed largely to amend earlier ones or to
incorporate bodies of proprietors.

　The passing of an Act of Parliament stood midway in the

---

[1] Houghton, *Collection for the Improvement of Husbandry and Trade*, ed. 1727,
ii. 285.

[2] 6 Geo. I, c. 27.   [3] Ibid., c. 28.
[4] Ibid., c. 29.   [5] Ibid., c. 30.
[6] 7 Geo. I, c. 8.   [7] Ibid., c. 10.
[8] Ibid., c. 15.   [9] Ibid., c. 17.
[10] 8 Geo. I, c. 14.   [11] *J. H. of C.* xix. 196.
[12] 'Weaver Navigation, 1699–1720', Add. MSS. 36914, f. 80.
[13] Ibid., f. 84.
[14] Ibid., f. 93. The Act was passed in the following session, 7 Geo. I, c. 10.

course of an economic enterprise; much activity had gone before and much was to come after. The Act was often the culmination of a long series of attempts spread over a period of as long as twenty years.[1] It was almost always the climax of a hard struggle between conflicting interests. Promoters met and discussed and issued statements of their case; opponents met and discussed and issued counter-statements. Both attempted to influence the public opinion of their neighbourhood, both collected petitions for or against the Bill, both made long, tiring journeys to give evidence before committees, both used the age-old weapons of local politics, influence, coercion, and misrepresentation. The cost of this promotion formed a considerable item in the general expenses of the undertaking. Richard Vernon claimed to have spent £2,000 in getting the Weaver Act, but this was admitted to be an exorbitant claim.[2] The Douglas Act of 1720 cost £900,[3] while that of a small, unopposed undertaking like Beverley Beck cost as much as £148 4s. 5d.[4] The Charity Commissioners, who were attempting to establish a right to the profits from the Tone, were prepared to allow the undertakers £350 for the Act,[5] which had in reality cost £528 15s. 11d. This sum included £123 11s. 1d. to sheriffs and juries 'and treating and entertaining them, and drinking themselves, and other such unjust, unnecessary expenses'.[6] In 1730 George Legh presented a bill for £380 3s. 10d. to the Weaver Commissioners for his expenses from 1726 to 1727. This was almost entirely for parliamentary activity. Legh drew up the petition from the Cheesemongers for 13s. 4d. and for the gentlemen and freeholders of Cheshire for 10s. He drew up a case for the Bill and had 400 printed for presentation to Members. He paid the doorkeepers of the Houses 10s. for distributing bills and cases.[7]

These petitions, which invariably formed a large item in

---

[1] The agitation for a Weaver Act lasted from 1699 to 1720.
[2] Cheshire MSS., River Weaver Commissioners, 1721–31; *Reasons Humbly Offered by the Trustees of Richard Vernon.*
[3] Wadsworth and Mann, *Cotton Trade*, p. 215.
[4] Beverley MSS., Beck Accounts.   [5] 6 Anne, c. 70.
[6] Toulmin, *Taunton*, pp. 395–6.
[7] Cheshire MSS., River Weaver Commissioners, 1721–31.

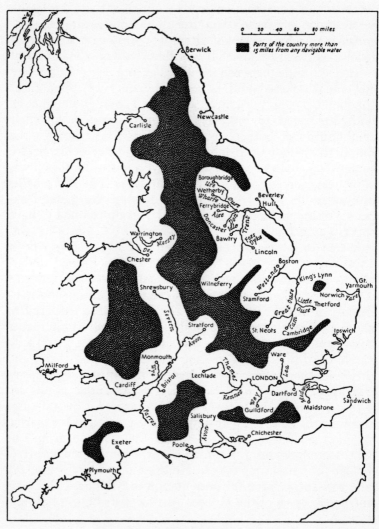

II. NAVIGABLE RIVERS, 1660–1700
Only the navigable parts of rivers are shown.

the promoters' expenses of a contested enterprise, are a valuable source of information on the reasons for and against an undertaking, but they can only be used with caution. They were not always a spontaneous expression of local feeling. On January 13th, 1696, Monmouth, in petitioning against the Bill for the Wye and Lug navigation, declared, 'the Mayor of the City of Hereford hath clandestinely prevailed upon William Williams, a poor Boatman, and several other poor men of the Town of Monmouth to subscribe a Paper, purporting their approbation of making the Rivers Wye and Lugg navigable'.[1] Similarly, in 1714, the High Sheriff of Derby and the gentlemen and merchants of Wirksworth declared that, among the petitions against the navigation of the Trent, 'there is One clandestinely obtained from some private Tradesmen in the Petitioners' Neighbourhood of Wirk-worth by Insinuations imposed on them'.[2] Here it is impossible to tell who was lying, but in other cases it is apparent that coercion and influence were at work.

In January 1723 Doncaster was nearing the end of a quarter of a century's agitation for a Bill for the navigation of the Don, when a petition against that Bill appeared in the town itself. The Corporation immediately investigated this unwelcome appearance. They found that some had signed the petition because they thought that the Bill would be prejudicial to their land or their market, that some had been unwarily drawn into signing it, whilst others had been actively coerced by a Dr. Eratt and a Mr. Cooke. The prime opposer was Dr. Eratt, whose interest in the matter is not clear. He had persuaded some to sign on the ground that their land would be prejudiced. Robert Ambler, a book-keeper to Mr. Simpson, refused to sign, and was told by Eratt that he was worth nothing. Worse still, Eratt had told Simpson that he would hinder Ambler's son and daughter from advancing in their trade and that Ambler himself was a 'vile pittiful fellow'. Robert Heaton, who also refused to sign, was informed by Eratt that he supposed he expected some benefit from his houses by the river, but he, Eratt, would see that he had none. Not unnaturally, Dr. Eratt's behaviour was

---

[1] *J. H. of C.* xi. 389; the petition referred to is in ibid. 387.
[2] Ibid. xvii. 609.

voted 'scandalous, vexatious and malicious', and it was
decided that members threatened with prosecution by Dr.
Eratt should be defended at the charge of the Corporation.
Then, with characteristic intolerance, the Corporation resolved
to take counsel's opinion to see whether members who had
signed the petition could not be fined or disfranchised.
But there the matter seems to have stopped.[1] It was a bad
case of coercion, but perhaps others found themselves in the
dilemma of 'Mr. Whitaker, senior, of the Angel', who signed
the petition for navigation, 'and as to signing the second
petition, he would not have done it, but that as he is in
publick business, he was loath to disoblige a great many
gentlemen who were opposed to the same'.[2]

Turning from the town to the country, the struggle for
the Act for the navigation of the Weaver gives a good, if
incomplete, picture of how the opposition was organized.
The Bill was opposed by the great landowners and their
tenants, who were also land carriers, and by certain of the
proprietors of the salt works. They were led by Sir Thomas
Aston, M.P. for Chester. On December 8th, 1709, Peter
Shakerley, Tory M.P. for Chester,[3] wrote from Westminster
to Aston, saying that he was getting support against the Bill.
He suggested that the best method of opposition was to
prevent subscriptions in the county. Lawton, from whose
pits coal was brought by land, should be written to, as well
as the Knights of the Shire, to oppose the Bill. Petitions
were to be obtained from the farmers who acted as land
carriers and from those who paid poor rates in all the town-
ships. 'The more Petitions the better (for one Petition will
not be so advantageous) but the words of each must be
varied', Shakerley concluded, and enclosed a draft petition
to show the necessary wording.[4] The opponents of the Bill
wrote to the gentlemen and inhabitants of Bucklow and
Macclesfield Hundreds pointing out how detrimental the Act
would be to their interests and desiring them to concur in
a petition against it.[5] Shakerley himself wrote to the Justices

---

[1] *Doncaster Records*, iv. 189–92.   [2] Ibid., p. 191.

[3] Hemingway, *Chester*, p. 207; for a pedigree of the family see Ormerod, *Chester*,
iii. 152.

[4] 'Weaver Navigation, 1699–1720', Add. MSS. 36914, ff. 34–5.

[5] Ibid., f. 20.

of the Peace and the Grand Jury of the Quarter Sessions at Northwich to prevent them giving a petition in favour of the Bill, and pointed out that the promoters had no intention of bringing the navigation up to Northwich itself.[1] On February 4th, 1710, Shakerley wrote to Aston pointing out that the promoters had printed their case. This was 'very Fallacious', but it would influence unthinking people and must be answered. He suggested answers which were to be printed and sent to Members.[2] These methods were apparently successful, for in 1711 the Bill was defeated.[3]

On the revival of the enterprise in 1720,[4] Charles Cholmondeley, one of the chief opponents, attempted to prove that the petition, upon which leave to bring in the Bill had been based, had been altered after it was signed.[5] When this proved unsuccessful, he wrote to Sir Thomas Aston, on February 5th, 1720, suggesting 'some little Subscription among ourselves' to carry on the opposition.[6] But Aston was incapacitated. 'The Condition I am in at present, by the Return of my Gout on Monday last', he wrote in reply, 'makes me uncapable of doing any Service in the present affair. Having neither Rest nor Ease, Day or Night.' He did not think there was much hope of a subscription unless it could be computed what the charge would amount to and how many would subscribe. None would subscribe 'to be at the charge of Opposition at Random'. He was not unwilling to contribute himself, 'but I would see how those will tax themselves who are likely to be the greatest Sufferers'.[7] He loved his neighbours so well, he concluded, that he would at any time subscribe more than the damage he would receive.[8] This time the opposition was in vain. The opponents were singularly unfortunate in their choice of witnesses. One 'young Lawley . . . was Sett first to the barr and terrible work hee made'; he refused to produce the map, 'butt talked idly of things of his own knowledge'. Neither

[1] Ibid., f. 40.   [2] Ibid., f. 44.   [3] *J. H. of C.* xvi. 538.
[4] A Bill was introduced in 1715, but it did not get beyond the committee stage. Hughes, *Studies in Administration and Finance*, pp. 260–1.
[5] 'Weaver Navigation, 1699–1720', Add. MSS. 36914, f. 63; *J. H. of C.* xix. 297.
[6] 'Weaver Navigation, 1699–1720', Add. MSS. 36914, f. 73.
[7] Ibid., f. 74.   [8] Ibid., f. 74 dorso.

he nor 'Old Lawley' would speak to be heard and the
Speaker had what they said repeated 'and was really very
angry'. 'In short', concluded Aston's correspondent, 'I
never saw two such fooles sett upp for wittneses in my life.'
He considered that they had quite altered the disposition of
the House.[1] But it was probably much more the speculative
atmosphere of the time that caused the Bill to pass than either
the incompetence of the witnesses or Aston's gout.[2]

These activities, besides showing the form of opposition,
do bring out the economic importance of the Member of
Parliament. Much has been written about his constitu-
tional position and his political activities, but little about the
part he played in the economic development of his country.
It is true his power was for ill as well as good. He could,
and did, oppose undertakings which were subsequently successful, but he was, after all, the representative of a certain
body of local opinion and had in some measure to conform
to that opinion. On March 1st, 1690, Thomas Foley wrote
to Sir Edward Harley: 'My father yesterday heard that at
Harold's Inn there had been a meeting of many freeholders,
and it was there passed not to choose any one who was for
making Wye navigable.' He considered this resolution due
to the influence of the Earl of Kent, whose ironworks were
threatened by the intended navigation.[3] In the election of
1710 the opponents of the Weaver navigation, dissatisfied
with the attitude taken by the county members, Crewe and
Booth, put up as candidates two of their number, Sir George
Warburton and Charles Cholmondeley, both of whom were
elected.[4] Similarly in Derbyshire, where the navigation of
the Derwent was favoured, it was said, 'whoever stood for
parliament-man and gave hopes for effecting of this, has
comonly been chosen'.[5] Peter Shakerley might oppose the
Weaver navigation, but he did not consider it inconsistent

---

[1] 'Weaver Navigation, 1699–1720', Add. MSS. 36914, f. 79.
[2] Hughes, *Studies in Administration and Finance*, p. 396, points out that the
opposition was weakened by a partial fusion of interest between the rock and white
salt traders.
[3] *H.M.C. Portland*, iii. 445.
[4] Hughes, *Studies in Administration and Finance*, p. 260.
[5] Houghton, *Collection for the Improvement of Husbandry and Trade*, ed. 1727,
i. 108.

to support the Douglas Bill at the same time. On January 20th, 1713, he wrote to George Kenyon enclosing a draft of a petition, 'as I conceive it will be propper enough for leave to bring in the Bill, it being signed by such Justices of Peace, gentlemen, and freeholders as had estates adjacent to the said river, from Wigan to Hesketh Bank'.[1] George Kenyon himself was Tory Member for Wigan from 1710 to 1714 and one of the Mersey and Irwell undertakers of 1721.[2]

It must indeed have facilitated the passage of Bills when the undertakers themselves were Members of Parliament. The Wye Act of 1696 included among its undertakers,[3] Sir Thomas Coningsby, M.P. for Leominster,[4] the Hon. Paul Foley, Speaker of the House of Commons,[5] Sir Edward Harley and his son Robert, both of whom had been associated with Herefordshire and Radnorshire as Members.[6] But Members more often acted as intermediaries between the promoters and the House. At York, in 1725, Edward Thompson, one of the City's Members, appears actually to have proposed the navigation scheme for the Ouse,[7] and he was certainly looked upon to defend the City's rights in the river.[8] Without support from Members, navigation schemes would naturally never have gone through the Houses, but that support was not the passive 'Aye', but the more active intervention of men interested in the economic development of their constituencies.[9]

It remains to be seen upon what grounds the promoters and opponents of these undertakings based their arguments in the innumerable petitions, statements of cases, and pamphlets which they issued. The supporters of improved river navigation based their case fundamentally on the necessity for cheaper carriage of goods and particularly of bulky goods. The City of Hereford in 1696 declared that cheaper carriage was essential, for goods were then 'mere Drugs in the Proprietors' Hands'.[10] Malmesbury[11] and Bristol[12] supported the navigation of the Stroudwater for the cheaper carriage of

---

[1] *H.M.C. Kenyon*, p. 450. [2] *V.C.H. Lancs.* v. 31.
[3] 7/8 Will. III, c. 14, sec. 2. [4] *D.N.B.* [5] Ibid. [6] Ibid.
[7] York MSS. House Book, 42, f. 61. [8] Ibid., f. 225.
[9] 'Don Navigation, 1697', Stowe MSS. 747, f. 84.
[10] *J. H. of C.* xi. 389. [11] Ibid. xxi. 509. [12] Ibid., p. 514.

coal; Wellington,[1] Boscombe, and Culmstock[2] supported that of the Tone for the same reason. The lead merchants and ironmongers of London petitioned for the Derwent Bill because of the high cost of land carriage of such 'ponderous commodities' as lead, iron, and millstones.[3] In 1740 it was said that the improvement of the Medway was essential for the cheaper carriage of timber for the Navy, for the excessive price of land carriage had caused people to grub up their trees and convert to tillage.[4] The Aire and Calder navigation Bill of 1699 was favoured for the cheaper carriage of cloth. The Company of Weavers of Kendal declared that they sent their cloth to London at a carriage rate of £1 8s. per pack; with the Aire and Calder navigation this would be reduced to 16s.[5] Even the opponents of this Bill admitted that it was customary to send cloth from Leeds to Hull by way of York and that the cost was 6s. per £100 worth of cloth by land from Leeds to York and 1s. 6d. by water from York to Hull.[6] These examples could be multiplied almost indefinitely,[7] for here the promoters had a genuine case. Even their opponents did not deny the fact that the land carriage of a ton of salt from Droitwich to Worcester, about 7 miles, was 5s., while the water carriage from Worcester to Bristol, about 77 miles, cost the same;[8] or that a ton of the same commodity cost 8s. from Northwich to Frodsham Bridge by land and only 3s. by water.[9]

Closely connected with this demand for cheaper carriage was the plea that river transport would preserve the highways. This was the dominant note in the petitions of Westbury, Hungerford, Bradford, and Trowbridge for the navigation of the Kennet in 1708 to 1709.[10] On March 24th, 1721, the lord and tenants of the manor of Rixton declared that if the Mersey and Irwell were made navigable they would save on the highway charges more than the value of the lands to be cut.[11] On the other hand, the Wey Act of 1671 granted Guildford a toll of 1d. per ton, as the highways to

1 *J. H. of C.* xiv. 402.   2 Ibid., p. 423.   3 Ibid. xi. 416; xii. 485.
4 Ibid. xxiii. 469.   5 Ibid. xii. 145.
6 *Reasons against the Bill for making the Rivers Ayre and Calder . . . Navigable.*
7 *J. H. of C.* xii. 76, 80, 485; xiv. 462, 467; xvi. 66, 69; xviii. 71; xix. 414, 495.
8 'Weaver Navigation, 1699–1720', Add. MSS. 36914, f. 10.
9 Ibid., f. 119.   10 *J. H. of C.* xvi. 53, 60, 62.   11 Ibid. xix. 493.

the town would be damaged by carts coming to the river.[1] The opponents of the Douglas Bill declared, in 1719, that the roads 'which lie near the River, will be much more cut, if this Navigation is carri'd on, than they are at present', by the carts and carriages bringing coal to the water side.[2] This was at least a tacit admission that the navigation would be well supported.

In the third place, the promoters of navigation made some attempt to gain the support of the agricultural interest. It was pointed out, not only that trade would be encouraged and so rents increased,[3] but also that land carriage was a precarious occupation incompatible with the best forms of husbandry.[4] 'Hinderly' men were said to owe for their oxen and to use many acres in feeding transport oxen which were, in any case, spoiled by land carriage. They had not the time to spread manure or till their land, and even hired others to do their ploughing.[5] On the other hand, it was shown that cheaper carriage of coal by water would lead to more lime being burned for use on the land,[6] a process which was said to have increased the value of the Hundreds of Wormelow and Greytree by £4,000 per annum.[7] This improvement of the land was the sole pretext for an Act of 1721 dealing with the Eden. The preamble declared:

that several Vast Tracts of Ground lying waste and uncultivated for want of water-carriage of coals, Lime and other Manure for that Purpose, renders it impossible for the said Inhabitants to burn Lime sufficient to lay on and improve the same, the Improvement whereof would employ, relieve and be very advantageous to the Poor, who, at present, are a very great Burthen to the Parishes near and adjoining to the said River.[8]

The provision of employment was a quite frequent point raised in favour of navigation. Petty considered as one way of employing the poor, 'The cutting and scowring of Rivers

---

[1] Manning and Bray, *Surrey*, iii, App. iii, lvii.
[2] *An Answer to the Reasons for Making the River Douglas Navigable.*
[3] *J. H. of C.* xi. 409.
[4] 'Derwent Navigation', Stowe MSS. 818, f. 85.
[5] 'Medway Navigation, 1600', Add. MSS. 34218, f. 39; *A Short Demonstration, That Navigation to Bedford is for the Benefit of Bedfordshire.*
[6] *J. H. of C.* xiv. 423.
[7] 'Wye Navigation, 1622–62', Add. MSS. 11052, f. 95.
[8] 8 Geo. I, c. 14, sec. 1.

into Navigable',[1] while Southwell thought that malefactors
and idle persons might be put to work on his canals, so
that there would be less danger 'from the distractions
and tumults, which may happen among poor and mutinous
people upon the want of commodities of necessary and daily
use'.[2] In 1700 Bury St. Edmunds favoured the navigation
of the Lark partly on the grounds that it would employ the
poor.[3] But when Edward Forde suggested that his project
for bringing a navigable river to London would find work
for 'a great multitude of poor labourers',[4] his opponent, Sir
Walter Roberts, answered in words that have a distinctly
modern ring, 'to set great multitudes of Labourers on work
is not simply good in it self, but quite contrary, unless the
Work which they are employed in, be good for the Common
Wealth'.[5]

Finally, the promoters appealed to the State on the
grounds of security; increased river navigation would provide
'additionall nurseryes for seamen'.[6] The opponents of the
Douglas navigation might declare, 'a Navigation of this Sort
cannot be accounted a Nursery for Seamen; nor can a few
Towers of flat-bottomed Boats and Coal-barges be of any
very great Service in the Navy',[7] but others pointed out that
the seamen, navigators, and watermen of the Thames 'doe
their Prince and Country often serve',[8] and that more would
be available if water transport were increased.[9] Nottingham
held that the navigation of the Derwent would not produce
one able seaman in twenty years,[10] but this was a minority
opinion.[11] The fact that river boats did not put out to sea
was held to be a disadvantage for training seamen in some
quarters,[12] but in others it was felt that men would learn

[1] Petty, *Works*, i. 29. Cf. Mandeville, *An Essay on Charity*, p. 364.
[2] Birch, *Royal Society*, iii. 211.
[3] *J. H. of C.* xiii. 62.
[4] Forde, *A Design for bringing a Navigable River*, ed. 1720, p. 4.
[5] Roberts, *An Answer to Mr Forde's Book*, ed. 1720, p. 17.
[6] 'Concerning making Rivers Navigable', Rawl. MSS. A 477.
[7] *An Answer to the Reasons for Making the River Douglas Navigable*.
[8] Taylor, *Thame Isis*, p. 16.
[9] Yarranton, *England's Improvement*, i. 140; Mathew, *Of the Opening of Rivers*,
p. 3.
[10] *J. H. of C.* xi. 38.
[11] Ibid. xi. 409, 499; xix. 589,
[12] Lloyd, *Papers relating to the . . . Wye and Lug*, p. 23.

rowing, sailing, and steering and 'their bodies are inured to the water, and they are not Sea-sick as other men be'.[1]

Against these alleged advantages were arrayed the counter-claims of a host of vested interests, of which the demands of certain towns that their economic life should not be jeopardized were perhaps the strongest. York, together with the towns dependent upon her and the seamen and merchants relying upon her trade, opposed the Aire and Calder Bills on the ground that any improvement of these rivers would draw away the tide from the Ouse.[2] The Don navigation was opposed on the same grounds,[3] for there the Dutch Cut had already taken away some of that tide, which had once been the cause of York's commercial greatness.[4] Bawtry opposed the navigation of the Derwent, for that would ruin its position as the chief town to which goods were brought by land from Derbyshire to be shipped down the Idle and so into the Trent.[5]

More interesting still is the opposition which came from the towns on those parts of the rivers which were already navigable. Thus Reading opposed the Kennet Bill in 1708,[6] Liverpool the earliest of the Mersey Bills,[7] and Monmouth the Wye navigation because corn was brought there on horseback and the market would be destroyed.[8] The reason for this type of opposition is clearly expressed in a petition from Ipswich against the Orwell Bill of 1719, 'for that the Importation and Exportation of Goods and Merchandizes, which has hitherto been at Ipswich, will, in a great measure, be carried to Stowmarket'.[9] In other words, a town which had hitherto been a market at the head of navigation might become a mere place through which boats passed without

---

[1] *A Short Demonstration, That Navigation to Bedford is for the Benefit of Bedfordshire.*

[2] *J. H. of C.* xii. 76, 98, 101, 126, 146.   [3] Ibid. xxiii. 455–6.

[4] Drake, *Eboracum*, p. 231; Sellers, 'York in the Sixteenth and Seventeenth Centuries', *E.H.R.* xii. 438. The opposition to the Don was neither consistent nor unanimous. On January 25th, 1723, seven people, including one alderman of York, said that they would not be prejudiced by the Don, 'If the Coales and other goods comeing from thence to this City be Locke Duty free' (York MSS., House Book 42, f. 30 dorso). In 1726 York petitioned for that navigation (*J. H. of L.* xii. 666).

[5] *J. H. of C.* xi. 410.   [6] Ibid. xvi. 53.   [7] *Liverpool Records*, i. 241.

[8] 'Survey of Wye and Lug', Add. MSS. 21567, f. 3 dorso; *J. H. of C.* xi. 389.

[9] *J. H. of C.* xix. 196.

stopping. Thus Maldon, in opposing the proposed navigation to Chelmsford in 1733, calculated that the 2,000 chaldrons of coals which went to Chelmsford and beyond used 1,500 wagons which spent 1s. each at Maldon, or £75 per annum altogether; the 600 tons of other goods used 400 wagons at 1s. per head, or £20 in all; the 2,600 tons of meal used 1,900 wagons at 1s., or £95 in all, making a total spent in the town of £190 per annum. There were also advantages to tradesmen from people attending the wagons to buy. With improved navigation the town might lose this, 'For it is presumed that the Bargemen who are to be imploy'd in it, will of course bring all their Provisions with them sufficient for each Voyage'. The borough would also lose a great part of its tolls by land and water, which were worth £110 per annum, and especially those from wharfage, for the goods would be unloaded directly from hoys to barges or vice versa.[1]

These towns did not content themselves with petitioning, but entered into a more active opposition, for which there was a financial side just as there was for promotion. When Liverpool opposed the Dee navigation in 1733, the Corporation employed a solicitor who sent in a bill for £240 15s.[2] The case of Nottingham may be taken as illustrative of the lengths to which corporations would go when they felt their interests at stake. Throughout the seventeenth century the Trent was navigable as far as that town, and the Corporation resolved that neither it nor its tributaries should be navigable above the Trent Bridges. In 1675 the Corporation began its long opposition by voting £10 to retain Counsel against the project for making the Trent navigable.[3] Twenty years later Derby took up its scheme for improving the navigation of the Derwent and began what was to prove a quarter of a century's almost continuous agitation. On December 16th, 1695, therefore, the Aldermen, the members of the Council, and burgesses of Nottingham were ordered to meet 'att Mistris Johnson's . . . to consult and draw up reasons to be

---

[1] *The Intended Navigation of the Chelmer.*
[2] *Liverpool Records,* ii. 92.
[3] *Nottingham Records,* v. 319. There is no other trace of this project, unless it were for the Derwent and not the Trent, *J. H. of C.* ix. 368.

presented to the Parlyament' against the Bill for the Derwent.[1]
On January 7th, 1696, these reasons were embodied in a
petition to the Commons, in which it was maintained that
the Bill would lessen the trade of Nottingham, Leicester,
and Loughborough, would ruin the Trent as a navigation,
lower the rents of lands, impoverish the land carriers, and
not breed one seaman in twenty years.[2] A fortnight later
the tradesmen and inhabitants of Nottingham proposed to
contribute a third of the cost of opposition, but the Corporation declared that if they would make this one-half, then
they, the Corporation, would pay the other half.[3] The Bill,
however, got no farther than the second reading.[4]

On the revival of the project in 1699, the Corporation
took still more drastic action. They agreed that all boats
from Wilne should be stopped at Trent Bridges, 'the said
River Trent beeinge Navigable noe further than the Trent
Bridges'. The arches of the bridge were to be chained and
stopped up 'to prevent the passage of the said Boates', and
any suits resulting from this were to be borne at the cost
of the Corporation. Three men were appointed to take the
names of persons who manned boats or haled, 'in order to
prosecute them for their trespassinge upon the Towne's
ground'.[5] On February 2nd, 1699, the Corporation sealed
a petition for the Commons and decided to write to Chesterfield, Mansfield, Warsop, Blythe, Retford, Lincoln, Boston,
Hull, and Newark for others,[6] but of this there was no need,
for on the 20th the Bill was rejected.[7]

Three years later Derby again petitioned for its Bill and
the Corporation of Nottingham resumed its opposition.
Members waited upon the Earl of Chesterfield and Sir
Thomas Willoughby and wrote to their representatives in
Parliament 'to use their utmost Endeavour to oppose the
Bill'. On November 30th, 1702, it was ordered 'that Mr.
Mayor and the severall Aldermen do take as many as they
think fitt along with them and go through their respective
wards and collect what money they can towards opposing

1 *Nottingham Records*, v. 391.
3 *Nottingham Records*, v. 391.
5 *Nottingham Records*, v. 398.
7 *J. H. of C.* xii. 519.

2 *J. H. of C.* xi. 381.
4 *J. H. of C.* xi. 377.
6 Ibid., p. 399 n.

the River Derwent'.[1] At the same time the Corporation voted
£40 for the same purpose.[2] A petition was sent to the Lords,[3]
and Mr. Alderman Smith and a Mr. Green were to go up
to London to prove it.[4] They, or their Counsel, Dodd,[5]
may have proved their case, for on February 1st, 1703, the
Bill was rejected by the Lords.[6] The Corporation still continued to collect funds and decided to wait upon the Earl of
Scarsdale 'about his bearing a proportionate charge'.[7] But
the navigation project lapsed for some time, and on February
11th, 1709, it was resolved that any money left over from
the opposition funds should be paid towards the cost of the
new fire engine.[8]

Five years later a new complication arose. In 1699 an Act
had been passed for improving the navigation from Wilden
Ferry to Burton-on-Trent.[9] This had not been wholly effective and so, in 1714, an attempt was made to get another Act
to make the former one more efficient.[10] Nottingham at once
voted £50 to oppose the Bill, for 'the Intent of the same
appears plainly to be to Ingrosse the Navigacion and Mono-
polize Trade between two or three persons to the prejudice
of the County in General and this Town in particular'.[11]
The Bill failed to pass. In 1717 the Corporation resumed its
opposition to the Derwent Bill by voting £100 to oppose it,[12]
but this was only to postpone the inevitable, and three years
later the Bill passed.[13] Finally, in 1742, the Corporation
voted £50 to tradesmen and navigators if they would spend
twice as much in opposing the Bill for making the Newark
branch of the Trent navigable, and they gave leave for people
interested to inspect such records and papers of the Corporation 'as may be of use in such Opposition'.[14] This Bill, too,
failed to pass. Thus for more than half a century Nottingham consistently opposed all attempts to improve the navigation of the Trent or its tributary, the Derwent. This town,
'one of the most pleasant and beautiful' in England, re-

[1] *Nottingham Records*, vi. 15.
[2] Ibid.
[3] *J. H. of L.* xvii. 246.
[4] *Nottingham Records*, vi. 16.
[5] *H.M.C. House of Lords*, N.S. v. 181.
[6] *J. H. of L.* xvii. 264.
[7] *Nottingham Records*, vi. 17.
[8] Ibid., p. 44.
[9] 10 Will. III, c. 26.
[10] *J. H. of C.* xvii. 607.
[11] *Nottingham Records*, vi. 60–1.
[12] Ibid., p. 63.
[13] 6 Geo. I, c. 27.
[14] *Nottingham Records*, vi. 175.

nowned for its horse racing and excellent ale,[1] dissipated its energy and its money in an attempt to maintain an economic exclusiveness worthy of a medieval gild.

Next in importance to the towns in their opposition to river improvements stood the agricultural interest. The petitions from the great landowners and their tenants reveal two main lines of hostility, the land and the market. It was held that the bargemen or their 'halers' would trample on the standing corn and grass and steal sheep, rabbits, and wood as they passed through the country-side.[2] If horses were used instead of men to tow the boats, then they would eat up the meadows.[3] More prevalent still was the view that river improvements necessitated raising the level of the water, with the result that the surroundings lands would be flooded. There was, of course, no objection to winter flooding, which was a recognized method of enriching land. The Bill for the Itchen of 1714 stipulated that the undertakers should make provision for watering the meadows in winter.[4] The destruction of weirs on the Wye was opposed because they caused that flooding which was essential to the land.[5] But flooding at other times was a different matter. The richest meadow lay along the river banks, and without it the rest of the farm was almost valueless. Charles Cholmondeley, in opposing the Weaver navigation, declared that he would lose meadow value £5,000 at 25 years' purchase and the loss to the farms would be £900 per annum;[6] it was impossible to dispose of the uplands of the farms without meadow to go with them.[7] There was doubtless much exaggeration in these estimates, but the fear of flooding was a constant pretext for opposition.[8]

---

[1] Defoe, *Tour*, ii. 547–50.

[2] 'Weaver Navigation, 1699–1720', Add. MSS. 36914, f. 95; *J. H. of C.* xiv. 81; xix. 479.   [3] *J. H. of C.* xix. 196.

[4] *Bromley Parliamentary Papers*, iii, no. 102. The Act for the Worsley, 10 Geo. II, c. 9, stipulated that the floodgates for flooding the land should be opened on request from Sept. 29th to March 25th.

[5] 'Wye Navigation, 1622–62', Add. MSS. 11052, f. 101.

[6] 'Weaver Navigation, 1699–1720', Add. MSS. 36914, f. 119 dorso.

[7] *J. H. of C.* xix. 252.

[8] Ibid. xv. 496; xvi. 534; xx. 140; *Reasons against the Bill for Making the River Douglas Navigable*. Somewhat similar objections were raised by landowners against canals and railways, Jackman, *Development of Transportation*, i. 396, ii. 497–9; Knowles, *Industrial and Commercial Revolutions*, p. 256.

With a fear for the land went a fear of increased competition in the local market with the opening up of new inland trade routes. It was in vain for Houghton to declare 'Have not the going down streams the advantage of the going up'?[1] and for Yarranton to point out that corn in Leicestershire was cheap, 'having no Navigable River near to carry it away'[2] and that the same applied to Warwickshire before the Avon was made navigable, where farmers 'were lockt up in the Inlands'.[3] Those who depended upon a good price for their corn felt their local monopoly threatened by river transport. Thus the gentlemen and landowners of Chippenham opposed the Bristol Avon navigation because it would bring in corn, butter, and cheese from remote parts and cause prices and rents to fall, besides discouraging the breeding of horses and throwing servants in husbandry out of employment.[4] The Grand Jury of the Assizes at Salisbury declared that corn brought from Bristol by horseback already flooded their market,[5] while the gentlemen and freeholders of Somerset pointed out that the value of land in Wales was low and therefore the competition with corn from such land unfair.[6] The case of the Avon was said to be different from that of the Wye and Lug where an outlet for corn was wanted,[7] and even the Wye and Lug undertaking was opposed because it would cause a glut of corn at Bristol.[8] Everywhere there was a feeling that corn would be brought in at cheaper rates than those at which the neighbouring farmer could afford to produce.[9]

Closely allied with the agricultural interest was that of the land carriers, who saw their employment threatened. The land carrier was necessarily something of a farmer just as the village shopkeeper to-day, who still uses a flat cart in preference to a motor van, has land upon which to feed his horse. More important still, the farmer was often a land carrier. Thus the

---

[1] Houghton, *Collection for the Improvement of Husbandry and Trade*, ed. 1727, ii. 286.

[2] Yarranton, *England's Improvement*, i. 117.　　　　　[3] Ibid., p. 123.

[4] *J. H. of C.* xi. 495.　　　　[5] Ibid., p. 514.　　　　[6] Ibid. xvii. 134.

[7] *The Case of making the River Avon . . . Navigable.*

[8] Lloyd, *Papers relating to the . . . Wye and Lug*, p. 23.

[9] *J. H. of C.* xi. 440; *A Short Demonstration, That Navigation to Bedford is for the Benefit of Bedfordshire.* The market argument was used by landowners near London against the turnpikes, Jackman, *Development of Transportation*, i. 413.

farmers and freeholders of Bucklow Hundred opposed the Weaver Bill because they employed themselves and their servants in carrying coals in summer, with which they supplied the wiches in winter,[1] while the farmers of Frodsham declared that land carriage alone enabled them to pay their rents.[2] This land carriage was valued at £17,000 per annum:[3] if the figure is anything more than a plausible guess, then the need for navigation is apparent. Yet, of all the petitions against navigation Bills, those from the land carriers were perhaps the most genuine, for they represent the protest of a class whose livelihood was threatened.[4] Some land carriers might, indeed, find employment in bringing goods to the river itself, others, with their horses, might become towers of boats, but many would suffer from the dislocation that inevitably follows the break-down of a monopoly.

Finally, a host of minor vested interests raised their voices. The shipmasters and carpenters of Stockwith, who owned, sailed, or made the ships on the Trent, protested against the navigation of the Derwent[5] and the Don.[6] The wharf-owners and the proprietors of waterworks at Reading opposed the Kennet navigation[7] and their opposition was supported by one Finch, a pensioner of a turnpike on the Reading road.[8] The innkeepers of Derby thought that the navigation of the Derwent would lower the price of corn and the farmers would therefore no longer attend the market;[9] the Company of Innholders of Bristol felt that the Avon navigation would stop people attending at Bristol to buy and sell.[10] Lastly, the millowners saw in the destruction of their weirs the destruction of the mill itself, and they, as in the case of the Bristol Avon, were supported by the bakers[11] and mealmen.[12] George Blagrave, who opposed the Kennet Bill in 1715, owned St. Giles, Minster, and Calcat Mills, which had cost

---

[1] *J. H. of C.* xviii. 169.   [2] Ibid. xix. 260.
[3] 'Weaver Navigation, 1699–1720', Add. MSS. 36914, f. 123.
[4] *J. H. of C.* xii. 414, 434–5.   [5] Ibid. xi. 416.
[6] Ibid. xx. 462.   [7] Ibid. xviii. 116, 125.
[8] *Answers to the (pretended) Reasons, Humbly Offer'd for making the River Kennet a Free River.*
[9] *J. H. of C.* xi. 449; and cf. xix. 234.   [10] Ibid. xiii. 92.
[11] Ibid. xi. 514.   [12] Ibid. xiii. 96.

him £3,000 and were let for £300 per annum. He, like others,[1] begged for a clause granting him compensation if the mills were damaged.[2]

How effective all these petitions were, either in assisting or hindering the passage of Bills, is a doubtful question. The long struggles necessary to obtain some of the Acts show that there was effective opposition somewhere, but the mere weight of petitions against a Bill was not necessarily sufficient to get it rejected. The Bill for the navigation of the Avon from Bristol to Bath in 1714 had sixteen petitions against it and only one in support of it, yet it passed.[3] These Acts, which were passed either because of or in spite of the petitions, were all similar in outline. They usually appointed the undertakers, who might be one man, as Henry Ashley who was to make the Lark navigable,[4] or a body of men as those for the Tone in 1699,[5] or a corporation as Bath,[6] or a company as that of the Cutlers of Hallamshire.[7] Sometimes the Acts merely stipulated who should appoint the undertakers, as the Chancellor and heads of Colleges, the Justices in Quarter Sessions and the Corporation of Cambridge for the Cam,[8] or the Lord Chancellor or the Lord Keeper of the Great Seal for the Wiltshire Avon.[9] In one case, that of the Nen, the commissioners were to appoint the original undertakers.[10] That was not the usual business of the commissioners, who were named in the Act and who included the chief gentry of the neighbourhood. Theirs was a work of general supervision. If the undertakers failed to agree with the proprietors of lands and mills over compensation, then the commissioners were to assess it. If their arbitration were refused, then the Sheriff should impanel a jury whose decision should be final. In some cases the commissioners had no power to determine charges without a jury,[11] in others there was no provision for a jury at all,[12] but here the Act might lay down the maximum number of years' purchase which might be

---

[1] J. H. of C. xix. 484; xxi. 509.
[2] Ibid. xviii. 126.
[3] 10 Anne, c. 2.
[4] 11 Will. III, c. 22, sec. 1.
[5] 10 Will. III, c. 8, sec. 1.
[6] 10 Anne, c. 2, sec. 1.
[7] 12 Geo. I, c. 38, sec. 1.
[8] 1 Anne S. 2, c. 11, sec. 1.
[9] 16/17 Car. II. P. A. Manby, *Collection of Statutes*, p. 271.
[10] 13 Anne, c. 19, sec. 2.
[11] 6 Geo. I, c. 27, sec. 3.
[12] 16/17 Car. II, P. A. Manby, *Collection of Statutes*, p. 271.

granted as compensation.[1] The commissioners had the power to fill up their ranks, but the new commissioners had usually to have property of annual value from £100[2] to £200[3] in the county wherein their duties lay. There was always a large body of commissioners, but the quorum was commonly about seven.

There is some evidence of the work of these commissioners, who in some ways resembled Turnpike Trustees.[4] The commissioners under the Douglas Act of 1720[5] seem first to have met on September 6th, 1738, at 'The Sign of the Wheat Sheafe', in Ormskirk, when they appointed fourteen new members of their Commission.[6] On March 12th, 1740, they met in Wigan and appointed two new undertakers in place of those named in the Act and drew up a warrant for the sheriff to empanel a jury to assess compensation. The jury reported their assessment on April 15th, 1740, and this was accepted and ordered to be paid by the undertakers. A new jury was ordered to be empanelled on February 23rd, 1741, but apparently never met. From then until 1752 the commissioners merely met and adjourned.[7] The Weaver Commissioners do not appear to have been much more active. From 1721 to 1727 they did nothing but elect new commissioners, but on October 25th, 1727, they elected John Daniel as an undertaker. About a year later they chose Philip Egerton, Roger Wilbraham, and Henry Wright as undertakers and, upon their resignation on October 7th, 1730, they substituted Thomas Eyre and Thomas Patten. Not until 1731 were they settling claims for compensation for trees and land cut.[8] From 1733 to 1741 they did nothing but audit accounts and elect new commissioners.[9]

With larger undertakings the commissioners' duties were perhaps more onerous. On January 2nd, 1736, the Dee Commissioners met at the Shire Hall in the Castle at Chester.

[1] 10 Geo. II, c. 33, sec. 4.
[2] 10 Will. III, c. 26, sec. 7.　　　　　　　　　[3] Ibid., c. 25, sec. 3.
[4] Jackman, *Development of Transportation*, i. 70, 433.
[5] 6 Geo. I, c. 28.
[6] Wigan Public Library MSS., Minute Book of the Douglas Commissioners, f. 1.
[7] Ibid., ff. 2–7.
[8] Cheshire MSS., River Weaver Commissioners, 1721–31.
[9] Ibid. 1733–41.

They received a report from six of their number, who had viewed the roads flooded by the navigation works, and ordered the undertakers to open certain drains and watercourses. They heard two witnesses in support of the claim of John Leach, John Dutton and Peter Machilt, joint tenants, who alleged damage value £25 to their lands, for which they could not agree with the undertakers, and ordered that amount to be paid if there were no appeal within six months. They granted £39 12s. 2d. damages to John Prescott, lessee of a warehouse at Chester, which represented the cost of carriage of cheese to where it could be shipped, as the navigation works had diverted the water so that it was impossible for boats to come up to the warehouse; a similar grant of £22 8s. 9d. was made to John Brookes. Finally, the commissioners received notice of a claim for lands cut at Saltney Marsh and discharged their clerk, Robert Jackson, for misbehaviour and appointed Robert Baxter in his place.[1] Here, at least, the commissioners were carrying out their duties to the full.

The Acts, too, usually laid down the maximum toll which was to be the undertakers' reward for their work. This was sometimes in the form of a flat rate, like the maximum of 5s. per ton on the Bristol Avon,[2] and sometimes a complicated scale of charges, like the forty-three different classes of goods for which toll was asked on Beverley Beck.[3] From these tolls there were almost always some exceptions. Landowners by the river banks might have pleasure boats free,[4] a privilege which was sometimes confined to 'Any Gentleman or Person of Quality'.[5] Riparian proprietors had usually the right to move manure, corn, straw, and hay from the various parts of their land free of toll.[6] Sometimes this exemption applied to mill owners carrying materials for the repair of their mills.[7] These restrictions of rates and exemptions from toll were not the only limitations on the power of undertakers. On the whole those powers were extensive and included the general right to enter upon land, to scour the river, and to

---

[1] Cheshire MSS., Dee Commissioners, 1736.
[2] 10 Anne, c. 2, sec. 11.
[3] 13 Geo. I, c. 4, sec. 4.
[4] 6 Geo. I, c. 27, sec. 24.
[5] 11 Will. III, c. 22, sec. 23.
[6] 6 Geo. I, c. 27, sec. 24.
[7] 11 Will. III, c. 22, sec. 15.

cut its banks subject to the payment of compensation. But there were sometimes serious limitations. The undertakers of the Eden could not 'straiten the River' otherwise than by making it deeper; they could make no new cuts.[1] Those of the Colne could only cut certain specified lands of the Earl of Kent and Nicholas Corselli.[2] The Lark undertakers could build no public wharf in Bury St. Edmunds without consent of the Corporation,[3] and the same applied to the Wiltshire Avon and Salisbury.[4] On the Stroudwater no boat was to pass along the river from August 14th to October 15th without the consent of the major part of the mill owners,[5] and there were nineteen mills.[6] On the Roding, free passage, after the payment of toll, through the floodgate at Barking Mill was only enforceable in time of flood.[7] Such restrictions were serious handicaps, but in some cases they were the price paid for the passing of the Act.

[1] 8 Geo. I, c. 14, sec. 2.
[2] 9 Will. III, c. 19, sec. 6.   [3] 11 Will. III, c. 22, sec. 22.
[4] 16/17 Car. II, P. A. Manby, *Collection of Statutes*, p. 273.
[5] 3 Geo. II, c. 13, sec. 19.
[6] *J. H. of C.* xxi. 437.   [7] 10 Geo. II, c. 33, sec. 2.

III

THE UNDERTAKERS

IN England men would have agreed only with the first half of the dictum, 'C'est ouvrage d'un grand Prince de rendre aisé le passage des mers, et de ioindre les fleuves pour le commerce des peuples'.[1] It was indeed held that the king 'is by his prerogative right the proper Judge, what river shalbe made and who shalbe undertakers', but this was only laid down in answer to a proposal that the freeholders in County Courts should nominate undertakers.[2] In granting Letters Patent the king did show himself the 'proper Judge', but the actual undertaking was always left to private or municipal enterprise. This was characteristic of the whole field of economic activity in seventeenth-century England. The Crown might grant a monopoly to the Company of Hostmen or the makers of glass, Parliament might grant a monopoly to the undertakers of the Colne or the Tone, but, except during a brief period when it administered the Crown lands, the State never entered directly into economic enterprises.[3]

Who, then, were the men responsible for river improvements during this period? Little need be said of those who owed their appointment as undertakers to an official capacity in another direction. Thus, under the Thames Act of 1623–4, the Lord Chancellor was to appoint four commissioners for the University and four for the City of Oxford from nominations of the Chancellor or Vice-Chancellor and Mayor and Aldermen respectively.[4] The University nominated William Pearse, D.D., Dean of Peterborough and Prebendary of Christ Church, John Bancroft, D.D., Master of University College, John Tolson, D.D., Provost of Oriel, and John Hawley, Doctor of Law, Principal of

---

[1] Coulon, *Les Rivières de France*, i. 76.

[2] 'Concerning making Rivers Navigable', Rawl. MSS. A 477.

[3] The relation of the State to the great trading companies (Clark, *Seventeenth Century*, pp. 32–3) was identical with that of the State to those engaged in river improvements.

[4] 21 Jac. I, c. 32, sec. 1.

Gloucester Hall; the City nominated Aldermen Potter, Harris, Wright, and Smith.[1] These men probably owed their appointment less to any interest they had in navigation than to their eminence in other directions, and it is misleading to call them 'adventurers' even in the technical sense of that word.[2] Similarly it is impossible to trace individually the personnel of all those corporations which were authorized to undertake river improvements. The more important corporations were undoubtedly composed of men of local eminence. Thus the eight aldermen of Leeds, who shared the undertaking of the Aire and Calder with the eight aldermen of Wakefield in 1699,[3] were all either past or future mayors. William Rooke was mayor in 1683,[4] Joshua Ibbetson was mayor in 1685 and married Mary, daughter of Christopher Brearey, Mayor of York.[5] John Dodgson was mayor in 1696.[6] Thomas Kitchingman married Mary, daughter of Thomas Driffield, a York merchant, and was mayor in 1688 and 1705, and in the following year bought New-Hall from the Hodgsons.[7] Henry Iveson, of Blackbank, near Leeds, was twice mayor, a Justice of the Peace for the West Riding, and High Sheriff of Yorkshire.[8] William Milner was mayor of Leeds in 1697 and married Mary, daughter of Joshua Ibbetson.[9] Finally, John Rontree and Thomas Lazenby were mayors in 1699 and 1700 respectively.[10] It was a combination of the commercial centre of High Street[11] and the civic quarter of Meadow Lane[12] that made the Aire and Calder navigable.

More interesting still was that body of men which was authorized to improve the Wye and Lug by an Act of 1696.[13] The work had been begun thirty years before by Sir William, Windsor, and Henry Sandys, but had been left incomplete.[14] The new body was to complete the work by means of a tax

---

[1] Twyne-Langbaine MSS. I; Salter, *Oxford Council Acts*, p. 325. The City appointed new commissioners to fill vacancies caused by death or resignation; Hobson and Salter, *Oxford Council Acts, 1626–65*, pp. 11, 52, 64, 129, 139, 321.

[2] Nef, *Coal Industry*, i. 259.   [3] 10 Will. III, c. 25, sec. 1.

[4] Thoresby, *Ducatus Leodiensis*, p. 263.   [5] Ibid., p. 146.

[6] Ibid., p. 263.   [7] Ibid., pp. 215, 264.

[8] Ibid., p. 103. His father, Lancelot Iveson, built three almshouses; ibid., p. 84.

[9] Ibid., p. 215.   [10] Ibid., p. 263.   [11] Defoe, *Tour*, ii. 611–12.

[12] Thoresby, *Ducatus Leodiensis*, p. 98.   [13] 7/8 Will. III, c. 14, sec. 2.

[14] Lloyd, *Papers relating to the . . . Wye and Lug*, p. 12.

levied on Herefordshire. They were not, therefore, undertakers in the ordinary sense, but rather trustees who were
to hold the river in trust for the good of the county.[1] This
new and imposing body was headed by the Bishop of
Hereford,[2] but its leading member appears to have been Sir
Thomas Coningsby.[3] This 'firm and unflinching Whig' was
'descended from an antient but impoverished family, possessed
of an extensive but burdened estate'.[4] He married Barbara,
daughter of Ferdinando Gorges, a Barbados merchant, and
throughout his life divided his time between political and local
strife. Coningsby was M.P. for Leominster, Chief Steward
of Hereford, Lord-Lieutenant of the County, Chief Justice
for Ireland, and Paymaster of the Forces. He was one of
the managers of the Sacheverell trial and moved the impeach-
ment of Harley, with whom a family feud had long existed.
His local connexions were no less strong and no less stormy.
His purchase of the Manor of Leominster from Major
Wildman for £3,060, led to lawsuits over the ejection of
freeholders, whom he held to be copyholders. At the same
time he engaged in a twenty years' suit with the Crown over
the right to present to the living of Leominster. The verdict
finally went against him. His interest in the Wye was
probably dictated by the fact that he owned Hampton Court
Mills and Weir.[5]

Others of these undertakers were equally interested. Lord
Chandos, sometime Ambassador at Constantinople, whose
son was M.P. for Hereford and spent £200,000 on his town
house, also possessed mills and weirs on the Wye.[6] The same
is true of Lord Scudamore, of the Scudamores of Holme Lacy,
who for generations were renowned for their horsemanship
and breed of horses.[7] The Foleys, two of whom figure among
the undertakers, had a different interest. Thomas Foley,
son of Thomas, of Willey Court, Worcestershire, was con-

---

[1] 7/8 Will. III, c. 14.
[2] For the Bishop's estates see Capes, ed. *Charters and Records of Hereford Cathe-
dral.*
[3] Townsend, *Leominster*, p. 188.   [4] Ibid., p. 157.
[5] 'Survey of Wye and Lug', Add. MSS. 21567, f. 7; *D.N.B.*; Townsend,
Leominster, pp. 157–67.
[6] 'Survey of Wye and Lug', Add. MSS. 21567, f. 4 dorso; *D.N.B.*
[7] Ibid., f. 5; *D.N.B.*

nected with the Stourbridge iron manufacture. The Honourable Paul Foley, M.P. for Hereford and Speaker of the Commons, had joined with Harley in proposing the establishment of a national land bank in 1696.[1] More important still, he possessed at least one forge and furnace on the Wye.[2] The enemies of navigation said that he possessed all but one and was using the pretext of navigation merely to get a monopoly by destroying the weirs which supplied the water to the Earl of Kent's forge.[3]

On the other hand, the Harleys, three of whom were among the undertakers, appear to have been comparatively disinterested. Sir Edward Harley of Brampton Bryan had been M.P. for Herefordshire before the Restoration. Of his sons, Edward was Recorder and then M.P. for Leominster, while Robert was High Sheriff of Herefordshire in 1689 and M.P. for Tregory and New Radnor successively.[4] John Dutton Colt, who was Mayor of Hereford at the time of the Act, was the son of George Colt, of Colt Hall, Suffolk, but he had married the daughter of John Booth, of Letton, Herefordshire, in 1670 and owned land and a house in Leominster.[5] He had been M.P. for Leominster for various years before 1696.[6]

It is obvious that all these men had the strongest local connexions, but it is equally obvious that they were not disinterested trustees. They had much to gain by administering an Act which, despite its safeguards, might be made to ruin the forge of a rival iron manufacturer, and which was intended to grant compensation for the removal of weirs which they themselves owned. The Act indeed appointed a body of commissioners to settle the yearly value of the weirs, which were to be bought out at not more than sixteen years' purchase, but if an ambiguous letter from James Morgan, one of the undertakers, to Coningsby, dated April 13th, 1696, means anything at all, it means that Coningsby was in a position to control the commissioners themselves.[7] Some of the weirs were bought out and Lord Chandos must have felt that he had got a good bargain when he received

[1] D.N.B.   [2] Lloyd, *Papers relating to the . . . Wye and Lug*, p. 29.
[3] Ibid., p. 27.   [4] D.N.B.   [5] Townsend, *Leominster*, p. 149.
[6] Ibid., p. 335.   [7] Ibid., p. 188.

£400 for Wilton Weir,[1] which, with its mills, was utterly decayed and not worth more than £10 per annum.[2]

Turning to those undertakers who acted neither as trustees nor as members of a corporation, it is apparent that they fall into two main classes, the country gentry and the town merchants. There are, indeed, exceptions who will hardly fit into either of these categories. Sir John Harington, who attempted to make the Avon navigable from Bath to Bristol,[3] was a wit and courtier, godson of Queen Elizabeth, translator of Ariosto's *Orlando Furioso*, and tutor to Prince Henry.[4] On the other hand, John Hore, of Newbury, one of the Kennet undertakers under the Act of 1715,[5] appears to have been primarily an engineer,[6] although he came of a family of maltsters.[7] He was employed on the Bristol Avon,[8] advanced a scheme for the Stroudwater,[9] and surveyed the Chelmer.[10] The body of undertakers responsible for the Tone under the Act of 1699 comprised seven gentlemen, seven clothiers, five merchants, two grocers, two fullers, two vintners, an ironmonger, a maltster, a dyer, a mercer, and a doctor of physic.[11] These men were all of the parishes of Taunton and Wilton and must have included the chief inhabitants of each. But such exceptions do not invalidate the general rule that the work was undertaken by either the landed gentry of the district or the prosperous merchants of the chief river towns.

The part played by the landed gentry was less than that by the merchant class, for the former spent much of their time in opposition to the river improvements of their day. But it must not be assumed that their activity was limited to opposition. John Malet, who made the Tone navigable under a Commission of the Great Seal of Charles I, was 'the last heir of an ancient baronial family'[12] which had resided

---

[1] Lloyd, *Papers relating to the . . . Wye and Lug*, p. 144.
[2] 'Survey of Wye and Lug', Add. MSS. 21567, f. 4 dorso.
[3] Mathew, *Of the Opening of Rivers*, p. 12.
[4] *D.N.B.*   [5] 1 Geo. I, P. A.
[6] For some notice of the Hore family see *V.C.H. Berkshire*, iii. 454; iv. 387.
[7] Thacker, *Kennet Country*, p. 317.
[8] Mavor, *Agriculture of Berkshire*, p. 438.
[9] *J. H. of C.* xxi. 437.
[10] *The Intended Navigation of the Chelmer*, p. 4.
[11] 10 Will. III, c. 8, sec. 1.   [12] Collinson, *Somerset*, i. 92.

in Somerset from the twelfth century.[1] He married Untia, daughter of Lord Hawley,[2] and his daughter Elizabeth married the Earl of Rochester. His three grand-daughters all married into the peerage.[3] Not all were as well connected as this. Henry Ashley, of Eaton Socon, Bedfordshire, who was actively concerned in the navigation of the Great Ouse[4] and was an undertaker for the Lark,[5] belonged to the class of smaller country gentlemen. In 1708 he sold his manor of Eaton to the Duke of Bedford,[6] perhaps as a result of his expenditure on river improvement.

The Sandys family, who were concerned in the Warwickshire Avon and the Wye, came originally from Lancashire.[7] By the seventeenth century they had become Worcestershire landowners. Sir William Sandys, of Fladbury, bought the manor of Miserden in Gloucestershire. Besides five daughters, he had three sons; Sir Myles, who died before his father, William, 'who settled in Kent and was called Water-work Sandys, from his taste in improvements of that kind', and Thomas, who died unmarried.[8] William made the Warwickshire Avon navigable[9] and proposed to improve the Teme,[10] but the work was checked by the Civil War.[11] In 1638 he was to share with John Child, a London merchant, the new farm of 1s. per chaldron on coals, but the agreement was cancelled.[12] Other members of the family were concerned in river navigation. In 1662 Sir William (as he had become) with his cousin Henry Sandys[13] and Windsor Sandys, grandson of his brother, Sir Myles, were appointed undertakers of the Wye and Lug,[14] a work which they never completed.[15] In 1670 Windsor Sandys had rights in the Wey,[16] while three

[1] Ibid., pp. 89–94. [2] Ibid., p. 92.
[3] Toulmin, *Taunton*, p. 384. [4] *H.M.C. House of Lords*, N.S. i. 49–51.
[5] 11 Will. III, c. 22, sec. 1. [6] *V.C.H. Bedfordshire*, iii. 191.
[7] Habington, *Worcestershire*, ii. 468.
[8] Rudder, *Gloucestershire*, p. 554 n. Atkyns was wrong in making William son of Sir Myles (*Glostershire*, p. 561); he was actually brother (Habington, *Worcestershire*, ii. 468).
[9] *Supra*, pp. 26–7. [10] *Cal. S.P.D., 1635–6*, p. 280; Rymer, *Foedera*, xx. 6.
[11] *V.C.H. Shropshire*, i. 425. [12] Nef, *Coal Industry*, ii. 280.
[13] His father was Sir Edwin Sandys, a leading member of the Virginia Company; Lipson, *Economic History*, iii. 188.
[14] Lloyd, *Papers relating to the . . . Wye and Lug*, p. 3.
[15] Ibid., p. 12; Pratt, *Inland Transport*, p. 131; 7/8 Will. III, c. 14, sec. 1.
[16] Exch. K. R. Wey Navigation Claims; Manning and Bray, *Surrey*, iii, App. iii, lvi.

years later a William, who was possibly Windsor's uncle, petitioned for a lease of the ballast office on the plea, 'through my experience I can improve the navigation of the river [the Thames] now much prejudiced by shelves'.[1] The Sandys did not retain their interest in the Warwickshire Avon, which passed to Lord Windsor, afterwards Earl of Plymouth. Lord Windsor, to whom Yarranton dedicated the first part of his *England's Improvement*, was typical of the scientifically minded peer of the seventeenth century. He was an undertaker of the Worcestershire Stour and Salwarpe in 1662,[2] and later, with others, continued Sandys's work on the Avon.[3] He settled his rights in the latter river upon his wife Ursula, to whom they were worth £400 per annum.[4]

Two final examples will suffice to show the part played by the nobility and landed proprietors. In 1699 William, Lord Paget was appointed undertaker of the upper Trent.[5] He was at that time Ambassador Extraordinary to Turkey,[6] and his son was empowered to act as his deputy.[7] He had strong local connexions with Staffordshire, of which he had been Lord-Lieutenant in 1688–9.[8] He was not only the Lord of the Manor of Burton-on-Trent, but was also actively interested in financing the colliery enterprises of the neighbourhood.[9] The Dane navigation of 1721 was undertaken by men who represented the best families of Cheshire. Sir Thomas Brooke, of Norton Priory, was Sheriff of Cheshire and Constable of Chester Castle.[10] Charles Cholmondeley, of Vale Royal,[11] was a great landowner[12] and possessed salt works worth more than £3,000.[13] Roger Wilbraham, of Nantwich, belonged to a local family of repute.[14] He was Deputy-Lieutenant of Cheshire in 1725[15] and one of the commis-

---

[1] *Cal. S.P.D., 1667–8*, p. 111.

[2] *H.M.C. House of Lords, 1692–3*, p. 387; *J. H. of C.* xiv. 70.

[3] Yarranton, *England's Improvement*, i. 189.   [4] *J. H. of C.* xi. 376.

[5] 10 Will. III, c. 26, sec. 1.   [6] *D.N.B.*   [7] 10 Will. III, c. 26, sec. 18.

[8] *D.N.B.*   [9] Nef, *Coal Industry*, i. 66, ii. 8.

[10] Ormerod, *Chester*, i. 685.   [11] Ibid. ii. 158.

[12] 'Weaver Navigation, 1699–1720', Add. MSS. 36914, f. 119 dorso; *J. H. of C.* xix. 252.

[13] 'Weaver Navigation, 1699–1720', Add. MSS. 36914, f. 121; *J. H. of L.* xxiii. 300; *J. H. of C.* xviii. 169. In the seventeenth century the Cholmondeleys had an iron forge on the Weaver, presumably for making the pans in which the brine was boiled; Hughes, *Studies in Administration and Finance*, p. 405.

[14] Ormerod, *Chester*, iii. 441.   [15] Hall, *Nantwich*, p. 438.

sioners under the Weaver Act of 1734.[1] Of the two remaining undertakers, Sir Richard Grosvenor was M.P. for Chester and had been Mayor of the City,[2] while James, Earl of Barrymore, was a Member for Wigan and had inherited a fortune from his first wife, Elizabeth, daughter of Lord Charles Clifford.[3] Other Cheshire county families were represented in similar enterprises by John Egerton,[4] a Weaver undertaker of 1721,[5] and Richard Manley,[6] a Dee undertaker of 1733.[7]

The share of the commercial class in the enterprises for river improvement was particularly strong in Lancashire in the early eighteenth century. It was only natural that this should be so. The expansion of trade[8] and the growth of industries, which demanded the transport of bulky commodities, was already creating that situation which eventually led to canal-building. But river preceded canal navigation, and in that it was the merchants, rather than the landowners and gentry, who were interested. They did not always show that interest openly. Thus the Douglas undertakers under the Act of 1720[9] were Thomas Steers, engineer of the new Liverpool docks, bailiff and mayor of that town,[10] and William Squire, Mayor of Liverpool in 1715.[11] But in the background was Squire's brother-in-law, Richard Norris, a Liverpool merchant and former Member for the borough. He was said to be entitled to one-third of the profits of the undertaking by a secret bargain.[12]

Typical of these enterprises undertaken and financed by the merchant class was the Mersey and Irwell undertaking of 1721. An Act of that year appointed thirty-eight men to improve the navigation of the river.[13] Of these, two were justices, three were Liverpool men, and thirty-three were of Manchester, mostly traders and including the chief linen

---

[1] Ibid., p. 265 n.   [2] Ormerod, *Chester*, ii. 841–3.
[3] Gibbs, ed. *Complete Peerage*, i. 445.
[4] Ormerod, *Chester*, ii. 217, 222–3.   [5] 7 Geo. I, c. 10, sec. 1.
[6] Ormerod, *Chester*, ii. 102–5; Hemingway, *Chester*, p. 171.
[7] 'Dee Navigation, 1733', Add. MSS. 11394, ff. 28–30.
[8] Defoe, *Tour*, ii. 670–1.   [9] 6 Geo. I, c. 28, sec. 1.
[10] Picton, *Memorials of Liverpool*, i. 553.
[11] Ibid. ii. 90. Squire was engaged in the salt trade from Liverpool, Hughes, *Studies in Administration and Finance*, p. 395.
[12] Wadsworth and Mann, *Cotton Trade*, p. 215.   [13] 7 Geo. I, c. 15, sec. 1.

drapers.[1] It is possible and instructive to consider these undertakers in greater detail. The two justices were George Kenyon, of Kenyon Peel Hall, and Oswald Mosley, of Ancoats. Kenyon was Tory member for Clitheroe from 1690-5 and Clerk of the Peace for Lancashire and Governor of the Isle of Man.[2] The Mosleys had bought Ancoats early in the seventeenth century and had connexions with the cloth trade. Oswald Mosley received the reversion of the manors of Rolleston and Manchester under the will of his father's cousin, Sir Edward Mosley.[3] His son, Sir Oswald, owned a horse mill at which the brewers of Salford ground their malt instead of at the Manchester Grammar School mills, a circumstance which led to a lengthy case which Sir Oswald lost;[4] he was also builder of the first Manchester Exchange.[5] The three Liverpool undertakers were Thomas Steers, the Douglas undertaker, who surveyed the Mersey and Irwell in 1712 'by order of the Gentlemen at Manchester'[6] and who was responsible for Liverpool's first dock and theatre,[7] Richard Gidart, former Mayor of Liverpool,[8] and Henry 'Trayford', who was probably the Trafford who was Corporation Treasurer in 1721 and Mayor in 1740.[9] The last two were merchants associated with Steers in other ventures[10] and both were shippers of salt from Liverpool.[11]

The thirty-three men of Manchester seem to have included the chief commercial families of the time. Amongst them was John Lees, of Clarksfield, near Oldham, of a family of bankers, cotton spinners, and coal-owners;[12] Oswald Ravald, of a family that went back in Manchester to the middle of the fifteenth century and who was probably the brother of Robert Ravald, a linen draper who died in 1718;[13] Samuel Clowes, a merchant who between 1721 and 1727 bought seven-eighths of the manor of Tyldesley for £3,485 and in

---

[1] Wadsworth and Mann, *Cotton Trade*, p. 219.
[2] *V.C.H. Lancs.* v. 31; cf. *H.M.C. Kenyon*, p. 464.
[3] *V.C.H. Lancs.* iv. 238, and see p. 232 for pedigree.
[4] Ibid. ii. 587.   [5] Axon, *Mosley Family*, p. 23.
[6] Steers, *A Map of the Rivers Mersey and Irwell.*
[7] Picton, *Memorials of Liverpool*, i. 553, ii. 91.
[8] Ibid. ii. 10.   [9] Ibid., p. 134.
[10] Wadsworth and Mann, *Cotton Trade*, p. 219.
[11] Hughes, *Studies in Administration and Finance*, pp. 395 n. 1507, 497.
[12] *V.C.H. Lancs.* v. 101.   [13] Ibid., iv. 221 n., 222 n.

1731 purchased the Chaddock Hall estate.[1] They included, too, Joseph Byrom, a wealthy mercer and purchaser of the manor of Byrom.[2] He was Borough-reeve of Manchester in 1703 and his son Josiah was probably a Worsley undertaker of 1737.[3] In 1722 a Joseph Byrom, of Salford, purchased Smithills Hall for £4,688, but this was probably a different branch of the family.[4] Joseph Yates, another undertaker, belonged to a family which came from Blackburn, where some were Presbyterians and mercers. He acquired Peel Hall through his wife Ellen, daughter of William Maghull, and was Governor of Blackburn Grammar School and High Sheriff of Lancashire. His son became a Judge of the King's Bench and was knighted.[5] James Lightbowne, another of the Manchester men, was probably the son of a barrister and Steward of Manchester Court, but the family were woollen drapers and owned estates in Moston.[6] Finally—for it is impossible to trace all the undertakers—two members of the Bayley family were represented. They were silk weavers and merchants in the seventeenth century[7] and James Bayley was 'one of the wealthiest Whigs in the town'.[8] His son Daniel purchased and rebuilt Hope Hall[9] and upon his death left £100 for apprenticing children of poor ministers and tradesmen being Protestant Dissenters.[10] It would be interesting to know how far the men engaged in this and similar undertakings came from that class of wealthy Nonconformists who directed their energies into economic rather than political or social life. Presbyterianism was stronger in Lancashire than elsewhere in England, and the Byrom, Houghton, Home, Nield, and Seddon families had all connexions with Nonconformity in the seventeenth and eighteenth centuries,[11] though it is impossible to prove directly that the members of these families, who were represented among the Mersey and Irwell undertakers, be-

[1] Ibid. iii. 441–2.   [2] Ibid. iv. 153.
[3] Parkinson, ed. *Literary Remains of John Byrom* (pedigree); 10 Geo. II, c. 9, sec. 1.
[4] *V.C.H. Lancs.* v. 14 n.   [5] Abram, *Blackburn*, pp. 408–9.
[6] *V.C.H. Lancs.* iv. 268 n.   [7] Axon, *Bayley Family*, pp. 20–1.
[8] Ibid., p. 4; *V.C.H. Lancs.* iv. 394.   [9] *V.C.H. Lancs.* iv. 394.
[10] Ibid. iv. 202 n.
[11] Nightingale, *Lancashire Nonconformity*, v. 3 n. 4, 39, 99, 110, 155–6.

longed to those religious bodies that stood outside the
Churches of England and Rome. But it is clear that the
undertakers of the Mersey and Irwell included the chief
trading families of that 'meer Village',[1] which was so much
greater than many towns.[2]

Where there is no obvious trading connexion, the undertakers appear to have been wealthy and respectable citizens.
The two Weaver undertakers of 1734, William Maisterson
and Thomas Williams, were both Charity Trustees for Nantwich[3] and both owned pews in the parish church which cost
£14 5s. each.[4] John Howe, of Guildford, a Wey undertaker
of 1651, and former Mayor of Guildford,[5] left £400, the
interest of which was to be cast lots for by two poor serving
maids who had lived for two years with credit in the same
family.[6] He also left a messuage for the use of the poor.[7]
Richard Cowslade, of Newbury, a Kennet undertaker by the
Act of 1715, gave land to educate and clothe ten more boys
in the charity school[8] and also left an endowment for the
organist of the parish church.[9] It is not therefore surprising
that his portrait hangs in the vestry as a benefactor of the
parish.[10] It is probable that these men had made their money
in trade before they became those benefactors whose memory
is so proudly preserved in the pages of the older local
histories.

The trading class undoubtedly played the greater part
in the river improvements of this period. Though some of
the work was done by corporations, they, too, were often
composed of the leading merchants of the town. The commercial class had, indeed, no monopoly. Just as colliery
finance and undertakings of the seventeenth century were
carried out by the landed families and the merchant class
within the towns,[11] so, too, the river improvements.

[1] Defoe, *Tour*, ii. 670.   [2] Ibid., p. 671.
[3] Hall, *Nantwich*, p. 264. Maisterson was a Justice of the Peace and a collector of
salt duties; Hughes, *Studies in Administration and Finance*, p. 389.
[4] Hall, *Nantwich*, p. 218. Thomas Williams was possibly the cheese-factor who
bought the lordship of Stoke from Edward Minshull in 1719; ibid., p. 351 n.
[5] Manning and Bray, *Surrey*, i. 39.
[6] Ibid., p. 82; *V.C.H. Surrey*, iii. 570.
[7] Manning and Bray, *Surrey*, i. 63.
[8] *V.C.H. Berkshire*, iv. 146.   [9] Ibid., p. 154.
[10] Ibid., p. 150.   [11] Nef, *Coal Industry*, ii. 3.

IV

FINANCE

THE financing of local enterprises in the seventeenth and early eighteenth centuries is an interesting if obscure subject. It has long been recognized that capitalist undertaking is not an essentially modern phenomenon, but the extent to which it had spread in what has been called the 'age of early capitalism', as opposed to that of *Hochkapitalismus*, has perhaps not been fully realized. This is particularly true of local finance in England, whether by individuals, by companies, or by corporations. The tendency to concentrate attention entirely upon London as the financial centre of the country and upon foreign trade as the sinews of the nation's strength has obscured the fact that the internal commerce of England was an essential part of its economic life, and that the organization of that commerce, particularly in the branch of transport, demanded an increasingly great capital expenditure. The improvement of internal means of communication dates back to before the Industrial Revolution, and the capitalist financing of river transport precedes the canals by more than a century.

It is true that an older tradition of finance, inherited from the methods of the Commissions of Sewers, lingered on well into the seventeenth century as the basis of certain river improvements. This was the district levy based on the assumption that all the inhabitants of a particular area would benefit from the improvement of the water transport within that area and should therefore share the immediate cost. Thus the Acts of 1605–6 and 1623–4 for the improvement of the Thames between Oxford and Burcot empowered the commissioners to assess and levy rates upon the inhabitants of the counties or towns which were to benefit from the improved navigation.[1] There is no evidence that these rates were ever assessed under the earlier Act, but they were under the later, though the University itself used a legacy of 2,000 marks, left to it by Sir Nicholas Kempe, towards the cost of

[1] 3 Jac. I, c. 20, sec. 2; 21 Jac. I, c. 32, sec. 3.

improving the river.[1] On July 29th, 1629, the Corporation
of Oxford, with a view to raising further taxation for improving the river, decided that the former taxation should
be reviewed. Those who were behindhand in payment, or
were under-taxed, or were new commoners to the city, should
be made to pay. There was to be a weekly tax on every
inhabitant of the city, able to pay, of not less than 1*d*. or more
than 6*d*., with a month's payment in advance for the ensuing
year. Ale-houses were to be taxed 'at a higher rate then
others of the like abilitie'.[2] Since the City was in debt over
the work, the yearly entertainments and banquets, usually
given when new officers were elected, were to be commuted
to money payments to be employed on the navigation undertaking. The Mayor was to pay £10, the Bailiffs £15 each,
the Chamberlain and Common Councillors £2 each on their
election days.[3]

These payments continued until 1634,[4] though in 1630
it was declared that if the commissioners did not proceed
with the work the money would be used for the new House
of Correction.[5] Neither the taxation nor the commutation
of entertainments appears to have been adequate. Between
Michaelmas 1632 and Michaelmas 1635 the City laid out
£300 on the navigation undertaking.[6] On March 20th,
1635, it was decided that not more than £300 should be
borrowed 'to pay the taxation on the navigation scheme
and also for payments of the City debts'.[7] Three years later
£100 of this was repaid, with interest, to Mr. Goodman, of
Sandford, as well as £30 which had been paid out by the
Mayor, but the whole sum had to be borrowed again as
the city was without funds.[8] About the same time £100
was repaid to Elizabeth Goodman, which had been borrowed

---

[1] 'Thames Navigation', Twyne-Langbaine MSS. I; Thacker, *Thames, General History*, p. 68; Clark, *Life and Times of Anthony Wood*, iv. 51.

[2] Hobson and Salter, *Oxford Council Acts, 1626–65*, p. 19.

[3] Ibid., p. 20.

[4] Ibid., pp. 21, 26, 28, 31, 36–7, 40–1, 44, 46, 49–50, 59. On September 29th, 1631, Edward Daniell, who had been chosen a member of the Common Council, refused to pay his £2 'to the barges', and was dismissed; ibid., p. 37. The same method of raising money was adopted at Exeter; Exeter MSS., Act Book, 1684–1731, f. 278.

[5] Hobson and Salter, *Oxford Council Acts, 1626–65*, p. 26.

[6] Ibid., pp. 417–18. [7] Ibid., p. 60. [8] Ibid., p. 80.

on St. Bartholomew's Day, 1635, for the river undertaking. Twenty pounds was also paid 'towards the forbearance thereof', which represented between 6 and 7 per cent.[1] Henceforth the city appears to have relied upon borrowing the money necessary for the maintenance of the navigation works. In 1647 it was decided to borrow £150 for this purpose.[2] Four years later £100 was borrowed.[3] On August 26th, 1659, £60, which had been borrowed from various persons, was repaid out of the city treasure.[4]

A similar method was adopted for improving the Wye and Lug. When three members of the Sandys family were appointed undertakers in 1662 they took over £1,300 which had been collected from the county for that purpose.[5] By the later Act of 1696 the undertakers were empowered to levy as much money in Herefordshire as the commissioners should think fit, but this was not to exceed £377 4s. 5d. a month or £4,526 13s. 1d. a year, and was not to extend beyond 1700. Commissioners, named in an Act of the same year for granting an aid,[6] were to collect these moneys. The undertakers were also empowered to borrow £16,000 at not more than 4 per cent.[7] This money, which was to be used primarily for buying up weirs, was apparently levied to its full extent. £18,000 was raised in the county of Hereford, and in 1727 much of this was still unspent.[8] A somewhat parallel instance is found in the case of the Trent. By an Act of 1699 William, Lord Paget was authorized to make the Trent navigable from Wilden Ferry to Burton-on-Trent. He was apparently to find the money himself, except that the commissioners could assess the inhabitants of Burton-on-Trent up to the sum of £600.[9] It is not clear whether the money was ever raised, but in 1714 Lord Paget himself had spent only £500.[10] These district levies were exceptional and ceased altogether by the eighteenth century. It was more usual for the Acts to empower the

[1] Ibid., p. 421.   [2] Ibid., pp. 147, 149.
[3] Ibid., p. 183.
[4] Ibid., p. 245.
[5] Lloyd, *Papers relating to the . . . Wye and Lug*, p. 10; 7/8 Will. III, c. 14, sec. 1.
[6] 7/8 Will. III, c. 5.   [7] Ibid., c. 14, sec. 23.
[8] 13 Geo. I, c. 34, sec. 4.   [9] 10 Will. III, c. 26, sec. 14.
[10] *Bromley Parliamentary Papers*, iii, no. 105.

undertakers to borrow money upon security of the tolls at a maximum rate of interest of 5[1] or 6 per cent.[2]

The earlier undertakers appear to have financed their enterprises out of their own resources. Of John Malet, the Tone undertaker, it was said, 'all persons concerned were satisfied out of his estate'.[3] Sandys spent between £20,000 and £40,000 on the Warwickshire Avon and impoverished himself.[4] Daniel Wigmore made the Welland navigable from Deeping to Stamford at a cost of £5,000 and left his rights in the work to his son-in-law, Charles Halford, to whom they were worth from £400 to £500 per annum.[5] Sir Bartholomew Shower, in defending the rights of Samuel Jemmatt, assignee of a Letters Patent from Spencer for improving the Great Ouse, declared, before the House of Lords, 'we sold £1,000 of land to get the Patent, and ruined our family'.[6] On the other hand, the undertakers of the Salwarpe under the Act of 1662 received salt water value £2,000 from the proprietors of the salt works at Droitwich to assist their work.[7] Even then Sir Timothy and Charles Baldwin, to whom they assigned their rights, spent a further £4,000 on the river, besides several thousands spent by others.[8] But capital was not yet concentrated sufficiently in the hands of individuals for one man to be responsible for the larger undertakings which marked the end of the seventeenth and the beginning of the eighteenth century. In 1714 an Act for the Nen had appointed commissioners who were to nominate an undertaker for the whole river.[9] Ten years later the commissioners reported that they were unable to get any one to do the whole work.[10] An Act was therefore passed allowing them to enter into several contracts for the undertaking.[11]

Where a body of men other than a corporation was responsible for an undertaking, it was usually constituted as a company, though of what exact type is not always certain.

---

[1] 13 Geo. I, c. 33, sec. 21.   [2] 10 Will. III, c. 8, sec. 3.
[3] Toulmin, *Taunton*, p. 383.
[4] *Cal. S.P.D.*, *1661–2*, p. 628; Bennett, *Tewkesbury*, p, 303; Habington, *Worcestershire*, ii. 469.
[5] *J. H. of C.* xi. 388.   [6] *H.M.C. House of Lords*, N.S. i. 49.
[7] Ibid., *1692–3*, p. 387.   [8] Ibid., p. 389.
[9] 13 Anne, c. 19.   [10] *J. H. of C.* xx. 370.   [11] 13 Geo. I, c. 19.

Some, indeed, were public joint-stock companies, a form
to which municipal enterprise ultimately tended. Thus the
'Company of the Proprietors of the Navigation of the River
Medway', incorporated under an Act of 1740, consisted of
forty-seven proprietors who were to raise the necessary
money among themselves. There were to be 300 shares
yielding not more than £30,000, and none was to hold more
than 10 shares. Any one not answering a call was to lose
what had been paid. Not until the navigation was completed
from Maidstone to Tonbridge for boats of 40 tons, could
these shares be sold.[1] The company, therefore, only became
a full public joint-stock concern on the completion of the
work.

The case of the Kennet is more obscure. A Private Act
of 1715 appointed seven undertakers,[2] who, by 1730, had
raised £44,603 as well as receiving £10,000 from duties.[3]
There is no evidence that the undertakers had formed a
public joint-stock company. It seems more probable that
the work was carried on by a partnership. The proprietors
could not sue for rates and duties unless their decision was
unanimous,[4] a handicap which was removed by an Act of
1730.[5] The same Act stipulated that each proprietor must
have a full one-thirty-second part or share in the navigation.
Yet another form was tried for financing the Weaver improvements. Under an Act of 1721, three undertakers were
appointed to carry out the work and fourteen men were
named, together with the amounts they would advance.
These amounts varied from £500 to £1,000 and totalled
£9,000, of which £2,500 was guaranteed by the undertakers.[6]
Interest at 6 per cent. was to be paid on this money, which
was gradually to be paid back and then the profits of the
navigation were to go towards repairing roads in Cheshire.[7]
This was in the form of a trust rather than a company,[8] but
the money was never actually advanced.[9] The work was

---

[1] 13 Geo. II, c. 26.   [2] 1 Geo. I, P.A.
[3] *J. H. of C.* xxi. 524.   [4] Ibid.   [5] 3 Geo. II, c. 35, sec. 3.
[6] Hughes, *Studies in Administration and Finance*, p. 263, n. 1073, confuses the
guarantors with the undertakers.   [7] 7 Geo. I, c. 10, secs. 24, 28.
[8] Wadsworth and Mann, *Cotton Trade*, p. 219.
[9] *Reasons Humbly Offered by the Trustees of Richard Vernon*, p. 2; *J. H. of C.*
xx. 639. Hughes, loc. cit., wrongly assumes that the money was actually subscribed.

III. NAVIGABLE RIVERS, 1724–7 (Defoe)

Only the navigable parts of rivers are shown.

ultimately done at a cost of £18,000 which was borrowed at 6 per cent.[1]

Not all this financing was above suspicion, and the chaos that could result either from carelessness or dishonesty is well illustrated by the case of the Wey. An Act of 1651 appointed the Mayor and approved men of Guildford or James Pitson, John Howe, John Waltham, and Richard Scotcher as undertakers.[2] The Mayor and approved men of Guildford and Waltham and Howe resigned their powers to Scotcher and Pitson, who took in Richard Darnelly and Sir Richard Weston, with whom the whole scheme had originated.[3] These four apparently formed a partnership, Weston advancing £3,000 and giving the lease of the manor of Sutton as security, Pitson, Scotcher, and Darnelly advancing £1,000 each.[4] The total capital of £6,000 was divided into twenty-four shares of £250 each.[5] Weston sold four of his shares to Pitson for £1,000 and two to Captain Blackwell and Mr. Crenbridge for £600.[6] He died in May 1652, having spent some £4,000 besides supplying timber value £2,000.[7] His son George continued the work and sold four of his six shares to Pitson.[8] The partners had two calls of £25 each on the shares and raised £1,200. Darnelly lent a further £1,000.[9] By November 1653 the work was finished, but, according to Scotcher's account, £3,366 5s. 5d. was still due to him.[10]

It is clear from the subsequent disputes that the work had been done by the simple method of not paying for it. It is unnecessary to go into the complicated details of the struggle which led up to the settlement of 1671, but in that year an Act vested the river in six trustees and appointed the two Chief Justices and the Chief Baron of the Exchequer to determine all claims.[11] A total of eighty-seven claims was sent in, which ranged from James Pitson's, who declared

[1] Cheshire MSS., River Weaver Commissioners, 1721–31.
[2] Firth and Rait, *Acts and Ordinances*, ii. 514.
[3] Scotcher, *River Wey Navigation*, p. 16.   [4] Ibid.
[5] Manning and Bray, *Surrey*, iii, App. iii. liv.
[6] Scotcher, *River Wey Navigation*, pp. 16–17.
[7] Manning and Bray, *Surrey*, iii, App. iii. liv.
[8] Scotcher, *River Wey Navigation*, p. 17.
[9] Ibid., p. 19.   [10] Ibid.
[11] Manning and Bray, *Surrey*, iii, App. iii. lvii.

that he had spent £14,000 and claimed sixteen shares in the river, besides the manor of Sutton, various locks, wharves, and lands, arrears of profit on the shares, and £1,045 15s. 4d. in money, to James Read's, who claimed £2 11s. for three loads of lime delivered in 1654 and 18s. for the carriage of two loads of timber.[1] The total capital sums claimed amounted to at least £67,478 8s. 5d., besides £473 11s. per annum for damage to land and sixty shares.[2] How all these claims were dealt with is not clear. Some were doubtless exaggerated, if not fictitious; the fixed number of shares, for example, had grown miraculously from twenty to sixty. But after making full allowance for misrepresentation and exaggeration, it is obvious that the finance of the whole undertaking was unsound.

The same must be said of the early Douglas scheme. In 1720 an Act appointed William Squire and Thomas Steers undertakers of the Douglas,[3] though in the background was Squire's brother-in-law, Richard Norris.[4] In June 1720, 1,200 shares of £5 each were issued against a quarter of the profits. Squire had the remaining interest vested in himself to dispose of as shares, from which the proceeds were to go to Steers, Norris, and himself. It is uncertain whether shares were ever issued against these three quarters.[5] The shares that were issued rose in a few days to £70 as a result of the South Sea speculation, but by August 18th they had fallen to £3 3s.[6] The shareholders declared that the scheme was impracticable and was only 'to make a Bubble thereof and to raise money from all such Unwary Persons as they could draw in'.[7] They accused Steers of making a mere pretence of effecting navigation. Steers attempted to justify his actions by pointing to the works completed, but what really happened to the £6,000 raised is, even at a charitable view, a matter for conjecture.[8] It is clear that the river was not made navigable until the scheme was taken up again in 1733 and work begun in 1738.[9] New undertakers were appointed

[1] Exch. K.R. Wey Navigation Claims.
[2] Ibid. Some of the entries are illegible.　　　　[3] 6 Geo. I, c. 28, sec. 1.
[4] Wadsworth and Mann, *Cotton Trade*, p. 215.　　　　[5] Ibid.
[6] Scott, *Joint-Stock Companies*, i. 419, 421.
[7] Wadsworth and Mann, *Cotton Trade*, p. 215.
[8] Ibid.　　　　　　　　　　　　　　　　　　[9] Ibid., p. 216.

in 1740, because those named in the Act had not finished in the prescribed time.[1]

Besides companies and partnerships, river improvements were sometimes undertaken by corporations. This does not imply that the money for financing them necessarily came from a different source from that which supplied companies or individuals. The Aldermen of Leeds and Wakefield were empowered to make the Aire and Calder navigable by an Act of 1699,[2] but the work was done 'at the Expence of several private merchants the Proprietors, without calling in the Assistance of the Nobility and Gentry as has been usual in like cases'.[3] Corporations, as to-day, had to borrow to finance their undertakings, but the early history of this municipal finance is a neglected subject.

Representative of the smaller type of municipal undertaking was the Beverley Beck improvement of the early eighteenth century. It is clear that the Corporation had always regarded the Beck as its own property and had levied rates on the inhabitants of Beverley for its upkeep.[4] At the end of the seventeenth century nearly £200 was spent on 'Beck Dressing'. The money was raised partly by gifts from prominent citizens, partly by collections through the wards, and partly by loans.[5] Financing by gift was the ideal from the Corporation point of view, for it implied no obligation to pay interest or refund principal. Thus, when the question of cleaning and deepening the Beck became acute about 1725, it was proposed 'that the charge of cleansing the said Beck be collected by a Voluntary Contribution and that the names of the Chief Benifactors and the sums they give be recorded on a Table to be set up in the Gild Hall of this Corporation'.[6] But the appeal to civic pride was an inadequate basis for obtaining the sums which were then necessary, and in 1727 an Act empowered the Corporation to levy tolls for goods passing along the Beck and to

---

[1] Wigan Public Library MSS., Minute Book of the Douglas Commissioners, f. 2.
[2] 10 Will. III, c. 25, sec. 1.
[3] Thoresby, *Ducatus Leodiensis*, p. 248.
[4] Beverley MSS., Minute Book, 1597–1642.
[5] 'Beverley Beck Navigation, 1699–1726', Lansdowne MSS. 896, f. 167; *Beverley Records*, p. 114.
[6] Ibid., f. 166 dorso.

borrow money 'with Legal Interest' on the security of these
duties.[1]

Between February 1727 and May 1731, when capital
expenditure appears to have ceased, £1,395 3s. 3½d. was
spent on the Beck, chiefly in payments to workmen and for
goods and interest on loans. In the same period the Corporation received £1,365 4s. 1d. on the Beck account. This included £282 6s. 6½d. in tolls for four years, a legacy of £200
left by Sir Ralph Warton 'to the Corporation for Knitting
Stockings', and diverted to navigation, and loans to the
extent of £900. The credit of the Corporation was good,
for it borrowed at from 4 to 4½ per cent. These borrowings
began with £100 in May 1727. On October 2nd of the
same year, £200 was to be borrowed at 4½ per cent., 'which
said several summes so to be borrowed the Town's Seal shall
pass to a security for repaying the same'. On December 19th
the Corporation itself lent the Beck account £28 12s. 5½d.
at 4½ per cent. Short-term loans between the Corporation in
its ordinary capacity and the Corporation as undertaker of
the Beck are an interesting feature of this financing.[2] On
September 11th, 1728, Mr. Habersham, the Town's Receiver, lent £50, and Mr. Harpham, the Minster Receiver,
the same amount, which was repaid on March 31st, 1729.
By November 1st, 1729, the Beck was indebted to the Corporation for £150, but by July 1730, £50 was paid back
and by November the remaining £100, but this was only
done by borrowing from individuals. When the period of
capital expenditure came to an end, the debts were all due
to individuals.[3] There was no attempt to repay the principal,[4]
for the Beck never made sufficient profit for that. From
1731 to 1742 the average annual profit, after deducting
expenses of upkeep and interest on loans, was £23 1s. 8d.[5]
By 1745 the Beck was again in a bad condition, due partly

---

[1] 13 Geo. I, c. 4, sec. 11.

[2] Their use was not confined to undertakings of this sort. On Sept. 13th, 1711,
the Chamberlain lent the foreman of the Workhouse Committee of Great Yarmouth
£100 without interest for six months, Great Yarmouth MSS., Assembly Book,
1701–18, f. 206.

[3] The source of this account is Beverley MSS., Beck Accounts (no foliation) and
Corporation Minute Book, 1707–36.

[4] *J. H. of C.* xxiv. 744.   [5] Beverley MSS., Beck Accounts.

to the difficulty in collecting the tolls, and a further £300 to £400 was needed.[1] An Act of the same year granted additional tolls towards meeting this necessary expenditure.[2]

Not unlike the Beverley Beck enterprise was the improvement of the Colne by the Corporation of Colchester, but there the evidence is less full. An Act of 1698 nominated the Corporation as undertaker with permission to mortgage the tolls for twenty-one years at 6 per cent.[3] On January 20th, 1699, it was decided that money should be borrowed at 6 per cent. from 'the bank of England or any other persons'.[4] The amount to be borrowed was £4,000.[5] Later the Corporation mortgaged its 'Milend' estate for £1,000 to pay various debts, which may or may not have included those of the navigation.[6] By 1707 more money was wanted[7] and was probably raised, for the appointment of a receiver of duties eighteen months later shows that the work was well advanced.[8] The duties, however, fell short of the sums required and in 1718 it was reported, 'there hath not been sufficient raised thereby either to perfect the said work or to pay the whole money borrowed for that Purpose'.[9] Another Act, therefore, continued the duties at half rates till 1740 and ordered the repayment of £1,200 to the executors of William Hewer, late of Clapham in Surrey.[10] There is a special interest attached to the last stipulation, partly because £1,200 was a large sum for one man to advance, and partly because William Hewer was chief clerk, friend, and executor of Samuel Pepys.[11] Pepys left Hewer £500 and the models of his ships,[12] so perhaps some of that wealth, for the increase of which the diarist yearly thanked God, found its way to the Corporation of Colchester. By 1740 Hewer's executors had been paid back and a lock costing £1,500 had been built.[13] Even then the commissioners had in their hands, or had due to them, £1,110, which yet another Act empowered them to lend on

---

1 *J. H. of C.* xxiv. 727, 744.
2 18 Geo. II, c. 13.   3 9 Will. III, c. 19.
4 Colchester MSS., Assembly Book, 1693–1712, f. 161.
5 Ibid., f. 172.   6 Ibid., f. 342.
7 Ibid., f. 357.   8 Ibid., f. 403.
9 5 Geo. I, c. 31, sec. 1.
10 5 Geo. I, c. 31.   11 *V.C.H. Surrey,* iv. 37.
12 Wheatley, *Pepysiana,* pp. 259, 264.   13 *J. H. of C.* xxiii. 451.

mortgage or lay out in the purchase of lands.[1] At the same time the tolls were reduced to one of 3*d*. per chaldron on coals.[2] This prosperity was short lived, for ten years later the lock was 'in a decaying condition' and the river 'much choked up'.[3] The powers of the Corporation as undertakers had ceased and arrears of duty could not be recovered. The navigation was therefore vested in the Justices of the East division of the County of Essex and in certain commissioners named in an Act which granted an additional duty of 3*d*. per chaldron on coal and gave permission for more money to be borrowed.[4]

There was nothing unusual in these enterprises starting as municipal undertakings and then passing out of the hands of the corporation into those of a company or individual. Thus the Corporation of Bath, which was appointed undertaker of the Avon in 1712,[5] did nothing at all, with the result that the work was carried out thirteen years later by private individuals.[6] The Corporation of Salisbury undertook to make the Wiltshire Avon navigable, but finally abandoned it to individuals on account of the expense.[7] This process was common where the undertaking ultimately demanded a large capital expenditure. An Act of 1700 empowered the Mayor, Aldermen, and Common Council of Chester to appoint seven commissioners, of whom the Mayor and two Justices should be three, to undertake the improvement of the Dee.[8] But the real undertaker was Francis Gell, a London merchant, who was to receive the tolls and the land reclaimed from the river as the price of his work.[9] Thirty-three years later, on the passing of another Act, the Corporation dropped out altogether. An engineer, Nathaniel Kinderley, or his assignees, was appointed undertaker,[10] but he merely got the Act in trust for others and proceeded to appoint a body of forty to finance the work.[11] Though some of these undertakers were local men, others came from as

[1] 13 Geo. II, c. 30, sec. 3.   [2] Ibid., sec. 2.
[3] 23 Geo. II, c. 19.   [4] Ibid.   [5] 10 Anne, c. 2, sec. 1.
[6] Latimer, *Annals of Bristol in the Eighteenth Century*, p. 95.
[7] H.M.C. *Various*, iv. 247–9.   [8] 11 Will. III, c. 24, sec. 9.
[9] *A Case, Relating to the making Navigable the River Dee.*
[10] 6 Geo. II, c. 30, sec. 1.
[11] 'Dee Navigation, 1733', Add. MSS. 11394, ff. 29–30.

far south as Southampton, as far west as Ireland, and as far
east as Great Yarmouth; they ranged from the Reverend
Doctor John King, Master of the Charterhouse, to Robert
Bowyer, baker, of Chester.[1] On April 9th, 1734, by a
quadruple indenture between Kinderley, Thomas Watts and
Richard Manley, Joseph Davis and William Parsons, and
ninety others (thirty-six of whom were undertakers nominated
by Kinderley, the remaining four 'not having paid any
Money to the said Undertaking'), it was agreed to raise a
joint stock of £40,000, divided into 400 shares of £100
each.[2] As in the case of the Medway, these shares could not
be sold until the work was completed.[3] By Deed Poll of
August 17th, 1736, and March 3rd, 1737, 30 per cent. was
advanced on the subscriptions, but this only brought in
£7,830 instead of the £12,000 which would have resulted
if all the calls had been met.[4] Finally, in 1741, the proprietors were united by Act into 'The Company of Proprietors
of the Undertaking for recovering and preserving the Navigation of the River Dee', with a capital of £52,000.[5]

Lastly, the case of the Don may be taken as illustrating
almost every aspect of local financing in this period. By an
Act of 1726 the Company of Cutlers of Hallamshire were
appointed undertakers of the Don from Holmstile in Doncaster to Tinsley;[6] by an Act of 1727 the Corporation of
Doncaster received similar powers for the part of the river
from Holmstile to Wilsick House.[7] Before the passing of
its Act, the Corporation of Doncaster had resolved that the
undertaking should be done by its members in their private
and not their corporate capacity, but it was finally decided
that fifty shares should be issued, of which the Corporation
in its corporate capacity should take ten.[8] The value of these
shares is, unfortunately, not known, but by 1731 Doncaster
had spent £3,774 0s. 9d.[9] Two years later it would appear
that the Corporation in its corporate capacity had spent about
£1,150.[10]

[1] Ibid.   [2] 14 Geo. II, c. 8, sec. 1.   [3] 6 Geo. II, c. 30, sec. 47.
[4] 14 Geo. II, c. 8, sec. 1.   [5] Ibid., sec. 2.
[6] 12 Geo. I, c. 38.   [7] 13 Geo. I, c. 20.
[8] Doncaster Records, iv. 199.   [9] J. H. of C. xxi. 673.
[10] By the Act of 1733 the Corporation received 10 shares of £115 each, and these
were allotted in proportion to the sums advanced, 6 Geo. II, c. 9, sec. 1.

At Sheffield two bodies were at work, the Company of Cutlers and the Town Trustees. The former began their financial operations by borrowing in return for annuities 'on terms which can hardly be justified as prudent finance'.[1] Thus Mrs. Ellen Cutler advanced £300 and received an annuity of £27 for life, but her age is not known.[2] The Company then resorted to ordinary loans, but they had difficulty in getting money. On June 25th, 1728, they 'spent considering where to get money, at twice, 6s'.[3] Meanwhile the Town Trustees had borrowed £1,750 at from 4½ to 5 per cent., chiefly in small amounts of from £100 to £200 each.[4] By 1728, £3,000 had been spent by both bodies together, and it was proposed to issue shares to cover that amount.[5] The issue was postponed until the following year, by which time the Cutlers had paid out £2,504 11s. 11½d. and the Town Trustees £2,752 3s. 11d.[6] These sums included money lent by the Cutlers and Town Trustees in their private capacities.[7] In 1729, a hundred shares of £55 each were issued, of which the Town Trustees took ten in their corporate and seven in their private capacity, while the Company of Cutlers took eight.[8] The remaining seventy-five shares were divided among forty-six people, who included six clergymen, six cutlers, three London merchants, two grocers, a jeweller, an apothecary, a surgeon, a carpenter, a mercer, and a baker.[9] Only seventy-five of the hundred shares were actually taken up.[10] Dividends were paid about 1731,[11] when Sheffield as a whole had laid out £8,692 7s. 2½d.[12]

Two years later came a complete reorganization with the amalgamation of the Doncaster and Sheffield enterprises, a step which had been considered as early as 1731.[13] A new company was formed by Act, 'The Company of Proprietors of the Navigation of the River Dun', with a capital of 150

---

[1] Leader, *Company of Cutlers*, p. 168. [2] Ibid.
[3] Ibid., p. 169.
[4] Leader, *Records of the Burgery of Sheffield*, pp. 356–7.
[5] Leader, *Company of Cutlers*, p. 169. [6] Ibid., p. 169 n.
[7] Cf. the allotment of 1733, 6 Geo. II, c. 9.
[8] Leader, *Company of Cutlers*, p. 169.
[9] Ibid., p. 170. [10] Ibid.
[11] Leader, *Records of the Burgery of Sheffield*, p. 361.
[12] *J. H. of C.* xxi. 673.
[13] *H.M.C. Portland*, vi. 37, 44.

shares of £115 each.[1] These shares were distributed to the corporations and individual contributors to the undertaking, 'in proportion to the several Sums of Money by them respectively advanced'. Thus the Company of Cutlers got six shares, the Corporation of Doncaster and the Town Trustees of Sheffield ten each, the Trustees of Holles Hospital two, and the remainder were distributed among sixty-five individuals.[2] These shares could not be sold or transferred without security for meeting the calls, which continued until 1763.[3] Whether they were a profitable form of investment is not clear, but in 1740, when £24,750 had been spent, the navigation was let for fourteen years at £1,200 per annum for the first seven years and £1,500 for the second seven,[4] which would give an average dividend of more than 5 per cent.

The financial history of the Don undertaking is symbolic of an age that was attempting to find the best mould into which to cast the capital of its economic enterprises. It was a period of experiment in the efficiency of different forms of organization. In that experiment the projects for improved river navigation played their part. Men became aware that the individual no longer either could or would bear the strain of sole financing, and that in his place must be evolved a more complex form of capitalist enterprise. It was largely a transition from undertakers who had the money to those who borrowed it. In that transition every different shade of organization was possible. The work might be done by a corporation on long-term loans as at Beverley, or by a family partnership as that of the three Sandys in 1662, or by an indefinable body of men as the Tone undertakers of 1699, or by companies of proprietors as those of the Dee, the Don, and the Medway. It was to the company form that organization tended as the demand for capital became greater. These companies appear usually to have been public joint stocks

---

[1] 6 Geo. II, c. 9. Leader (*Company of Cutlers*, pp. 170–1) antedates this Act by three years and so makes a complicated situation still more complex. He shows, for example, that dividends were paid in 1731 (*Records of the Burgery of Sheffield*, p. lvii; *Company of Cutlers*, p. 171), and assumes that these were on shares in the 'Company of Proprietors', whereas they can only have been on those of the earlier company of 1729. [2] 6 Geo II, c. 9, sec. 1.

[3] Leader, *Records of the Burgery of Sheffield*, p. lviii. The call of that year was the 58th. [4] *J. H. of C.* xxiii. 441.

with two qualities which differentiate them from those of to-day. The shares could often not be sold until the work was finished, a precaution made necessary partly by the nature of the undertaking and partly by the second factor, namely, the system of making 'calls' on shares instead of issuing additional ones as the need for capital increased. But the fundamental feature of these joint stocks was the same as at the present time, the drawing of capital from an ever-increasing circle of investors whose connexion with the undertaking was solely the cash nexus of dividends.

How much capital was thus tapped and spent on river improvements? It is impossible to say. In the absence of statistics an estimate becomes mere guess-work, and, on the other hand, the addition of sums known to have been spent results in an under-statement, for the evidence is incomplete. It is possible to trace, more or less accurately, the expenditure of £376,650 during the period from 1600 to 1750. That this is not the whole expenditure is obvious. It does not include, for example, money spent on the Aire and Calder, the navigation of which was let for £3,200 per annum in 1744,[1] or on the Derwent, the Great Ouse, the Bristol Avon, and the Dane. It includes only partial expenditure on the Douglas, the Thames, and the Foss Dyke. Compared with the sums later spent on canals,[2] this figure may appear paltry, but much canal expenditure was uneconomic, whereas, except for the Douglas and the Wey, the money invested in river improvements seems to have been fairly well spent. In any case, river improvements offered a field for investment at a time when 'companies of men' were 'so eager to enter into joint-stocks for improvement of any thing that appears reasonable'.[3]

---

[1] *J. H. of C.* xxiv. 578.
[2] £13,205,117 by 1825, Jackman, *Development of Transportation*, i. 419.
[3] Houghton, *Collection for the Improvement of Husbandry and Trade*, ed. 1727, i. 87.

V
ENGINEERS AND ENGINEERING

IT cannot be said that the river improvements of this period were inspired by any great advance in technical knowledge. There was, indeed, some interest shown in the more theoretical side of hydrodynamics, chiefly through Italian influence.[1] In 1618 Castelli, a pupil of Galileo, had emphasized the importance of velocity as well as breadth and depth in measuring moving water. His book, *Della misura dell'acque correnti*, was translated into English after the Restoration.[2] Later Guglielmini had studied the motion of water down inclined planes,[3] but even towards the end of the century, the English were considering it an important factor in river navigation, 'by how much the more slimy and gross a water is, by so much can it carry the heavier burdens'.[4]

On the more practical side the seventeenth century produced no Brindley. Indeed, it has been asserted 'Engineers there were none, except those who used petards for military purposes'.[5] It is doubtful whether this is true even in the strictest sense of the word 'engineer'. Admittedly it is difficult to assign men to their proper professions in the seventeenth century. The mathematician merged into the surveyor and probably the surveyor into the engineer. Sir Jonas Moore did everything from writing mathematical treatises to founding the Royal Observatory, surveying the Great Level of the Fens, and studying the connexion of the Cam and the Thames.[6] Edmund Custis, who in 1673 removed the wrecked colliers from the Tyne by blowing them up, could almost certainly be described as an engineer.[7] The same may be said of Samuel Fortrey, grandson of a refugee from Lille, who became what might be called manag-

---

[1] For the general progress of mathematical studies see Clark, *Seventeenth Century*, ch. xiv.

[2] By Thomas Salusbury under the title, *Of the Mensuration of Running Water*.

[3] Wheeler, *Tidal Rivers*, p. 2.   [4] Heylin, *Cosmography*, i. 23.

[5] Trevelyan, *England under the Stuarts*, p. 53.

[6] *Cal. S.P.D.*, *1665–6*, p. 57; *D.N.B.*

[7] *Cal. S.P.D.*, *1673*, pp. 519–20; *1673–5*, p. 285; Hollar, *Engraving of the Tyne*, 1673.

ing director of the Wiltshire Avon undertaking in 1675.[1] Although 'one of the Gentlemen of his Majesties most Honourable Privy Chamber',[2] Fortrey was 'well versed and expert' in affairs of navigation and hired his services to the Corporation of Lincoln for cleansing the Foss Dyke. After the Corporation had spent £500, Fortrey was to bear one-third of the expense and receive one-third of the profit and to 'afford his best advice, direction and assistance according to the best of his skill and knowledge'.[3] Sir Hugh Middleton, the New River undertaker,[4] Sir Edward Forde, who devised an engine for raising water into the higher streets of London,[5] and Sir Richard Weston, who canalized the Wey,[6] must all bear the title of engineer.

By the eighteenth century that title had become a common-place in the field of river improvement. Witnesses who discussed locks and cuts before Committees of the Commons were often described as engineers.[7] There is, unfortunately, little evidence on the social status or financial position of these men. As early as 1675 Fortrey had demanded £500 as his salary for carrying out the Wiltshire Avon works. This sum was to be paid in instalments of £50 a quarter for five quarters and then the remainder when the work was finished.[8] This would appear to be an excessive charge, but Fortrey's services were certainly retained.[9] In 1722 Robert Wilson received only £2 7s. for surveying the Don from Sheffield to Doncaster,[10] but about the same time William Palmer, a more important man, was receiving large sums for surveying, though it is not clear how much was for himself and how much for expenses.[11] Palmer was also in charge of the works on the Yorkshire Ouse and received £50 for his expenses of surveying there in 1725. The following year he received ten guineas for attending a Parliamentary Committee to give evidence.[12] On the whole he appears to have had a substantial and well-paid position. The engineer who

[1] *Cal. S.P.D.*, 1675–6, p. 331.
[2] Fortrey, *England's Interest and Improvement*, title-page.
[3] Lincoln MSS., Box 29, 660.   [4] *D.N.B.*
[5] Ibid; Smiles, *Lives of the Engineers*, pp. 73–116.   [6] *D.N.B.*
[7] *J. H. of C.* xxii. 661; xxiv. 599.   [8] *H.M.C. Various*, iv. 247.
[9] Ibid.   [10] Leader, *Records of the Burgery of Sheffield*, p. 167.
[11] Ibid., pp. 350, 353.   [12] York MSS., Chamberlains' Accounts, vol. 33.

was responsible for removing obstructions from the Bristol Avon at Hungroad in 1745 received £1 10s. per week, compared with the 18s. given to the watermen and the 12s. to the labourers.[1] Thomas Redforth, who in 1728 was appointed 'expenditor' of the Don navigation and appears to have been manager and treasurer, received £50 per annum, 'he finding himselfe an Horse and bearing his own Charges'.[2] John Hore, who carried out the works on the Kennet from 1718 to 1723, received 'for his Skill, Pains and Trouble . . . only £60 per annum', but he was also appointed surveyor of the river and wharfinger at Newbury for life.[3] Finally, Daniel Dunnell, who succeeded William Baily as engineer for the Exeter canal improvements in 1699, received a salary of £3 a week.[4]

At the same time there arose a class of engineer pamphleteers who were prepared to give their opinion on the technical problems of their day and occupation. Controversy tended to centre round two subjects. The first was a largely academic question of how much fall was necessary for water to flow at all. Thomas Badeslade maintained that a drop of 6 inches in a mile was essential for a river or canal,[5] whilst John Grundy held that 4 inches were sufficient.[6] Despite their complicated mathematical proofs, they were both wrong for neither 4 nor 6 inches were essential.[7] The second question was more important, for it centred round the action of the tides upon the lower reaches of a tidal river. It was apparently held that special qualifications were necessary for dealing with tidal, as opposed to non-tidal, rivers. Grundy maintained that the engineer for the former must be a good mathematician, able to take surveys and levels and draw maps; he must understand natural philosophy and the laws of motion; he must be able to account for the rainfall and

---

[1] Latimer, *Annals of Bristol in the Eighteenth Century*, p. 254. The Beverley Beck labourers of 1726 received about 1s. 3d. a day, Beverley MSS., Beck Accounts.

[2] Leader, *Company of Cutlers*, p. 169.

[3] Thacker, *Kennet Country*, p. 318.

[4] Exeter MSS., Extracts from the Chamber Act Book.

[5] Badeslade, *The New Cut Canal*, pp. 9–11.

[6] Grundy, *Philosophical and Mathematical Reasons*, pp. 10–14; cf. also his *An Examination and Refutation of Mr Badeslade's New-Cut Canal*.

[7] On the lower reaches of the Danube and the Mississippi the surface inclination is only ¼in. to the mile, Wheeler, *Tidal Rivers*, p. 47.

the force of the backwater; finally, he must be capable of inventing engines.[1] If Grundy were correct, then all early eighteenth-century river engineers possessed these qualifications, for they all threw themselves into the dispute as to whether tides were or were not beneficial to navigation. One school of thought held that the tides brought up sand into the mouths of rivers, which they deposited on the ebb; the other maintained that the ebb tide combined with the land flood, scoured out the bed of the river, and carried away much more sand than the tides brought.

For a century the controversy centred round the Great Ouse and its important port of King's Lynn. The problem was brought into prominence there by the drainage works, in connexion with which a dam and sluices were built across the river at Denver in 1650–1.[2] This at once prevented the flow of the tide up the river. The building of the dam met with the approval of men like Dugdale[3] and Dodson[4] whose interest was primarily in fen draining, but it was opposed by the inhabitants of the river towns.[5] The opposition was unavailing, but in 1713 the dam was destroyed by flood.[6] In spite of this, the river continued to silt up and controversy revived about 1720.[7] In 1724 Charles Bridgman reported that the decay in navigation was due to the tides, which not only brought up sands, but widened the river and so made it shallower.[8] He proposed to check the tides at King's Lynn by means of a sluice and to cut a new mouth for the Ouse.[9] These suggested remedies were opposed by King's Lynn[10] and John Armstrong.[11] The latter, who had the support of Badeslade,[12] proposed to take up the remains of Denver Dam to allow the tides to flow freely and, at the

1 Grundy, *Philosophical and Mathematical Reasons*, Preface; cf. Badeslade, *A Scheme for Draining*, p. 3.
2 Badeslade, *Ancient and Present State of the Navigation*, pp. 51–2.
3 Dugdale, *Imbanking*, p. 178.
4 Dodson, *Designe for the present Draining*, p. 4.
5 Badeslade, *Ancient and Present State of the Navigation*, pp. 54–6.
6 Ibid., p. 91.
7 Kinderley, *The Present State of Navigation*, 1721.
8 Bridgman, *Report of the Present State of the Great Level of the Fens*, pp. 2–4.
9 Ibid., pp. 11–13.
10 *An Answer . . . to A Report of the Present State of the Great Level of the Fens.*
11 *Report, with Proposals for Draining the Fens.*
12 Badeslade, *Ancient and Present State of the Navigation*, pp. 91, 102–3.

same time, to close the New Bedford River, which had cut
off a curve in the Ouse as part of the drainage scheme of
1649.[1] By these means he hoped to unite the land floods
with the ebbing tides as a scouring agent.[2] None of these
schemes was carried out. Twenty-one years later, Elstobb
was demanding the removal of the foundations of Denver
Dam,[3] while Labelye was attacking the sands and tides.[4]
A similar controversy centred round the works on the Dee,
which were attacked by both Badeslade and Grundy on the
ground that the new cut destroyed the cleansing action of
the tides.[5]

These controversies which centred round the Great Ouse
and the Dee did not produce the mere theoretical speculation which inspired the seventeenth-century pamphleteers.
They enlisted the best brains of the navigation engineers
of the time, men such as Kinderley, who was responsible
for the new cut at Chester,[6] and Labelye, the engineer of
Westminster Bridge.[7] How did these men and those who
came before them carry their theories into practice? What
were the obstacles which they had to overcome? When the
Acts speak of a river being 'choaked up'[8] or 'utterly un-
passable'[9] they appear usually to mean that the navigation
was impaired by sands, tree trunks, broken banks, and
weirs.[10] The engineers then acted on the principle, 'Widen
a Channel, and you weaken its Current; straiten, and you
strengthen it: The first feeds and fills up the Channel, the
last grinds and deepens it.'[11] Thus in 1725 Captain Perry,
who had gained his engineering experience in the employment of Peter the Great,[12] suggested flood-gates and sluices
for overcoming the shallows of the Yorkshire Ouse, but his

---

1 Armstrong, *Report, with Proposals for Draining the Fens*, p. 16.
2 Ibid., p. 17.
3 *Pernicious Consequences of Replacing Denver Dam and Sluices*, p. 18.
4 *Result of a View of the Great Level of the Fens*, pp. 55-6.
5 Badeslade, *Reasons Humbly offer'd to the consideration of the Publick; New Cut
Canal*; Grundy, *Philosophical and Mathematical Reasons*.
6 *J. H. of C.* xxi. 813.   7 *D.N.B.*
8 9 Will. III, c. 19, sec. 1; 13 Geo. I, c. 4.
9 11 Will. III, c. 22, sec. 1.
10 'Medway Navigation, 1627', Add. MSS. 34105, ff. 188-92; Taylor, *Thame
Isis; Norris Papers*, pp. 37-8.
11 *The Case of Augustin Woollaston.*
12 Perry, *The State of Russia; D.N.B.*

plan was rejected for that of William Palmer, who proposed
to contract the river into a channel 90 feet wide and so
deepen it.[1] Palmer was put in charge to execute his plan.[2]

Some idea of the actual methods employed can be gained
from the suggested schemes for cleansing Beverley Beck,
which appear to date from about 1726. John Warburton
proposed to cleanse the Beck and deepen it by $1\frac{1}{2}$ feet by
using the tide as a flushing agent.[3] An engine boat, 'after the
manner of those used in Holland and Flanders', was to draw
up weeds and loosen mud. This was to cost £10 and the
labour of men and horses for working it the same amount.
A 'Lock, or Floodgate' near the Great Bridge was to form
a reservoir to collect water at every tide, which was to flush
out the Beck at low tide. This would cost £60, while a smaller
flood-gate near the Little Bridge, to scour the space between
the bridges, would cost £10. Finally, cleaning and planting
willows on the banks to prevent them from being washed
into the stream would cost £20.[4] This scheme was opposed
by 'Mr. P.', who agreed that it was easy and cheap, but he
felt that there was not sufficient strength of tide to drive out
the sludge.[5] An alternative scheme was put forward by Mr.
Lelham for deepening the Beck by $3\frac{1}{2}$ feet at a cost of £369
12s., or £1 8s. a rood. His method is not clear, but £50 was
to be spent in 'Jettying the Banks with Piles and Brushwood'
and £40 for a lighter to take rubbish away. A final £35 was
to go for 'makeing a Jinn to be fixt in the lighter for deepening the beck if the water cannot be conveniently turned
another way'.[6] The planting of willows or hedges was a
recognized method of protecting banks even as it is to-day.
About 1695, it was suggested that a shallow caused by
Hancock weir on the Wye might be narrowed 'with a Hedge,
on Each side [of] the stream'.[7] The banks of the Great

---

[1] Drake, *Eboracum*, p. 232.

[2] York MSS., Chamberlains' Accounts, vol. 34.

[3] Nearly a century before, Christian Derickson had taken out a Patent for a
spring door on the land side of sluices in sandy rivers for the forcible scouring and
maintaining the outfall (1634), *Abridgments of Specifications relating to Harbours,
Docks, and Canals*, p. 4.

[4] 'Beverley Beck Navigation, 1699–1726', Lansdowne MSS. 896, ff. 164, 166.

[5] Ibid., f. 163. 'Mr P.' was probably William Palmer.

[6] Ibid., f. 167.

[7] 'Survey of Wye and Lug', Add. MSS. 21567, f. 5 and cf. f. 6.

Ouse in 1749 were defended by faggots and wood called
'Counter Shores', towards the preservation of which the landowners paid a common charge or 'Acre-shot'.[1]

What the engine boats were it is impossible to say. Innumerable Patents were taken out for machines for cleansing
rivers, chiefly the Thames, during this period. On July 16th,
1618, John Gilbert took out a Patent for a water-plough for
taking up sand and gravel.[2] Thirteen years later the Patent
was surrendered and taken out again by Gilbert and James
Freese at a rent of £6 13s. 4d. per annum.[3] The king
requested the Mayor and Court of Aldermen to use the
gravel taken up from the Thames as ballast,[4] but they replied
that the engines of Gilbert and Freese 'do much hurt to the
river by taking up gravel from the firm ground and making
great holes',[5] which was at least a proof of the efficiency of
the machines. Somewhat similar Patents were granted to
John Shotbolte,[6] Simon Hill, and Sir John Christopher Van
Berg.[7] In 1673 Lewis Bayly patented an engine, the drawing of which shows scoops on the circumference of a wheel.[8]
Here the principle was getting much nearer that of the
modern dredger. A variant of this was Israel Pownoll's
device for scoops, buckets, or vessels on the end of a pole.[9]
It is doubtful whether many of these devices were put into
practice.[10] Baskerville, it is true, wrote, 'As we rode along
by the river to Yarmouth we saw an engine in the river to
take up mud in shallow places as the people told us'.[11] But
in 1676, when it was found that the channel of the Thames
had silted up 3 feet since the Restoration, Harris declared,
'If this be the Case, and the usual Method of clearing the

---

[1] *J. H. of C.* xxv. 786.

[2] *Abridgments of Specifications relating to Harbours, Docks, and Canals*, p. 1; Rymer, *Foedera*, xvii. 112–15.

[3] *Cal. S.P.D., 1631–3*, p. 99; Rymer, *Foedera*, xix. 305–9.

[4] Overall, *Indexes to the series of records known as the Remembrancia*, viii. 149.

[5] *Cal. S.P.D., 1631–3*, p. 433.

[6] *Abridgments of Specifications relating to Harbours, Docks, and Canals*, p. 2.

[7] Ibid., p. 4.   [8] Ibid., pp. 6–7.   [9] Ibid., p. 8.

[10] In June 1720 two companies were formed for dredging rivers and harbours, but they probably suffered the fate of most South Sea schemes, Scott, *Joint-Stock Companies*, iii. 452, 456.

[11] *H.M.C. Portland*, ii. 268. In 1712 an engine for cleansing Great Yarmouth haven was to cost £328, Great Yarmouth MSS., Assembly Book, 1701–18, f. 226 dorso.

Bottom (by only Two Men in a Lighter) should be found, as it seems to be, insufficient for that Purpose, it will behove the Government to take more speedy care about it'.[1] As late as 1745 the expenditure for the removal of obstructions in the Bristol Avon at Hungroad included 18s. 8d. for a pair of iron tongs to get up large stones.[2]

There is no doubt that the greatest obstacles to navigation were neither stones nor mud, but were the weirs and the mills which they served. These barriers or dams served two, often interconnected, purposes. Firstly, they were used as fish garths or kiddles for the breeding and capture of fish. Thus Wall and Ash Weirs on the Wye, belonging to the Duke of Bedford, were rented by a Mr. Waitte of London who received fish from them by horseback.[3] The fishing in the New Weir, on the same river, was valued at £100 per annum.[4] These weirs also led to the excessive destruction of fish and prevented salmon from ascending rivers.[5] It was said of the Wye that, before the erection of weirs, fresh salmon and other fish were so plentiful 'that hired Servants would condition with their Masters not to eat such fish above three meales in the weeke'.[6] Secondly, weirs raised the level of water for the supply of mills and were sometimes used to give winter flooding to the land.[7] Their destruction implied the ruin of the grist, paper, and fulling mills which they served.[8] Thus Taylor considered that the weirs on the Wiltshire Avon would have to be compounded for,[9] while the mill-owners on the Aire and Calder begged the undertakers to purchase or farm their mills.[10] These weirs were often formidable barriers. Monmouth Weir was 11 feet high 'built of Loose Stone, great and small confusedly thrown together, with cubbs of Stakes and Boughs of Trees platted together to stay the stones there; upon this loose confused stone there is raised a hedge with many great

[1] Harris, *Kent*, p. 258.
[2] Latimer, *Annals of Bristol in the Eighteenth Century*, p. 254.
[3] 'Survey of Wye and Lug', Add. MSS. 21567, f. 2.
[4] Ibid., f. 3 dorso.   [5] Ibid., f. 3.
[6] 'Wye Navigation, 1622-62', Add. MSS. 11052, f. 96.
[7] Ibid., f. 101.   [8] *J. H. of C.* xi. 470.
[9] Taylor, *A Discovery by Sea*, p. 26.
[10] *J. H. of C.* xii. 117.

stakes and small poles of about 5 feet high above the stone'.[1]
The Medway weirs of 1600 were from 6 to 8 feet high.[2] These
weirs were not only barriers themselves but caused shallows
below them.[3] It is not surprising, therefore, that boats had
sometimes to unload before they could get past a weir and
reload on the other side.[4] On the Thames the barges used
'Lightening-boats', which took goods out of them, 'for their
Passage through the several Locks, Weirs and Shoal-Waters'.[5]

On the other hand, it must not be assumed that weirs
served no purpose useful to navigation.[6] They banked up
water which they could let down upon occasion by a sluice
device, and it was upon these 'flashes' of water that the barges
passed over the shallows. Weirs thus contrived were what
seventeenth-century writers meant by the word 'lock'. They
were thus described by Plot,

... provided the fall of the Water be not great, a Lock will suffice, which
is made up only of bars of wood called Rimers, set perpendicularly to
the bottom of the passage (which are more or less according to its
breadth) and Lock-gates put down between every two of them, or
boards put athwart them, which will keep a head of water as well as
the Turn-pike for the passage of a Barge, but must be pulled up at its
arrival, and the water let go till there is an abatement of the fall, before
the boat may pass either down or upwards; which, with the stream, is
not without violent precipitation; and against it, at many places, not
without the help of a Capstan at Land, and sometimes neither of them
without imminent danger.[7]

Taylor had found similar weirs on the Thames which he
described, together with their capstans or 'Crabbs', to show
that weirs need not necessarily stop the passage of boats.[8]
This system was in use in France in the eighteenth century,
where 'partout les pertuis gardèrent jusqu'en 1773, un
système d'ouverture et de fermeture très compliqué, très
long et dangereux'. These 'pertuis' were shut by a series of
horizontal beams which were let fall, one on top of another,

[1] 'Survey of Wye and Lug', Add. MSS. 21567, f. 3.
[2] 'Medway Navigation, 1600', Add. MSS. 34218, f. 38.
[3] 'Survey of Wye and Lug', Add. MSS. 21567 passim.
[4] The Case of the River Derwent in respect of Navigation.
[5] J. H. of C. xxi. 790.
[6] 'Sir Clement Edmondes's Report on the Outfalls of Ouse and Nen, 1618',
Tanner MSS. 74, f. 201 dorso.
[7] Plot, Oxfordshire, p. 233.   [8] Taylor, Taylor's Last Voyage, p. 12.

into grooves, or by vertical pieces of wood called 'aiguilles'.[1]
In England these flash weirs remained until almost the
present time.[2]

It was not a good system, for it involved danger and delay.
The owners of mills might refuse flashes from their weirs,
either because they wanted the water themselves, or merely
to extort excessive charges for the passage of boats. In 1666
the owner of Tottenham Mill on the Lea refused water with
the result that barges lay aground for fourteen days.[3] On
the Thames it was not unusual for barges to lie aground
for a month or six weeks, during which time the bargemaster
was forced to maintain his crew.[4] Since flashes were in-
dispensable, the mill- or weir-owners charged excessive prices
for them. Their exorbitant demands for passing the Thames
weirs interfered with trade and led to the passing of Acts to
protect the bargemasters.[5] What were the alternatives to
this 'baneful practice'[6] of 'flashing'? The weirs, of course,
could simply be removed, but that was merely to take away
a necessity of navigation without putting anything in its place.
When the weirs on the Wye were bought out and demolished
it 'occasioned great Shoals and other Inconveniences whereby
the Navigation of the said River is much obstructed'.[7] The
real solution lay in the replacement of the weirs by the
modern form of lock which raises and lowers boats within
an enclosed basin.

It is not the place here to give the history of what, to
avoid confusion, must be called the pound lock. Holland
has been called 'the nursery of the lock-system',[8] but there
seems little doubt that the pound lock originated in Italy in
the early part of the fifteenth century. It was perhaps part
of the scientific side of the Renaissance spirit of inventiveness

---

[1] Letaconnoux, *Les Voies de communication en France au xviii° siècle*, p. 141.

[2] Clark, *Seventeenth Century*, p. 51. In 1908 Lord Desborough described the
flash weir as follows: 'The flash lock is a sort of weir right across; you pull out
the centre sluice until you lower the whole water in the river above, supposing you
are going up the reach. Then the barge goes through and they very often have to
wait some time; you shut these sluices behind and you have to wait an hour or two
until the river rises again.' *Canals and Waterways*, Third Report, iii. 339.

[3] *Papers . . . relating to the Navigation on the River Lea*, p. 12.

[4] Yarranton, *England's Improvement*, i. 188.

[5] *Infra*, pp. 118–19.   [6] Jackman, *Development of Transportation*, i. 431.

[7] *J. H. of C.* xx. 784.   [8] Bates, *Touring in 1600*, p. 83.

that inspired their use by Philippe Marie Visconti in 1440.[1]
They do not appear to have crossed the Alps into France
until the end of the sixteenth or the beginning of the seventeenth century.[2] Of the time of the Revolution it has been
said 'les écluses à sas, en usage sur les canaux de la Flandre
sont presque inconnues dans le reste de la France'.[3] In
England, the older tradition that pound locks were first
introduced from Holland by Sir Richard Weston in 1645[4]
is unfounded. It is probable that the English copied the
Dutch in this, as in much else, but the earliest traceable
pound locks in England date from about 1564. These were
on the canal at Exeter, constructed by John Trew, and were
undoubtedly genuine pound locks.[5] Unlike the modern
common type, their lower gates were single,[6] which was the
usual form in Holland.[7] It is probable that, ten years later,
the lock at Waltham on the Lea was a pound lock.[8]

The pound lock was obviously known in England. How
far was its use extended as part of the river improvements
of the seventeenth century? It has been said of the Act of
1623–4,[9] 'the shining distinction of this Act is that it in-
augurated the system of modern locks upon the Thames'.[10]
These modern locks were the turnpikes at Iffley, Sandford,
and Swift Ditch. Two at least were built by 1632, for
Taylor relates,

> From Oxford two miles Ifley distant is,
> And there a new turne pike doth stand amisse,
> Another is at Stanford.[11]

[1] Sieveking, 'Origin and Early History of Locks', *The Field*, April 10th, 1915;
cf. Andreossy, *Histoire du Canal du Midi*, Introduction, p. xx, where the *écluse à
doubles portes* is definitely attributed to the Italians. For pictures of seventeenth-
century Italian pound locks, see Zonca, *Novo teatro*, and Coronelli, *Viaggi*, i. 84.

[2] Renard and Weulersse, *Life and Work*, p. 139, declare 'the first locks built in
France date from 1575'. Sieveking, 'Origin and Early History of Locks', *The Field*,
April 10th, 1915, and Belidor, *Architecture Hydraulique*, iv. 357, say that the first
French pound locks were built on the Canal de Briare.

[3] Sée, *L'Évolution commerciale et industrielle*, p. 206.

[4] James and Malcomb, *Agriculture of Surrey*, p. 9; Brayley, *Surrey*, i. 170 n., ii. 19.

[5] De la Garde, *Memoir of the Canal of Exeter*, p. 94; Fleming and Brocklehurst,
History of Engineering, p. 61; Forbes and Ashford, *Our Waterways*, p. 95.

[6] 'Thames Navigation', Twyne-Langbaine MSS. I.

[7] Ray, *Observations Topographical*, pp. 3–4.

[8] Sieveking, 'Origin and Early History of Locks', *The Field*, April 10th, 1915.

[9] 21 Jac. I, c. 32.   [10] Thacker, *Thames, General History*, p. 67.

[11] Taylor, *Thame Isis*, p. 17.

Scale and legend

0   20   40   60   80 miles

········· Rivers, or parts of rivers, For which Improvement Acts were passed

Map labels

Eden

York
Leeds
Beverley
Wakefield
Aire
Wigan
Worsley
Manchester
Don
Sheffield
Idle
E. Retford
Lincoln
Witham
Chester
Weaver
Middlewich
Nantwich
Derby
Derwent
Trent
Burton
Fossdyke
Welland
Nen
Norwich
Yare
Waveney
St. Ives
Cam
Little Ouse
Great Ouse
Lark
Bury St. Edmunds
Northampton
Cambridge
Sudbury
Stour
Hereford
Wye
Severn
Avon
Stour
Colchester
Oxford
Hertford
Burcot
Thames
Lea
Stroud
Frowdwater
Kennel
Newbury
Wey
Mole
Medway
Guildford
Avon
Bath
Salisbury
Itchen
Parret
Tone
Taunton
Avon
Wey

IV. RIVER ACTS, 1600–1750

It is clear, partly from the higher tolls charged for passing these turnpikes—1*s.* 8*d.* as opposed to the weirs' 6*d.*[1]— and partly from the high cost of upkeep—Sandford cost £155 to repair in 1647[2]— that these turnpikes were not the ordinary seventeenth-century lock. The evidence of Plot proves conclusively that they were pound locks of the modern sort. 'Hither also belong', he wrote, 'the Locks and Turn-pikes made upon the River Isis, the 21 of King James, when it was made navigable from Oxford to Bercot'.[3] He described the lock with its flash and then proceeded:

But where the declivity of the Channel, and fall of the water is so great, that few barges could live in the passage of them, there we have Turn-pikes, whereof there are three between Oxford and Bercot; one at Ifley, another at Sanford, and a third at Culham in the Swift-ditch, which was cut at that time when the River was made navigable; and are all thus contrived. First, there are placed a great pair of Folding doors, or Flood-gates of Timber across the River, that open against the stream and shut with it, not so as to come even in a straight line, but in an obtuse angle, the better to resist and bear the weight of the water, which by how much the greater it is, by so much the closer are the gates pressed; in each of which Flood-gates there is a sluce to let the water through at pleasure, without opening the gates themselves. Within these there is a large square taken out of the river, built up at each side with Free-stone, big enough to receive the largest barge afloat; and at the other end another pair of Flood-gates, opening and shutting, and having sluces like the former. Which is the whole Fabrick of a Turn-pike.[4]

Plot finally described how these turnpikes worked, which was exactly in the modern manner.[5] It would be interesting to know whence the inspiration for these pound locks came. About the time of the Act, Twyne visited Exeter and brought back a plan of the pound lock there. This he showed to the Thames Commissioners, 'but . . . the carpenters had newly begun their sluces here another waye and so it was not heeded'.[6] It is possible that the 'another waye' merely meant

[1] 'Thames Navigation', Twyne-Langbaine MSS. I.
[2] Thacker, *Thames, General History*, p. 79.
[3] Plot, *Oxfordshire*, p. 232.   [4] Ibid., p. 233.
[5] Ibid., pp. 233–4. Professor Clark was wrong, therefore, in believing that until the time of Charles II there were only weirs on the Thames, *Seventeenth Century*, p. 51.
[6] 'Thames Navigation', Twyne-Langbaine MSS. I. This is probably the earliest existing plan of an English pound lock.

that the Thames turnpikes had double doors at both ends, whereas the Exeter had a single door at the lower end. It seems probable that there were other pound locks in England for the Thames Commissioners to copy.

There seems little doubt that the use of the pound lock spread in the seventeenth century, but the whole question is rendered difficult by defective terminology. The use of the word 'lock' cannot be accepted as evidence. Pepys, for example, called the dangerous rush of water between the piers of London Bridge 'the lock'.[1] Nor is it safe to assume that a turnpike, as applied to a river, meant a pound lock. Yarranton, in his proposal for improving New Haven in Sussex, suggested 'two Turnpikes to be made in the River, to let down flashes of water upon all necessary occasions'.[2] As late as 1738 the 'Turnpike or Tumbling Bay' in Manifold Ditch described a mere sluice to keep up the level of the water.[3] On the other hand, pound locks were used in the improvement of the Wey navigation[4] and were introduced on to the Wye by Sandys in 1662, but there they were not a success.[5] In 1698 William Baily agreed to build at the northern entrance of Exeter Canal,

One large Lock or Sluce, the Upper Gates of which shall be Nineteen Foot high and the Walls or Sydes thereof shall be made with Stone and shall be in length above the Gates of the said Sluce, Twenty Seaven Foot and in length below the said Gates Thirty Foot and shall be Twelve Foot Thick att the Bottome and Six Foot Thick att the Top thereof, the Same to Rise Gradually; and that in the Upper Apron of the Gates of the said Sluce or Lock shall be laid One plate of Cast of Iron in length the whole Sweepe of the said Gates and that each and every of the Said Gates shall have One wheele of Brasse att the Outer Corner thereof, which wheele shall Turne upon the said plate of Iron and keepe the said Gates from Dragging; and that the said double Lock or Sluce shall be in breadth Six and Twenty Foot[6] and the Walls well Ioyned and layed with Tarrass in the Outer Ioynts thereof and shall contayne in the whole Two paire of Gates, Fower

[1] Pepys, *Diary*, i. 164.   [2] Yarranton, *England's Improvement*, i. 99.
[3] 'Bill for the Lea, 1738', Rawl. MSS. C 192.
[4] Ray, *Observations Topographical*, p. 3.
[5] Lloyd, *Papers relating to the . . . Wye and Lug*, p. 12; Pratt, *Inland Transport*, p. 131.
[6] i.e. the entrance to the lock was to be 26 feet wide, while the actual breadth of the basin was 75 feet.

Walls and Two Aprons. . . . The said Double Lock or Sluice shall be in length between the Upper and lower Gates thereof Three Hundred and Fifty foot and in breadth in the body of the said Lock Seaventy and Five Foot for att least Two hundred Foot in length to be measur'd upon the Surface of the Water when there shall be Fowerteenth Foot depth of water upon the Apron of the Upper Gate and shall be in breadth att the Bottome thereof Fifty Foot between the said Bankes.[1]

About 1700 it was estimated that £1,382 would be necessary to complete the lock gates, £181 to dig out the pool, and £605 to wall it.[2]

In the eighteenth century the use of the pound lock became more common.[3] In 1718 the Kennet was improved by John Hore on the pound-lock system;[4] the same man may have introduced them on to the Stroudwater in 1730.[5] The Don Acts of 1733[6] and 1741[7] show that the river had been rendered navigable by the use of pound locks. The lock on the Colne, which cost £1,500 to build and £120 per annum to maintain,[8] must have been more than a mere flash weir.

It is true the pound lock did not win universal acceptance. About 1725 Defoe thought that the proposed Forth–Clyde Canal would only need flashes 'to push on the Vessels this way and that, as Occasion requir'd, not to stop them to raise or let fall, as in the Case of Locks on other Rivers'.[9] As late as 1743 the opposition to the navigation of the Newark branch of the Trent was based partly on the fact that locks would be necessary. 'The Inconveniences of Locks must be borne with in Rivers which cannot be otherwise navigable', declared the opponents, who supported the system of flashes then in use. It was held that pound locks wasted water, for whereas ten to twelve boats could go up a flash, only one or two could pass through a lock at once; the pound locks were held to freeze more quickly and thaw more slowly.[10] Much of this was probably mere prejudice against the scheme in

---

[1] Exeter MSS., Misc. Deeds, 156.   [2] Oliver, *Exeter*, ed. 1861, p. 260.
[3] This is shown indirectly by the Acts which made the destruction of 'locks' a felony, 1 Geo. II, S. 2, c. 19; 6 Geo. II, c. 33; 8 Geo. II, c. 20.
[4] Mavor, *Agriculture of Berkshire*, pp. 438–9.
[5] *J. H. of C.* xx. 437.   [6] 6 Geo. II, c. 9, sec. 31.
[7] 13 Geo. II, c. 11, sec. 23.   [8] *J. H. of C.* xxiii. 451.
[9] Defoe, *Tour*, ii. 755.
[10] *Objections to the Bill for making the Branch of the Trent running by Newark Navigable*; cf. *Observations of Mr Grundy, Junior.*

general, but it helps to explain why flash weirs continued in use so long.

The invention of the pound lock was almost as important for economic development as the discovery of steam power. Without it the canal-building of the Industrial Revolution would have been impossible. Short canals, in the technical sense of navigable cuts with artificial water-supplies, were built in Wales in the early eighteenth century. In 1700 Sir Humphrey Mackworth was said to have had a canal at Neath 'and placed his Floodgates and Sluices so convenient, that a ship of 100 tun may come up the Canal'. Later, from 1740 to 1751, a canal was constructed to convey iron and other products from the Ynysgerwn Rolling and Tin Mills to 'the old works at Aberdylais'.[1] Such canals were exceptional during this period, but river improvement did imply the canalization of rivers. Engineers supported the digging of new cuts rather than the improving of the old channel of the river. Thus Hore suggested an $8\frac{1}{4}$-mile cut, 23 feet wide and 5 feet deep, for the Stroudwater scheme of 1730,[2] and a cut costing £12,870, rather than an improvement of the old stream costing £9,355, for the Chelmer in the same year.[3] These were theoretical schemes rather than practical achievements, but the Dee was given a new channel between 1733 and 1737. This cut was somewhere between $8\frac{1}{2}$[4] and 10 miles[5] long and cost about £48,000.[6] In other rivers both cuts and the old channel were used. Thus the Mersey was canalized by cutting off the bends,[7] a course suggested for the Yorkshire Ouse.[8] The Wey, too, was clearly canalized under the Act of 1651, for in 1671 Thomas Cressy and Thomas Tyndall claimed 'severall parts of the cutt or Navi-

[1] Davies, *Economic History of South Wales*, p. 94.

[2] *J. H. of C.* xxi. 437. This was possibly intended to be a genuine canal, for Hore spoke of a 4-in. pipe supplying the water.

[3] *Intended Navigation of the Chelmer*, p. 12.

[4] *Canals and Waterways*, Second Report, iii. 1. There the width is given as 360–500 feet at high water.

[5] *J. H. of C.* xxiii. 597.

[6] 14 Geo. I, c. 8, sec. 1. There seems little truth in Postlethwayte's account of the 'canal' costing £739 4s. a mile and running for 20 miles, *Dictionary*, ii, 'Rivers'.

[7] Aikin, *Description of the Country . . . round Manchester*, p. 106; Jackman, *Development of Transportation*, i. 355.

[8] Drake, *Eboracum*, p. 232.

gable pass called the River Wye', while William Dickinson claimed rights in cuts 7 miles long; others even referred to the river as 'the Aqueduct'.[1] Thus in the direction of technical skill and accomplishments the river improvements of this period paved the way for the canal-building of the late eighteenth century.

[1] Exch. K.R. Wey Navigation Claims.

VI

THE MEANS OF CONVEYANCE

(i) THE BOATS

BOATS, no less than men, evolve a local character of their own. Hence, what may be true of the river vessels of one part of the country may be untrue of those of another part. It is only possible to generalize broadly on the different types of boats which plied on the English rivers during this period. With one type we are not concerned at all, namely, those which Pepys used so regularly when travelling to his work or to his pleasures. The wherries which plied for hire on the Thames formed an integral part of London life, but their story has been told elsewhere.[1] To the foreigner, indeed, the barge was 'a Sort of Pleasure-Boat, at one End of which is a little Room handsomely painted and cover'd, with a Table in the Middle and Benches round it'.[2] These barges played a great part in state and civic functions, but their economic importance was negligible.

The more commercially important river-boats appear to have been sailing-barges of every shape and size. They were usually square rigged with a single square sail, such as is used on some canal barges to-day.[3] This was the older and clumsier form of rigging, which was essential for ocean-going vessels, but which was largely superseded for river-boats, especially in Holland, by the fore and aft rig.[4] The latter was not unknown in England,[5] but its introduction appears to have been slow.[6] The boats themselves ranged from

[1] Humpherus, *Company of Watermen*.
[2] Misson, *Memoirs and Observations*, p. 11.
[3] The evidence for this is derived from contemporary illustrations, Cotton MSS., Augustine, I. 79 (map of the Great Ouse); Stukeley, *Itinerarium*, plates of Boston and London; Deering, *Nottinghamia*, plate 'A South Prospect of the Town of Nottingham'; Thoresby, *Ducatus Leodiensis*, plate 'The Prospect of Leeds from the Kinostrop road'; Buck, *Antiquities*, i, 'The South West View of Sion Abbey', iii, *passim*; Kip, *Britannia Illustrata*, i, plates of London; Hind, *Hollar*, plates xxii, xxiii, li (107).   [4] Chatterton, *Fore and Aft Craft*, pp. 47–9.
[5] Drake, *Eboracum*, plate 'A South West View of the City of York'; Buck, *Antiquities*, i, 'The South View of the Tower of London'; Kip, *Britannia Illustrata*, i, plates of London.
[6] Chatterton, *Fore and Aft Craft*, p. 161.

rectangular punt-like structures of almost unbelievable ugli-
ness[1] to the more graceful curves of the modern shape of
barge.[2] The latter were wider and more rounded at stern and
bow than the Navicello, the river-boat of the Arno, the use
of which Dummer advocated for English rivers.[3]

The boats appear to have been largely open with the goods
piled up without covering.[4] Some had a sort of canvas shelter
at either bow or stern, but this appears to have been for the
use of the crew.[5] More adequate protection was not unknown. The farmers of the Corporation's right of passage
in Beverley Beck in 1689 had to maintain two boats of which
one was 'to be a close decked boat'.[6] At Stourbridge Fair in
1700, the boats on the Cam had booths on them and 'Rooms
and secret Retirements, all covered above for the conveniency
of Strangers which resort thither'.[7] As the river vessels
increased in size so they became more elaborate. The lighters
on the Great Ouse increased from 40 to 130 tons burden, and
whereas the smaller ones had only a 'Hair cloth or Tilt' for
covering, several of the larger ones had decks, 'which are
very necessary for preserving severall Sorts of Goods, particularly Salt, Flour and Corn'.[8]

The boats of the Severn and the Thames stood in a class
apart. In 1758 it was said that two kinds of vessels were used
on the Severn, 'the lesser kind are called barges and frigates,
being from 40 to 60 feet in length, have a single mast, square

[1] Deering, *Nottinghamia*, plate 'A South Prospect of the Town of Nottingham';
Thoresby, *Ducatus Leodiensis*, plate 'The Prospect of Leeds from the Kinostrop
road'; Buck, *Antiquities*, i, 'The South West View of Sion Abbey'; iii, plates of
Leeds and Guildford; Kip, *Britannia Illustrata*, i, plates of London.

[2] Stukeley, *Itinerarium*, plate of Boston.

[3] 'Dummer's Voyage into the Mediterranean Seas, 1685', Kings MSS. 40, ff.
142-3.

[4] Drake, *Eboracum*, plate 'York from near the confluence of the River Ouse and
Foss'; Thoresby, *Ducatus Leodiensis*, plate 'The Prospect of Leeds from the Kinostrop road'.

[5] Deering, *Nottinghamia*, plate 'A South Prospect of the Town of Nottingham';
Kip, *Britannia Illustrata*, i, plate of Lambeth; Hind, *Hollar*, plate lviii (116).

[6] *Beverley Records*, p. 179.   [7] Brome, *Travels*, p. 67.

[8] *J. H. of C.* xxv. 787. The later canal barges had often only tarpaulin covering,
Jackman, *Development of Transportation*, i. 441. See Buck, *Antiquities*, iii, 'The
South East Prospect of the City of Norwich', for early boats with considerable
covering. In the seventeenth century 'Tilt cloths for Barge-men' were made at
Witney, Plot, *Oxfordshire*, p. 279, quoted Plummer, *The Witney Blanket Industry*,
pp. 4-5.

sail, and carry from 20 to 40 tons; the trows, or larger vessels, are from 40 to 80 tons burden: these have a main and top mast, about 80 feet high, with square sails, and some have mizen masts; they are generally from 16 to 20 feet wide and 60 in length'.[1]   The trows usually carried a square sail and a square topsail on the mainmast and a lateen sail on the mizen.[2] They thus combined the square rig with the fore and aft. The size of these trows had probably been increasing, for in 1657 a trow built by the State to carry timber from the Forest of Dean to Shirehampton had a burden of only 20 tons.[3] On the Thames, the great western barges were 'remarkable for the Length of the Vessel, and the Burthen they carry, and yet the little Water they draw; in a word, some of these Barges carry above a Thousand Quarter of Malt at a Time, and yet do not draw Two Foot of Water'.[4] They were sailing barges with 'broad Sails'.[5] In 1695 the Company of Watermen complained that these barges blocked up the public stairs and led to great contentions, tending to a breach of the peace.[6] Half a century later these barges were charged with obstructing navigation by being over-built and over-loaded and drawing too much water. They had even rafts of timber tied to their sides.[7] They may, indeed, have been too large for the river, for they had to use 'Lightening-boats', which lightened their loads for passage through weirs and over shoals.[8] In 1751 an Act appointed commissioners to make orders relating to the size and draught of boats on the Thames, and no boat was to draw more than 4 feet of water.[9]

There seems no doubt that the western barges were larger, on the whole, than the boats on other rivers. The size was

[1] *Gentleman's Magazine*, 1758, p. 277. For the later history of the trows see *The Mariners' Mirror*, July 1912, pp. 201–5 (R. Morton Nance, 'Trows, Past and Present'); for a sketch of a seventeenth-century trow see ibid., July 1913, p. 219.

[2] Carr, *Sailing Barges*, p. 137.   [3] *Cal. S.P.D., 1657–8*, p. 56.

[4] Defoe, *Tour*, i. 348. In 1720 barges of 50 tons were said to go to Lechlade and of 90 tons to Oxford, Cox, *Magna Britannia*, i. 117.

[5] Defoe, *Tour*, ed. 1742, i. 229.

[6] Humpherus, *Company of Watermen*, i. 401.

[7] Griffiths, *An Essay*, pp. 16–17. In 1747 the bargemasters, petitioning against the new bridge to be built at Walton-on-Thames, declared that they navigated 'very large barges', which the bridge would put in danger of sinking, *J. H. of C* xxv. 303.

[8] *J. H. of C.* xx. 790.

[9] 24 Geo. II, c. 8. The Act of 1726 for the Don laid down that boats were not to draw more than 3 feet except in time of flood, 13 Geo. I, c. 20, sec. 8.

everywhere dictated by the question of the draught which the river could take. Thus, in 1749, it was reported of the Great Ouse 'that the Tide and Current of the said River having of late Years been of greater Force and Rapidity than formerly ... the Size of the Lighters and Vessels used therein' had also increased from 40 to about 130 tons.[1] On the Yorkshire Ouse the reverse process was at work. Sea-going vessels of 100 tons had reached York in the time of Charles II,[2] but with the decay of the river these had fallen to about 70 tons by the eighteenth century.[3] At the other end of the scale was the flat-bottomed boat of 4 tons drawing 1 foot 4 inches of water, which could ascend the Wye to Hereford,[4] and the suggested boats of 10 tons for which the Wiltshire Avon was to be made navigable.[5] The largest boat passing along the Foss Dyke from Michaelmas 1714 to Michaelmas 1715 carried only 18 tons.[6] If it is possible to generalize at all, then it would appear that boats on rivers, other than the Thames and Severn, had usually a burden of between 20 and 40 tons.[7]

Though river-boats were almost invariably sailing-vessels, they were not entirely dependent upon the wind for their motive power. There were, as Petty said, 'Some for Oars, some for Poles, some for Sails, and some for draught by Men or Horses'.[8] The obvious omission from this list is any mechanical means of propulsion. That, indeed, did not get beyond the experimental or even the theoretical stage. In 1618 David Ramsey, a page of the King's Bedchamber, took out a Patent to put into use engines 'and to make boats for carriages running upon the water as swift in calmes, and more safe in stormes, than boats full sailed in great windes'.[9] After the Restoration 'a way how to make a Boat work it

[1] *J. H. of C.* xxv. 733, 787.   [2] *H.M.C. Portland,* ii. 40.
[3] Macky, *Journey through England,* ii. 212; Defoe, *Tour,* ii. 639.
[4] 'Wye Navigation, 1622–62', Add. MSS. 11052, f. 95.
[5] *H.M.C. Various,* iv. 247.   [6] Lincoln MSS., Foss Dyke Tolls.
[7] 'Survey of Wye and Lug', Add. MSS. 21567, ff. 3–4; Cheshire MSS. Book of Tonnage Duties (1740–69); Mathew, *Mediterranean Passage . . . from London to Bristol,* dedication; *H.M.C. Portland,* ii. 270; Habington, *Worcestershire,* ii. 468; *J. H. of C.* xx. 140; xxii. 786, 803; 13 Geo. II, c. 26.
[8] Petty, *Works,* i. 260.
[9] Rymer, *Foedera,* xvii. 121–3; Boulton, *Pageant of Transport,* p. 91; Woodcroft, *Steam Navigation,* pp. 3–4.

self against Wind and Tide' formed part of the Marquis of Worcester's project of 1661.[1] Twenty years later, it was reported from Rochester that an engine had been carried into the Medway 'worked by the help of horses', which would 'tow up and down the river any ship the king has, against wind or tide or both'.[2] About the same time Petty was evolving a plan for a paddle boat.[3] It was not until the eighteenth century that the use of steam was seriously considered as the motive power for boats. Hull's machine, worked by steam and atmospheric pressure on a vacuum,[4] and Savery's marine engine, improved by Newcomen and finally used by Papin,[5] were early attempts to utilize a force which did not become of importance until after this period.

In the absence of more mechanical means the only alternative when the wind failed was to use men or horses. Both were used. In 1635 it was said that barges were hauled up to Shrewsbury by strength of men 'with much strain, force and pains'.[6] At the end of the century they were hauled to Worcester 'by strength of men 6 or 8 at a tyme'.[7] These 'halers' were employed on the Thames,[8] the Lea,[9] the Derwent,[10] and the Exe,[11] and probably on almost all rivers. Their use continued into the nineteenth century[12] when they were gradually displaced by horses and steam-driven barges. It is surprising that men were not superseded more quickly, for horses were used in the early part of the seventeenth century. They towed boats on the Great Ouse before the period of the Fen drainage[13] and were a familiar sight to the English traveller in Holland.[14] In France, in the sixteenth century, an edict of Henry IV had established relays of horses on the roads and towing-paths; horses for towing could be hired at

[1] Dircks, *Worcester*, p. 558.   [2] *H.M.C.* vii. 406.
[3] Fitzmaurice, *Life of Petty*, p. 122; cf. Dircks, *Worcester*, pp. 409–10, and Woodcroft, *Steam Navigation*, p. 9.
[4] Hull, *A Description and Draught of a new-invented Machine*; Woodcroft, *Steam Navigation*, pp. 11–12; Kennedy, *Steam Navigation*, p. 3.
[5] Kennedy, *Steam Navigation*, p. 2.   [6] Brereton, *Travels*, p. 187.
[7] Fiennes, *Through England on a Side Saddle*, p. 196.
[8] Buck, *Antiquities*, iii (Reading).   [9] Salmon, *Hertfordshire*, p. 2.
[10] Buck, *Antiquities*, iii (Derby).   [11] Ibid. (Exeter).
[12] Plymley, *Agriculture of Shropshire*, p. 82; Priestley, *Historical Account of the Navigable Rivers*, p. 46.   [13] *News from the Fens*, p. 6.
[14] Brereton, *Travels*, pp. 18–19; Evelyn, *Diary*, p. 25.

25 *sols tournois* a day, together with the feeding which was
valued at 10 *sols*.[1] The English attempted nothing as
systematic as this, but the use of horses appears to have
spread and to have brought with it new economic problems.
Horses required a stronger and more clearly defined towing-
path than men. About 1723 £150 was spent in building
fifty bridges and twenty gates for horse-towing along the
Yorkshire Derwent; and besides that a rent had to be paid
for the towing-path.[2] Landowners frowned upon the passing of horses through their land and this was sometimes
forbidden in the Acts. The Wey Act of 1651 allowed
towing by men only,[3] but it is clear from the claims of 1671
that horses were used.[4] By the Bristol Avon there was to be
a towing-path for men only.[5] The use of horses led to exactions by the proprietors of the lands through which the
horses passed. In 1730 it was said that towing-paths along
the Thames used to be free for men, but towing 'requires
such Numbers of Men as renders it very chargeable', therefore it was 'found much more convenient to tow with
Horses', but the owners and occupiers of land 'oblige the
Barge Masters to pay such Sums of Money for the Passage
of the said Horses, as, if not regulated and ascertained, will
lessen the Navigation'.[6] An Act proceeded to appoint commissioners, part of whose duty was to regulate the rents
charged for towing-paths.[7]

Towing by horses was undoubtedly much cheaper than by
men. In 1723 a witness for the Yorkshire Derwent Bill
declared that he towed 4 miles for 1s. with a horse, which
formerly would be done by four men at a cost of 4s. 'and a
Drink'.[8] Of the Thames in 1730 it was said, 'upwards of

---

[1] Pigeonneau, *Histoire du commerce de la France*, ii. 295. The system was never
completed, ibid., p. 397. In France oxen were sometimes used, Avenel, *Histoire
économique de la propriété*, vii. 94.

[2] *J. H. of C.* xx. 141.   [3] Firth and Rait, *Acts and Ordinances*, ii. 516.

[4] Exch. K.R. Wey Navigation Claims (Sir John Wyrley's claim).

[5] 10 Anne, c. 2, sec. 12. An advocate of the Derwent (Derby) navigation declared
that the Bill 'allows Haleing only by Men and not with Horses', *Case of the River
Derwent in respect of Navigation*.

[6] 3 Geo. II, c. 11, sec. 1.   [7] 3 Geo. II, c. 11.

[8] *J. H. of C.* xx. 140. In 1726 it cost £2 10s. to tow a barge from Newbury to
Reading and back, but it is not clear whether men or horses were used, G.W.R.
MSS., Canal Relics, 15, No. 3.

Three score Men are now employed to each Barge to tow it, when six Horses might be sufficient for that Purpose'.[1] When the size of vessels increased, towing by horses became a necessity. Thus for the large lighters on the Great Ouse, horses were essential. In places where the river was broad, towing required four-score fathom of line 'which the Strength of Men could never draw tight'. Not only were the lighters as large as western barges, but they were towed in gangs of nine or ten tied together, under the charge of a 'Bridgman' whose business it was to pilot them up the river.[2] With this practice horses were essential.

Towing by men or horses was necessarily slow, but probably not slower than the prevailing methods of land carriage. It was said to take three or four days to tow 50 miles on the Welland in 1619,[3] but in 1654 it was possible to go from King's Lynn to Cambridge with horses in twenty hours.[4] On the eighteenth-century canals the rate was only $2\frac{1}{2}$ miles per hour.[5] Until the advent of railways water transport compared favourably in speed with any other form of goods carriage.

The information on river-boats of this period is scattered and incomplete. There was no general register of these boats until 1795, when an Act[6] made national that registration and numbering of boats which had been enforced locally by various river-improvement Acts,[7] in order to trace boats responsible for damage. Where were the boats built, and how much did they cost? It seems certain that they were built locally by the rivers for which they were intended. Thus the boats for the Yorkshire Ouse were built at Selby, Wistow, Stillingfleet, Naburn, Fulford, and Cawood.[8] The

---

[1] *J. H. of C.* xxi. 427.

[2] Ibid. xxv. 787, 837. Buck, *Antiquities*, iii, 'The South East Prospect of the City of Ely', shows a gang of four lighters. In 1909 it was said that the towing-path along the Great Ouse had stiles over which the horses had to be taught to jump, *Canals and Waterways*, Third Report, v, part ii. 141.

[3] Wheeler, *Fens*, p. 121.   [4] *News from the Fens*, p. 15.

[5] Clapham, *Economic History*, i. 84. In 1641 Taylor took four days to get from London to Oxford in his 'Scullers boate', *Taylor's Last Voyage*, p. 11. In 1809 barges took three and a half days from Oxford to London and six from London to Oxford, Mavor, *Agriculture of Berkshire*, p. 531.

[6] 35 Geo. III, c. 58.   [7] e.g. 4/5 Anne, c. 2, sec. 26.

[8] *H.M.C. House of Lords*, N.S. iii. 211–12; Pococke, *Travels*, i. 173.

ship carpenters of Cawood petitioned against the Aire and Calder navigation on the ground that it would drain water from the small rivers by which they got their timber.[1] York, too, had its shipbuilding, for an order of the Corporation, dated January 28th, 1736, declared 'leave be not at any time hereafter given to anyone to build Boats, Keels, Ships or other Vessels upon the Bank of the River Owze near the Ferry Boat at Northstreet postern. The Bank there being shrunk and damaged by such Building and the road much spoiled besides the damage done to passengers on horseback by their horses being affrighted.'[2] Boats for the Trent coal trade were built at Newark,[3] while East and West Stockwith, Misterton, and Butterwick had their ship carpenters and rope- and sail-makers.[4]

On the Thames, John Davis was a boat-builder at Oxford in 1730, and in that year he leased a cottage by the river at 1s. a year rent and a pullet.[5] At Rotherhithe in 1716, Thomas Bevois, a boat-builder, took Andrew Cuzmin as apprentice for five years at a premium of £80.[6] The following year, Daniel Woodden of Lambeth, boat-builder, took Ivan Schipiloff as apprentice for five years at £55, while Thomas Dyson, boat- and barge-builder of the same place, took Juan Schirisoff for the term of three years seven months for £30.[7] At Thames Ditton in 1721 Richard Cockman, a barge-maker, apprenticed his son to a Hampton-upon-Thames baker for £10.[8] Some of these men may have been builders of state barges or passenger wherries, but others may have been responsible for the west country barges. Severn trows were built at Tewkesbury,[9] and probably at Gloucester and Worcester as well.

The cost of these boats is hard to determine. In 1600 an interesting comparison was made between the capital outlay

[1] *J. H. of C.* xii. 98.
[2] York MSS., House Book, 42, f. 201.
[3] *H.M.C. Middleton,* p. 177.
[4] *J. H. of C.* xi. 416; *J. H. of L.* xvii. 255.
[5] Salter, *Oxford City Properties,* p. 101. Cf. Salter, *Cartulary of Oseney Abbey,* ii. 531, for the lease of a house by another boat-builder of Oxford, Thomas Dewy, in 1740.
[6] *Surrey Apprenticeships,* Surrey Record Society, x. 47.
[7] Ibid., p. 151. The Russian names suggest a connexion with Peter the Great.
[8] Ibid., p. 37.   [9] *Cal. S.P.D., 1629-31,* p. 445.

and the yearly charges of land and water carriage in the Medway valley. The estimate was as follows:

Cart and Oxen (6 oxen, 2 horses) cost £34 9s. 8d.
Yearly cost of these   .   . £12 16s. (presumably depreciation).
Other yearly charges .   . £27   (including pasture and hay, £24).
Servants' wages .   .   . £10
Total yearly charges .   . £49 16s.

The cart would carry two loads per day in summer for 4s. 4d. and one load per day in winter for 4s.

'The Boateman with his Implements'

Boat	£4 6s.	8d.
Oars	6s.	
Tow line	1s.	
'Setting staves and boat hook' . . .	1s.	8d.
	£4 15s.	4d.

Yearly cost:

Boat with 10s. a year spent on it will last 8 years.	£1 6s.	8d.
Oars last two years	3s.	
Tow line, &c.	2s.	8d.
	£1 12s.	4d.

One man in summer and two in winter will get their livings.[1]

This estimate was not without bias and the cost of the boat seems small, but in 1681 a boat built at the charge of the Dean and Chapter of Wells and Robert Pope, gentleman, for repairing the sea-wall at Burnham and Huntspill, cost only £6.[2] On the other hand, a Sunderland keel, fully equipped, was said to be worth £100 in 1618,[3] and a ballast lighter of 40 tons was valued at £250 at Harwich in 1659.[4] In the eighteenth century a lighter to take away rubbish from Beverley Beck was estimated to cost £50,[5] but a boat bought on August 8th, 1734, possibly for that purpose, cost only £12 2s.[6] The price would naturally vary with the tonnage. A boat of 6 tons on Loch Garry in 1728, built for the use of the ironworks, floated away and was 'dashed to pieces down

[1] 'Medway Navigation, 1600', Add. MSS. 34218, ff. 40–1.
[2] H.M.C. Wells, ii. 445.   [3] Nef, Coal Industry, i. 388.
[4] Cal. S.P.D., 1658–9, p. 293.
[5] 'Beverley Beck Navigation, 1699–1726', Lansdowne MSS. 896, f. 167.
[6] Beverley MSS., Beck Accounts.

a Precipice where the Water falls'. Its loss was reckoned at
£24.[1] In 1758 a Severn trow of from 40 to 80 tons, new
and completely rigged, was worth £300.[2] A good proportion
of this sum was probably taken up by the masts and sails. A
committee that reported on the removal of obstructions in
the Avon at Hungroad in 1745 declared that a boat to carry
35 tons would cost £25, but if 'the sand &c. that shall be
taken up be delivered in Kingroad then the vessel will want
a mast and sail, which will cost £20'.[3] Thus the mast and
sail were to cost 44 per cent. of the entire price of the boat.
This may have been exceptional, but there seems little doubt
that a fully equipped river-boat was a quite valuable possession during this period.

(ii) THE BOATMEN

River transport employed two large classes of men, between which contemporaries did not trouble to distinguish.
There were those who towed the boats, the 'halers', and those
who actually navigated them. The former must have had an
arduous form of employment, comparable to that of unload-
ing colliers in the Thames. In times of extreme drought or
heavy floods, or when mill-owners refused flashes, the 'halers'
must have been thrown out of work. It would be interesting
to know whether these men were recruited locally at various
stages as the barge passed, say from London to Oxford, or
whether they were hired for the whole voyage. The former
seems probable, as it would do away with the difficulty of
accommodating the men at night. If that were so, 'haling'
would be only one of the many employments of the casual
labourer. Even the leading of towing horses could be difficult and dangerous work. Before the Fen drainage, horses
led by boys towed the boats on the Great Ouse and they were
often forced to go up to their middles in water. When they
came to a dike or slough, 'they were fain to take in the boy
and the Horses into the Boat, and set them out again when
they were past it, which was no small hindrance and loss of

---

[1] Fell, *Early Iron Industry of Furness*, p. 360.
[2] *Gentleman's Magazine*, 1758, p. 277. In 1906 a Birmingham canal barge of
25–30 tons cost £65 and lasted from 15 to 20 years, *Canals and Waterways*, First
Report, i, part ii. 224.
[3] Latimer, *Annals of Bristol in the Eighteenth Century*, p. 254.

time, besides the death of so many Boyes and Horses with this unreasonable dealing'.[1] After the Fen drainage, boys and horses continued to tow, and for some reason, perhaps the tides, they worked in the night time.[2] About a century later boys who seem actually to have pulled the boats along Beverley Beck were receiving 6*d*. a day. Two boys worked to each boat.[3]

The men who worked on the barge, rather than the bank, required skill as well as strength. It was they who sailed the boat when the wind allowed or sometimes punted it along with ashen poles and 'incredible dexterity'.[4] About the middle of the seventeenth century it was reckoned that three men were required per 10 tons,[5] but in 1720 vessels of 40 tons on the Weaver only required that number.[6] At the end of the eighteenth century *The True Briton* of Abingdon, 122 tons burden, had a master, one man as 'steersman and Cost-bearer', four men as bargemen and navigators, and a boy to do errands.[7] *The Toll Dish* of 43 tons had three men as crew.[8]

It is dangerous to attempt to judge the character of a class of men who lived two or three centuries ago. If the present can look impartially on the past, the past could not look impartially upon itself. Those who opposed river improvements made the character of the men who towed or navigated the barges one of the grounds of their opposition. They were held to be 'seldom of the better Sort',[9] or 'but a fewe dronken and beggerley fellowes', who would steal 'Hennes, Geese, Duckes, Piggs, Swannes, Eggs, Woode and all other such Commodytes'.[10] It was felt that 'lawless bargemen . . . who have so easy a way of escaping the Constable'[11] had special facilities for stealing fruit or rabbits or wood.[12] It was in vain

---

[1] *News from the Fens*, p. 6.   [2] Ibid., p. 15.

[3] Beverley MSS., Beck Accounts.

[4] Mavor, *Agriculture of Berkshire*, p. 432; cf. Kip, *Britannia Illustrata*, i, plate of Lambeth.

[5] 'Wye Navigation, 1622–62', Add. MSS. 11052, f. 95 dorso.

[6] 'Weaver Navigation, 1699–1720', Add. MSS. 36914, f. 118.

[7] *Abingdon Records*, App. p. xli.   [8] Ibid., p. xlii.

[9] 'Derwent Navigation', Stowe MSS. 818, f. 85.

[10] 'Medway Navigation, 1600', Add. MSS. 34218, f. 37.

[11] Lloyd, *Papers relating to the . . . Wye and Lug*, p. 23.

[12] 'Wye Navigation, 1622–62', Add. MSS. 11052, f. 101.

that their defenders pointed out that if, for example, the
'halers' stole a sheep they would have to bring it back to the
boat, and people turned to look at the boats. They had, therefore, less opportunity of stealing than others.[1] They were
still considered 'very lewed and ill-disposed people'.[2] The
river-improvement Acts usually made the master of the vessel
answerable for the damage done by his boat and 'by the rude
and disorderly persons rowing and manageing the said
barges'.[3] Even the bargeman's almost legendary powers of
invective are traceable to this period. In 1654 it was said of
the watermen on the Great Ouse 'that for all the good you
do them, you must expect nothing but railing; which is so
customarie amongst them, that they cannot forbear one
another'.[4] More than half a century later Saussure declared:
'Most bargemen are very skilful in this mode of warfare
[verbal]; they use singular and even quite extraordinary
terms, and generally very coarse and dirty ones, and I cannot
explain them to you.'[5]

How far was this bad reputation justified? The bargemen
certainly figured quite prominently in the Quarter Sessions
records. In 1619 John Greene of Ware, bargeman, was
presented at Hertford for keeping an ale-house without a
licence.[6] Seven years later Gregory Stevens appeared before
the Mayor of Reading for abusing the Constables and
Churchwarden in service time, 'he beinge drinkinge with a
bargeman in his house'.[7] Bargemen appeared in bastardy
cases[8] and were ordered to be whipped for larceny.[9] Some
of the things with which they were charged arose directly or
indirectly from the nature of their work. Thus Henley
bargemen cut loose and used a boat belonging to John Hall
'and left her loose uppon the River'.[10] Bargemen at Hertford

---

[1] 'Derwent Navigation', Stowe MSS. 818, f. 85.

[2] 'Weaver Navigation, 1699–1720', Add. MSS. 36914, f. 119.

[3] 6/7 Will. and Mary, c. 16, sec. 8; cf. 10 Will. III, c. 25, sec. 6; 6 Geo. I, c. 27,
sec. 19.   [4] News from the Fens, p. 7.

[5] Saussure, Foreign View, p. 95. In 1701 an order of the Company of Watermen
forbade 'immodest, obscene and lewd expressions' under pain of a fine of 2s. 6d.,
Binnell, A Description of the River Thames, pp. 162–3.

[6] Hertford County Records, v. 4.

[7] Reading Records, ii. 297.   [8] Ibid. iii. 187.

[9] Hertford County Records, vii. 105, 233, 234.

[10] Reading Records, iii. 248.

stole eels[1] and were presented for working on Sundays.[2] The damaging of ferry-boats and their ropes, which stretched across the river and so hindered navigation, was a frequent offence among Trent bargemen.[3]

The loose material lying about ship-building yards appears to have presented special temptation to theft. On December 23rd, 1651, Richard Harris, bargeman, petitioned the Council of State for delivery of his barge and tackle. He was employed by the State in fetching timber from the west to Deptford and Woolwich; 'upon the last occasion he was absent from his barge, having much business to attend to in London, and his men, availing themselves of his absence, took some plank and cordage out of the yard at Woolwich, and fled, but the barge was stayed at Deptford'.[4] Thomas Scott, who supported the petition, declared that the stoppage of the barge had been sufficient punishment and if it were not restored Harris would become a charge on the parish.[5] Whether the Navy Commissioners accepted this plea is unknown. About the same time Peter Pett wrote to the Admiralty Committee, 'we have sent a bargeman caught stealing iron, to be tried for his life, but the greatest punishment will be burning in the hand. I wish there could be some other punishment found out than hanging, but without exemplary justice, we shall not stop these incorrigible people'.[6] On August 5th, 1665, Pepys ordered 'six or eight bargemen to be whipped, who had last night stolen some of the King's cordage from out of the yard'.[7]

Finally, there were thefts from the actual cargoes of the barges. In 1632, at Reading, eight men, 'servantes to William Conwaye, master of the barge called the Dooves of Readinge', brought the barge to the wharf with 17 barrels of beef and other provisions for Sir Henry Wallop. Next morning one of the barrels was missing and two pieces of beef were found in the house of Edward Terant, one of the eight, who denied the theft. John Cole, another of the eight, explained that the head of one of the barrels flew off and

---

[1] *Hertford County Records*, i. 103; iv. 240.

[2] Ibid. iv. 123; the Act against this was passed on July 29th, 1641, *J. H. of C.* ii. 229.   [3] *Nottingham County Records*, p. 80.

[4] *Cal. S.P.D.*, 1651–2, p. 75.   [5] Ibid., pp. 75–6.

[6] Ibid., 1650, p. 492.   [7] Pepys, *Diary*, i. 614.

some pieces of meat fell out. These they 'delivered to Edward Terant intending to be merrye therewith'. Though others affirmed this story they were bound to appear at the next sessions, where their fate is unknown.[1]

These cases, if they prove anything at all, merely show that bargemen were typical of their age. Pepys gives the more pleasant side of the picture. Returning from Deptford he did not hesitate to take into his boat 'for company, a man that desired a passage—a certain western bargeman, with whom I had good sport, talking of the old woman of Woolwich, and telling him the whole story'.[2] On May 14th, 1669, the Pepys family went by water to Fulham, 'talking and singing, and playing the rogue with the Western bargemen about the women of Woolwich, which mads them'.[3] This was not the only time they made 'sport with the Westerne bargees'.[4] Rather than to condemn a class for the crimes of a few, it is wiser to conclude in the words of an anonymous pamphleteer, 'I know many water-men, and I know them to be like other men, some very honest men, and some Knaves'.[5]

Contemporaries who attacked bargemen as a class held that they were not only 'ill-disposed people',[6] but were 'very probably Beggars too'.[7] Unfortunately the evidence of their economic position is very scanty. Except for the watermen and lightermen of London they were not organized in companies or regulated by Act. The western bargemen were expressly excluded from those Acts which enforced apprenticeship or otherwise regulated Thames watermen.[8] There were certain difficulties and dangers in the bargeman's life which were economically disadvantageous. Thus in March 1623, when a Reading barge overset and nine people lost their lives, the goods were claimed as deodand.[9] Fifty years later the leases of Iffley, Sandford, and Swift Ditch

---

[1] *Reading Records,* iii. 165–7.
[2] Pepys, *Diary,* ii. 520. The story is unfortunately lost.
[3] Ibid., p. 691.   [4] Ibid., p. 696.
[5] *A Short Demonstration, That Navigation to Bedford is for the Benefit of Bedfordshire.*
[6] 'Weaver Navigation, 1699–1720', Add. MSS. 36914, f. 119 dorso.
[7] Ibid., f. 120.   [8] 1 Jac. I, c. 16, sec. 1; 4 Geo. II, c. 24, sec. 1.
[9] *H.M.C.* xi, App. vii. 183.

turnpikes contained the stipulation that if the owner of a boat doing damage could not be found, then the owners of all boats passing five hours before or after should contribute towards the repair of the damage. If they refused, then their boats could be denied passage.[1] Trade was liable to be interrupted, not only by flood and drought, but also by the presence of plague. In 1625, because of the plague in London, it was forbidden to bring goods or people from there to Reading.[2] If the bargemen went to London they were to stay there.[3]

Finally, bargemen were liable to be impressed, especially if they worked on the larger rivers like the Thames, the Severn, or the Great Ouse. London watermen in particular suffered from this,[4] and even Pepys thought it 'a great tyranny'.[5] The press-gang did not confine its attention to London watermen. In 1665 Thomas Campe of Ware was impressed out of his barge at London and served for two years against the Dutch. Twenty years later he sought to be admitted as a pensioner in the room of William Church of Ware, deceased.[6] William Jennings, who received 1s. 'for beating the Drume when the sea soulders were prest' at Gloucester in 1637, may possibly have been instrumental in disturbing the lives of many trowmen.[7] In 1666 watermen were pressed on the Severn and sent to Bristol.[8] During the Third Dutch War fifty men were impressed at Chepstow,[9] but the Mayor of Bristol requested the release of two 'who are owners of two trows that constantly use betwixt this and Worcester'. Their departure to the Navy 'would be a very great hindrance to the trade of this city'. The request ended with the rather ominous suggestion that one of the men could himself be used in pressing seamen.[10] Though the danger of

1 'Thames Navigation', Twyne-Langbaine MSS. I.

2 *Reading Records*, ii. 244.

3 Ibid., p. 245. Bargemen and watermen themselves were supposed to be 'not at all or rarely infected with the Plague', Baynard, *Cold Bathing*, p. 233.

4 *Cal. S.P.D.*, *1658-9*, p. 44, an order for pressing 500 watermen; ibid., *1664-5*, p. 187, 1,700 watermen at sea; ibid., *1671-2*, p. 75, an order to impress 1,000 watermen.

5 Pepys, *Diary*, ii. 59.   6 *Hertford County Records*, i. 365.

7 Gloucester MSS., Chamberlains' Accounts, 1633-53, f. 42.

8 *Cal. S.P.D.*, *1665-6*, p. 540.

9 Ibid., *1671-2*, p. 495.   10 Ibid., p. 534.

impressment was less than in the case of sea-going vessels, it was nevertheless a real one.

Details of the ordinary economic life of these bargemen are scanty. On the Medway in 1600 it was said that a boat-man 'dothe Labour very ill yf his dayes worke be not worth him xvjd.':[1] on the Bristol Avon in 1745 a waterman earned 18s. a week,[2] but between these two facts there is an almost complete blank. Few bargemen would be as fortunate as those on the three west-country barges, who passed the Queen in the summer-house of the Royal Garden at Rich-mond in 1731 and, upon giving her three cheers, were rewarded with three guineas.[3] There is indeed a definite statement as to the poverty of bargemen. An Act of 1671 for consolidating the Wey navigation granted a toll of 1d. a ton to Guildford to pay for the upkeep of the roads damaged by carts coming to the river and also because 'the Corpora-tion and Inhabitants would be burthened with poor more than before the Navigation, by the poverty of the bargemen, their families and others occasioned by the Navigation'.[4] If this statement were true in general, there were notable ex-ceptions. John Williams, a bargeman of Stoke, provided timber, stones, and other material for wharves on the Wey to the value of £408 11s. 1d., a sum which was owing to him in 1671.[5] After the Restoration the proprietors of the naviga-tion vested their monopoly of carriage in Henry Goldwyer, bargeman, of Guildford and William Bromfield, who repaired damage valued at £200 which had been done by other boats.[6]

It is clear that bargemen were not always the beggarly people their opponents made them out to be. On the Lea the bargemen themselves took a lease of Waltham Lock and collected the dues for passing through it.[7] In 1710 'Francis Philpe, Boatman in Pembroke' shared with Sam Barren, master of the *William and Jane* of Milford, a coasting trade bond of £200; William Evans, another boatman, shared a

1 'Medway Navigation, 1600', Add. MSS. 34218, f. 40.
2 Latimer, *Annals of Bristol in the Eighteenth Century*, p. 254.
3 Thacker, *Thames Highway, Locks and Weirs*, p. 488.
4 Manning and Bray, *Surrey*, iii, App. iii, lvii.
5 Exch. K.R. Wey Navigation Claims.
6 Ibid.
7 'Suit concerning Waltham Lock', Add. MSS. 33576, f. 36.

bond of £20.[1] At Oxford, in 1667, William Giles, a boatman, took a lease of a piece of ground near the South Bridge
for forty years at a rent of 1s. and 2 capons per annum. He
promised to erect a house on the land within three years.
This house was 'The Anchor', an inn which remained in
the hands of bargemen for a century. In 1683 it was occupied
by Nicholas Hooper, boatmaster; in 1741 Richard Hooper,
a bargemaster, renewed the lease at a fine of £12.[2] In
the seventeenth century 35 St. Aldate's was occupied by
Nicholas Cully, a boatman, at the not inconsiderable rent
of £1 2s. and 2 capons per annum.[3] William Pemmerton,
another Oxford boatman, spent £45 in repairing a house in
1699,[4] while twenty years later, Thomas Gardner, bargeman,
leased a tenement in the Fishrow for forty years with a fine
of £3 and a rent of 9s. and a capon or 2s. 6d. per annum.[5]

Finally, bargemen earned sufficient to be able to apprentice
their sons. On May 1st, 1712, John Johnson, son of Henry,
late of Guildford, bargemaster, was apprenticed to a London
tailor for £10.[6] Three years later, Hugh Moth, son of a
Guildford bargeman, was bound to a cooper for £10: his
brother, John Moth, was bound to the same trade for £13
two years later.[7] Thus this Guildford bargeman could lay
out £23 within two years for the apprenticeship of his sons.
John Collins, son of another Guildford bargeman, was
apprenticed to a local mason in 1718 for a premium of £5.[8]
The bargemasters themselves took apprentices, for in 1663
Edward Taney was apprenticed to Nicholas Taney an Oxford waterman.[9]

Some picture of the life of a late seventeenth- or early
eighteenth-century bargeman can be gained from Jonathan
Brown's account of himself, which he gave to Edmund
Calamy whose spiritual guidance he was seeking. Brown
had no notion either of his father or mother, but was put out to nurse
by he knew not whom, while very young. His nurse was kind to him,

---

[1] Exch. K.R. Port Books, 1320/5.
[2] Salter, *Oxford City Properties*, pp. 104–5.   [3] Ibid., p. 106.
[4] Salter, *Cartulary of Oseney Abbey*, ii. 504.
[5] Ibid., p. 496. For further evidence of house rents, see ibid., p. 527; iii. 20–1.
[6] *Surrey Apprenticeships*, Surrey Record Society, x. 98.
[7] Ibid., p. 123.   [8] Ibid., p. 39.
[9] Hobson and Salter, *Oxford Council Acts, 1626–65*, p. 302.

and put him, when six or seven years of age, to a barge-master that plied between Ware and London. While a child, he was employed in such little services as he was capable of; and, as he grew up, approving himself diligent and faithful, he was commended and trusted, and wanted not either for meat, drink or clothes. With this barge-master he continued until twenty-five years of age. . . . His master had a kindness for him, and much favoured him, though his fellow-servants and others seemed to bear an ill will to him, because he would not speak and act as they did.

Because of his religious doubts, Brown ran away, first to his old nurse and then to his cousin, a pipe maker. The bargemaster sought him out and offered him a quarter of the barge, which was worth £80, 'hull and tackle all together'. The offer was refused, but after serving seven years' apprenticeship with his cousin, Brown turned again to the water. At first he worked in barges and lighters as a servant to others, but 'living thriftily and saving all he could, and Providence favouring him, he at length, in process of time, got first a smaller vessel of his own, and then a larger, till he came and settled at Westminster, where he had an established reputation as an honest man, and was worth money'.[1]

It is dangerous to generalize from such scanty evidence, but, on the whole, there appear to have been three classes engaged in the actual transport of goods. At the head was the bargemaster who probably owned the barge and either carried goods for others or acted as a merchant himself. His position usually demanded some capital and was perhaps economically favourable. Below him were the crew, composed either of paid bargemen or possibly of partners with a share in the boat. Their position was less secure, but many were men of substance. Finally came the 'halers', probably casual labourers of the lowest class.

[1] Calamy, *An Historical Account of My Own Life*, ii. 122–7.

THE COST OF CARRIAGE AND CARGOES

THE economic justification of all the river improvements of this period was the cheaper carriage of commodities and especially those of a bulky nature. Land carriage was not only expensive but was subject to increasing restrictions. The age of the turnpike coincided with an attempt to fit the wagons to the roads rather than the roads to the wagons. Restrictions on the number of horses per wagon and their arrangement within the traces and minimum limitations of the breadth of tyre on the wheels[1] were a confession that the highways were unable to keep pace with the increased demand for the movement of heavy goods. The use of rivers meant an escape from these restrictions, though the rather rare limitation of draught of the river-boats to some extent corresponded to the maximum load of the highway Acts.[2] On the other hand, the river traffic was subject to two restrictions, one differing from, and the other corresponding to, those of road transport. River transport could be, and sometimes was, monopolized by law, whereas the roads were free for all. Secondly, it was subject to the payments of tolls not unlike the turnpike tolls.

Monopoly was the characteristic recompense for those river improvements undertaken under Letters Patent.[3] Thus Bath in 1619 was given the sole right of carrying goods and passengers on the Avon at rates to be agreed upon;[4] Henry Lambe was granted a monopoly of water carriage from Bury St. Edmunds to Mildenhall, but only after he had stated his rates.[5] This principle was continued by some of the Acts of Parliament. In 1651 the Wey undertakers were to run barges and take a fixed carriage rate.[6] These barges were

---

[1] 14 Car. II, c. 6; 22 Car. II, c. 12; 7/8 Will. III, c. 29; 5 Geo. I, c. 12.

[2] Cf. 14 Car. II, c. 6, sec. 8.

[3] Except in the case of the Soar, *supra*, p. 26.

[4] S.P.D. Warrants, x, July 16th, 1619.

[5] *Cal. S.P.D., 1637–8*, 323. For the Warwickshire Avon, Sandys was granted 'the benefit of the Water Carriages, as in such cases is usual', Rymer, *Foedera*, xx. 6.

[6] Firth and Rait, *Acts and Ordinances*, ii. 515.

built and the bargemen paid by the week, though in 1657
£190 was due to the towers.[1] After the Restoration the
undertakers granted their monopoly to Henry Goodwyer
and William Bromfield. Apparently they leased out parts
of the barges, for in 1671 John Skarvill, citizen and distiller
of London, claimed a quarter of a barge and a quarter of all
the profits of 'one Barge of the usuall Burthen' for nineteen
years from January 1665. Skarvill had leased this quarter
from John Rawcliffe for £325, which indicates that the trade
on the Wey was considerable.[2] Similar monopolies were
granted on the Wiltshire Avon[3] and the Wye[4] and proposed
for the Salwarpe[5] and the Nen.[6] In 1740 an Act for the
Medway allowed the proprietors to run their own boats and
take toll from others—here they were competitors and not
monopolists.[7] It seems doubtful whether this permission
was really necessary. Undertakers of river improvements
were not forbidden to be public carriers, as were early canal
proprietors.[8] Thus in 1746 Roger Holt sold to his brother a
moiety of one thirty-eighth share in the Douglas, which
included the navigation and 'a Like undivided part or share
of all the Boats, Barges and other Vessels now trading upon
the said River which belong to the proprietors or undertakers'.[9] But there is nothing in the Douglas Act[10] permitting
the undertakers to run their own boats. Similarly, the Kennet
undertakers used their own boats on their navigation, apparently without express authority, but they lost heavily and
soon dropped the practice.[11]

Occasionally a monopoly was based, not on statute, but
on prescriptive right. Thus the Corporation of Beverley
claimed a monopoly of traffic on the Beck. They paid a rent
of £4 per annum to the Crown for a cut through the manor
of Cottingham Richmond, and leased the passage of the
Beck for £5 per annum in order to cover this expense.[12] No

---

[1] Scotcher, *Origin of the River Wey Navigation*, p. 20.
[2] Exch. K.R. Wey Navigation Claims.   [3] 16/17 Car. II, P.A.
[4] Lloyd, *Papers relating to the . . . Wye and Lug*, p. 6; cf. 7/8 Will. III, c. 14,
sec. 1.   [5] *H.M.C. House of Lords*, 1692–3, p. 387.
[6] Ibid., p. 284.   [7] 13 Geo. II, c. 26, sec. 23.
[8] Jackman, *Development of Transportation*, i. 434–5.
[9] Wigan Public Library MSS., Capt. Case Deeds, No. 28, Portfolio Misc. Docs.
No. 6.   [10] 6 Geo. I, c. 28.
[11] Thacker, *Kennet Country*, p. 320.   [12] *Beverley Records*, pp. 114, 144.

goods were to be sent except in vessels provided by the tenant of the Corporation, who was to maintain two good and sufficient boats and take in goods at reasonable times.[1] By the beginning of the eighteenth century this system appears to have been replaced by one of taking tolls, which were double in the case of non-freemen;[2] but even after the passing of Acts which gave statutory authority to the tolls, the Corporation retained its right to farm out two market boats.[3]

That monopoly could have its effect on carriage rates is well illustrated in the case of the Trent. In 1699 an Act empowered Lord Paget to improve the navigation of the Trent from Wilden Ferry to Burton. A final clause of that Act declared that no wharves or warehouses should be erected on the navigation without the consent of the commissioners.[4] Lord Paget assigned his power as undertaker to one Hayne. Hayne owned the only wharf at Burton and refused to allow others to be erected. The commissioners appear to have taken no action at all. At Wilden a boatmaster, Fosbrook, owned the ferry-boat and rented a warehouse, 'and the said Fosbrook not only receives and carries Goods to Gainsborough, and back for Merchants &c. that employ his Boats, but is a considerable Merchant himself'. Fosbrook insisted that his wharf was private, which none could use unless they used his boats. According to the opponents of these men, 'Hayne and Fosbrook agreed to ingross the whole Navigation to their own Boats'. It was useless for Nottingham boats to go higher than Nottingham itself, as there was no wharf to land or take in goods (except Hayne's and Fosbrook's, where they were refused) and they could build no wharf without Hayne's permission. The result was 'the River being so monopolized Hayne and Fosbrook took their own Rates for Carriage, Wharfage, Warehouse-room &c. to the great Abuse of the Act and the Oppression of the Country and Fosbrook ingross'd the Markets also by keeping back other Merchants Goods at his Warehouse till his own were sold'. When the Nottingham boats attempted to go up the

---

[1] *Beverley Records*, p. 179.   [2] Ibid., p. 114.
[3] Beverley MSS., Corporation Minute Book, 1736-53 (copy).
[4] 10 Will. III, c. 26, sec. 22.

river Fosbrook stopped them with his ferry-boat and rope.
He made a boom of boats across the river and defended it
with forty or fifty men. Finally, Chancery issued an In-
junction for the removal of obstructions on the river. Hayne
and Fosbrook appear to have attempted to avoid this by
getting an Act to confirm their powers, but the Bill never
passed.[1]

A similar type of monopoly was created by the Mersey
and Irwell Navigation Co., which owned nearly all the warehouses in Manchester on the banks of the navigation. Though
the company was limited in the amount of tonnage duty
it could levy, there was no limit to what it could charge
for the use of the warehouses. Thus it was able to put the
warehouse charges up so high that it drove all the other
carriers off the river and so monopolized the trade.[2]

The second great factor in carriage rates was the tolls,
without which the improvements in river navigation could
never have been carried out. The Acts laid down the
maximum tolls, which varied enormously according to the
estimated cost of the undertaking. The Aire and Calder
Act of 1699 fixed the maximum rate at 10s. a ton from
October 1st to May 1st and at 16s. a ton from May 1st to
October 1st.[3] That was for the full distance from Leeds or
Wakefield to Weeland. The Derbyshire Derwent and the
Idle Acts of 1720 fixed 1s. per ton as the maximum.[4] It
is unlikely that the maxima were always imposed, for some
were exorbitant. From Maningtree to Sudbury 5s. a London
chaldron could be imposed on coal,[5] from Mildenhall to
Bury St. Edmunds 3s. 2d.[6] From the Ouse to New Malton
8s. a ton on all goods could be levied.[7] On the Dee the tonnage rates were sufficiently high to discourage trade and had
to be reduced.[8] These tolls were at least regulated and levied
for an economic purpose. Only in rare instances do they
appear to have checked trade.

---

[1] This case is given at length in *Reasons humbly offer'd against the Bill for . . .
making Navigable the River Trent.*
[2] Jackman, *Development of Transportation*, ii. 517.
[3] 10 Will. III, c. 25, sec. 4.
[4] 6 Geo. I, c. 27, sec. 8; 6 Geo. I, c. 30, sec. 6.
[5] 4/5 Anne, c. 2, sec. 8.   [6] 11 Will. III, c. 22, sec. 13.
[7] 1 Anne, c. 14, sec. 5.   [8] 17 Geo. II, c. 28.

More dangerous were the tolls exacted by mill- and weir-owners, for which there might be no statutory limit. These never attained in England the proportions which they did in France, where, despite a Royal Ordinance of 1669 suppressing tolls *sans titres*, there were eighty-four in Dauphiné alone twenty years later.[1] In England the Thames was the only river to suffer severely from these exactions. As early as 1623 barges passing through the nineteen locks between Burcot and London paid £2 0s. 2d.[2] Throughout the century the rates increased until, in 1694, an Act appointed Justices of the Peace as commissioners to fix the rates taken by occupiers of weirs, having regard to the ancient rate and the cost of repair.[3] In the following year the charges of thirteen locks were reduced to 19s. 4d. by a Session at Abingdon.[4] When the Act expired the rates increased again. The charges at sixteen locks, fixed by the Justices of the Peace at £2 19s., were raised to £8 19s., and it was said that barge-masters had been forced to lay down their businesses.[5] Petitions for an Act to revive the one of 1694, from the inhabitants of Berkshire, the Mayor and Corporation of Oxford, and the Chancellor of the University, pointed out that the occupiers of locks exacted double or treble the sums fixed by the Justices, besides the new exactions for the use of towing-paths.[6] Abingdon Corporation voted £30 towards the expense of getting an Act which was finally passed in 1730.[7] This Act declared that the owners of locks and weirs from Cricklade to London 'exact such exorbitant Sums of Money . . . as tend greatly to the Discouragement of the Navigation, and the enhancing the Prices of Water-Carriage'. It therefore appointed commissioners to fix the rates to be taken by occupiers of locks and proprietors of towing-paths and also the charges for water carriage.[8] Unfortunately, as with the 1694 Act, its operation was limited to nine years,

---

[1] Avenel, *Histoire économique de la propriété*, vii. 195; Boissonade, *Colbert*, p. 91. For Germany in the nineteenth century, see Clapham, *Economic Development of France and Germany*, p. 109.

[2] Thacker, *Thames, General History*, p. 98.   [3] 6/7 Will. and Mary, c. 16.

[4] *H.M.C. House of Lords*, N.S. i. 548.

[5] *The Case of the Barge-Masters and others, Navigating on the Rivers of Isis and Thames.*   [6] *J. H. of C.* xx. 775; 790; xxi. 417.

[7] *Abingdon Records*, p. 192.   [8] 3 Geo. II, c. 11.

and on the expiration of that term charges again rose. In 1746 a barge from Lechlade to London paid £13 15s. 6d. in lock dues and from Oxford to London £12 18s., though this was only in summer for flashes when the water was low.[1] The result of these exactions was further petitions[2] and yet another Act, passed in 1751, which largely revived the powers of its predecessors.[3] These dues were not confined to the Thames. On the Lea, for example, there were constant conflicts over the charges for barges passing Waltham Lock and Ware Mills,[4] but nowhere was the problem so acute or so likely to affect the rates of water carriage as upon the chief river of the kingdom.

In spite of these disadvantages, there is no doubt that water carriage by river was infinitely cheaper than land carriage by road. According to Sir Robert Southwell, wheel carriage was twelve times dearer than inland water carriage,[5] but this was possibly an exaggeration. The saving was greatest where the distances were long, as on the Thames, the Trent, or the Severn. In 1603, 104 'pairs of salsamenta' were sent by water from London to Burcot for 16s. 8d., while the short land carriage from Burcot to Oxford cost 7s. 8d.[6] More than thirty years later the 'King's Rate' for the carriage of coal from London to Wallingford or Burcot for the making of saltpetre was only 5s. a ton, but the bargemen were demanding 15s. as necessary because of the lock dues.[7] At the end of the century it was said, with exaggeration, that it was possible to bring 300 miles down the Thames for 10d. goods which cost 3s. for the 30 miles by land from Hitchin to London.[8] In 1729 the carriage of a chaldron of coal from London to Abingdon by water cost 15s.;[9] ten years later it cost 18s.[10] This works out at just over 1d. per ton per mile, a rate which land carriage could not even approach. The

---

[1] Griffiths, *An Essay*, p. 162.

[2] *J. H. of C.* xxv. 767. [3] 24 Geo. II, c. 8.

[4] Add. MSS. 33576, f. 63; *Papers . . . relating to the Navigation on the River Lea*, pp. 7–16. [5] Birch, *Royal Society*, iii. 208.

[6] Rogers, *History of Agriculture and Prices*, vi. 656.

[7] *Cal. S.P.D., 1636–7*, p. 252; Hedges, *Wallingford*, ii. 129; Thacker, *Thames, General History*, pp. 98–100.

[8] Houghton, *Collection for the Improvement of Husbandry and Trade*, ed. 1727, ii. 285. [9] *J. H. of C.* xxi. 417.

[10] Ibid. xxiii. 313; cf. Defoe, *Complete English Tradesman*, ii. 172.

same is true of carriage rates on the Trent. About 1605, coal
from Nottingham to Gainsborough cost 3s. a ton and from
Gainsborough to Hull 2s.[1] Ten years later glass cost 7s. a
ton from Nottingham to Hull.[2] At the beginning of the
eighteenth century it was said that the land carriage from
Derby to Wilne was twice the water carriage from Wilne
to Gainsborough[3] and that a ton of cheese by land from
Derby to Wilne cost 6s. to 7s. and from Wilne to London
by water only £1.[4] Under monopolistic conditions, the
freight from Nottingham to Burton-on-Trent by the river
was 14s. to 15s. a ton, and even this was less than the land
carriage.[5]

On the Severn in 1635, Sir William Brereton sent by a
trowman from Bristol to Shrewsbury a firkin of old soap,
three dozen stone bottles, chiefly filled with wine, and a
cloak-bag, for half a crown.[6] Not quite a century later a ton of
salt by water from Worcester to Bristol cost 5s., or less than
1d. a mile.[7] In 1758 the freight from Shrewsbury to Bristol
by the Severn was 10s. a ton and from Bristol to Shrewsbury 15s.[8] When in 1667 the bringing of coal from King's
Lynn to London by river and land carriage was discussed,
it was estimated that the freight by water from King's Lynn
to Cambridge would be 4s. a London chaldron, while the
shorter distance by land from Cambridge to Ware would cost
from £1 to £1 5s. the chaldron.[9] In 1696 a London chaldron
of coal could be brought by the Ouse from King's Lynn to
St Ives for 3s., or about two-thirds of a penny per ton per
mile.[10] Nine years later, evidence before a Parliamentary
Committee showed that, from May Day to Michaelmas, the
freight from King's Lynn to St. Ives by water was 4s. a
chaldron of 40 bushels, and that coal bought in King's Lynn

---

[1] *H.M.C. Middleton*, p. 172.　　　　　　　　[2] Ibid., p. 501.
[3] *The Case of the River Derwent in respect of Navigation*; cf. Houghton, *Collection
for the Improvement of Husbandry and Trade*, ed. 1727, i. 117, where the carriage
by land from Derby to Wilne is said to be as much as by water from Wilne to Hull.
[4] 'Derwent Navigation', Stowe MSS. 818, f. 84.
[5] *Reasons humbly offer'd against the Bill for . . . making Navigable the River Trent.*
[6] Brereton, *Travels*, p. 178.
[7] 'Weaver Navigation, 1699–1720', Add. MSS. 36914, f. 119.
[8] *Gentleman's Magazine*, 1758, p. 277.
[9] *Cal. S.P.D.*, 1667, p. 268.
[10] Badeslade, *The Ancient and the Present State of the Navigation*, p. 70.

for £1 6s. 6d. a London chaldron could be sold in Bedford for £1 17s. 6d.[1]

It must be admitted that there were exceptions to these cheap rates. The Wey Act of 1651 allowed the undertakers to charge 4s. a ton from Guildford to Weybridge, a distance of some 15 miles.[2] The Idle Act of 1720 fixed the freight from East Retford to Bawtry at 8s. a ton from September 25th to March 23rd, and at 6s. a ton for the rest of the year,[3] a rate varying from 9½d. to 7d. per ton per mile. The supporters of the Chelmer navigation admitted that the freight from Maldon to Chelmsford, a distance of 13 miles, would be 4s. per London chaldron of coal, but the land carriers' interest did not deny that the existing rate by land was 8s.[4] In 1741 John Eyes, surveyor, giving evidence before a committee which was considering a petition for extending the Calder navigation to Halifax, declared that the water carriage of a ton of wool from Halifax to Wakefield would be 9s. This was a high rate, but here again the cost of land carriage was greater, being 15s. a ton.[5]

Three facts emerge clearly from the available evidence on carriage rates. Firstly, high rates were practically confined to small rivers or the upper reaches of larger rivers, which it was probably uneconomic to make navigable. Secondly, in spite of the meandering of rivers,[6] water carriage was universally much cheaper than land,[7] a fact which even the land carriers' interest never denied. Lastly, over long distances the rate of carriage by water was usually as low as 1d. per ton per mile.

It remains to be seen what goods were carried and in what quantities, but first there is the question of passengers. The promoters of river navigation never put forward the carriage of passengers as a justification for their schemes. There was never in England anything corresponding to the

---

[1] *J. H. of C.* xiv. 510.

[2] Firth and Rait, *Acts and Ordinances*, ii. 515.

[3] 6 Geo. I, c. 30, sec. 6.

[4] *The Intended Navigation of the Chelmer*, pp. 7–8.

[5] *J. H. of C.* xxiii. 608.

[6] Especially the Wye, Add. MSS. 11052, f. 95 dorso.

[7] Besides the evidence given, see Add. MSS. 34218, f. 40; Yarranton, *England's Improvement*, i. 42; *J. H. of C.* xxi. 438; xxii. 438.

system at work in France. There the *coches d'eau* operating
on the Seine, the Marne, the Rhône, the Loire, and the
Garonne were leased to *fermiers* such as the Marquis de
Vallavon and the Marquis de Caumartin, who were bound
to maintain the tariffs fixed by the State.[1] By these means it
was possible to go from Paris to Rouen in 4 days at a cost of
36 francs.[2] Besides these there were the *bateaux de poste*,
the masters of which received free 'les religieux mendicants
et ce qui regardait les affaires du Roi'. Not very propitiously
there were fixed to the masts alms-boxes for the poor, 'qui
prieront Dieu pour ceux qui s'embarqueront'. On the Loire
were *les cabanes* or *petites maisons flottantes*, on the Saône,
vessels with cabins and saloons, but on the Rhône the boats
were 'sales, sombres et malodorantes'.[3] A foreigner in England would never have thought of travelling in the manner
Evelyn did on the Continent. In 1641 he went from Antwerp to Brussels by water and from Brussels to Bruges on
the canal cut by the Marquis of Spinola.[4] Three years later
he went down the Loire from Orleans to Blois, 'the passage
and the river being both very pleasant',[5] and down the Rhône
to Vienne and so to Tain.[6] In 1646 he passed from Geneva
to Lyon by the Rhône, though he had to buy the boat, 'for
it could not be brought back against the stream of the
Rhône'.[7]

In England it seems to have been assumed that passengers
would be carried on the rivers. The Patent to Bath in 1619
speaks of passengers as well as goods,[8] while the Act of 1712
allowed a toll of 6*d.* for each person passing along the river.[9]
Similarly, the Wey Act of 1651 fixed the fare from Guildford
to London at not more than 1*s.*,[10] while the Wye Act of 1662
stipulated for the undertakers to fit boats for passengers to
go weekly from Hereford to Bristol.[11] On the other hand,

[1] Boissonade, *Colbert*, pp. 91, 168.

[2] Avenel, *Histoire économique de la propriété*, vii. 92. For a less favourable view
of the *coches d'eau*, see Sée, *L'Évolution commerciale et industrielle*, pp. 207–8.

[3] Avenel, *Histoire économique de la propriété*, vii. 93–4.

[4] Evelyn, *Diary*, pp. 25, 27.   [5] Ibid., p. 58.

[6] Ibid., p. 68.   [7] Ibid., p. 231.

[8] S.P.D. Warrants, x, July 16th, 1619.

[9] 10 Anne, c. 2, sec. 11.

[10] Firth and Rait, *Acts and Ordinances*, ii. 515.

[11] Lloyd, *Papers relating to the . . . Wye and Lug*, p. 6.

there is little evidence that people did travel by water. London and Bristol[1] had their watermen and their wherries, the latter were even taken from London to Cambridge on wagons to row people up and down the Cam from the town to Stourbridge Fair.[2] Wherries, too, apparently carried passengers between Norwich and Great Yarmouth.[3] People seem to have gone from London to Reading by the Thames,[4] and there is record of a boat with two men and twelve women capsizing in the Taff at Cardiff in 1614.[5] Others may, perhaps, have made journeys like that described by Sir John Percival in a letter to Robert Southwell, dated June 1665.

> We are at length got to Gloucester and that necessity which forced us to make use of a barge, which has proved a providence to us, for I was so bad that no coach or wain could have been endured. The barge was a feather bed to me, but having reached this city, and my wife being not well pleased any longer with the tediousness of her conveyance, we go by coach to the Bath.[6]

It is almost as difficult to get details of the carriage of goods as it is of the carriage of passengers. Here it is only possible to give some idea, from direct and indirect evidence, of the bulk of trade done. There seems no doubt that, of individual commodities, coal was the most important. River-borne coal had an advantage over sea-borne, for it was duty free.[7] It had been estimated that from 1681 to 1690 a quarter of a million tons of coal per annum were shipped by river.[8] Some idea of the relative importance of the rivers engaged in these shipments can be gained from the distribution of the collectors of the proposed tax on river-borne coal in 1695. Out of eighteen collectors, the Tyne, Newark, Nottingham, Sunderland, and Lincoln were to have one each, Hull was to have six, and Worcester seven.[9] Thus the Severn was reckoned the most important, and indeed its valley has been called 'the principal river market for coal in the

---

[1] Fiennes, *Through England on a Side Saddle*, p. 200; cf. Defoe, *Complete English Tradesman*, ii. 75, where he says that the Thames alone had wherries and watermen.

[2] Defoe, *Tour*, i. 84. [3] Carr, *Sailing Barges*, pp. 130–1.

[4] *Reading Records*, ii. 242. [5] *Records of Cardiff*, ii. 169.

[6] *H.M.C. Egmont*, ii. 13.

[7] *H.M.C. House of Lords*, N.S. iii. 213; Defoe, *Tour*, ii. 615.

[8] Nef, *Coal Industry*, i. 79.

[9] Treasury Board Papers, xxxiv, f. 233.

British Isles'.[1] Most of this coal came from the collieries around Broseley and Benthall and, by the beginning of the eighteenth century, about 100,000 tons per annum seem to have been carried down the river.[2] In 1696 Ursula, Countess of Plymouth, in petitioning against the tax on river-borne coal, declared that she drew £400 per annum from the Warwickshire Avon, which was derived from duties on coal brought down the Severn and up the Avon.[3] This coal trade had flourished from the time that Sandys first made the Avon navigable.[4]

The group of rivers flowing into the Yorkshire Ouse was second only to the Severn in importance in carrying coal. Until the navigation of the Aire and Calder was improved, York itself received coal by water from Newcastle.[5] Later the Aire and Calder developed a trade in coal, wool, and cloth which is well illustrated by the fact that, in 1744, the navigation was let for £3,200 per annum.[6] Even a small place like Beverley received, from June 1st, 1730, to May 31st, 1731, 1,465 chaldrons, or about 2,000 tons, of coal by water.[7] The Trent was an important coal-carrying river throughout this period. As early as 1605 a scheme had been drawn up for shipping 3,000 tons per annum from Nottingham to London.[8] From 1613 to 1614 Fosbrook shipped from Nottingham to Newark 2,111 rooks, or from 2,111 to 3,050 tons, of coal from Willoughby's colliery alone.[9] At the same time coal was being sent from Strelley colliery, which was let for £3,300 per annum.[10] In the eighteenth century Trent coal was going down the Foss Dyke to Lincoln: from Michaelmas 1716 to Michaelmas 1724, 9,501 tons of coal, or about 1,357 per annum, were unloaded at Lincoln.[11]

The rivers to which collectors were to be appointed were

[1] Nef, *Coal Industry*, i. 65.

[2] *An Answer as well to a Paper, intituled Reasons wherefore the making Navigable of the Rivers Stower and Salwerpe* ...; cf. *Gentleman's Magazine*, 1758, p. 277; Nef, *Coal Industry*, i. 65.   [3] *J. H. of C.* xi. 376.

[4] Habington, *Worcestershire*, ii. 469.   [5] Nef, *Coal Industry*, i. 102.

[6] *J. H. of C.* xxiv. 578; cf. Defoe, *Tour*, ii. 615.

[7] Beverley MSS., Toll Book I.   [8] *H.M.C. Middleton*, p. 172.

[9] Ibid., p. 177. The rook weighed from 1 to 1½ tons, Nef, *Coal Industry*, ii. App. C.   [10] *H.M.C. Middleton*, p. 176.

[11] Lincoln MSS., Foss Dyke Tolls.

not the only ones on which the coal trade was important. Before the 5s. per chaldron tax on sea-borne coal, a small river like the Welland was producing from £400 to £500 per annum from duties which were derived largely from an annual importation of 3,000 London chaldrons of coal. Even after the imposition of the tax, from 1702 to 1706, about 2,000 London chaldrons per annum passed up the river.[1] The Great Ouse, too, had a considerable coal trade,[2] but statistics are lacking. Much of the 16,546 Newcastle chaldrons, which King's Lynn imported from Xmas 1682 to Xmas 1683, must have passed up the river;[3] the same is true of the Yare and the 14,228 Newcastle chaldrons of coal imported by Great Yarmouth in the same period.[4] On the Thames, it was estimated in 1769 that 80,000 London chaldrons of coal went farther up the river than the metropolis, though only 3,000 chaldrons got as far as Abingdon.[5]

Agricultural produce and timber are even more difficult to treat statistically. Corn went up the Trent in exchange for the coal which came down it.[6] There was also a considerable downward traffic in timber[7] and cheese, of which 4,000 tons per annum of the latter were said to go to Hull.[8] Small quantities of corn passed along the Foss Dyke, amounting to 5,471 quarters from Michaelmas 1716 to Michaelmas 1724.[9] King's Lynn supplied 'ten counties in part with corn and salt',[10] of which the bulk of the former was brought down the Great Ouse in 'great Quantities'.[11] Barges from Ware to London were said, in 1698, to carry 3,744 tons of malt a year,[12] while 4,000 loads of timber passed down the Wey in 1664.[13] The agricultural produce of the Thames valley passed down 'the most beautiful River in Europe'[14] to feed

---

[1] *Mr Halford's Case; J. H. of C.* xi. 388.

[2] *J. H. of C.* xxv. 787; *H.M.C. Portland,* ii. 263.

[3] Exch. K.R. Port Books, 200/5. The Newcastle chaldron was about 53 cwt.; Nef, *Coal Industry,* ii. App. C.   [4] Ibid.

[5] *Report from the Committee appointed . . . to consider the Bill for extending the Coventry Canal to Oxford.*   [6] *Cal. S.P.D., 1629–31,* p. 548.

[7] Ibid., *1667–8,* p. 506; ibid., *1670,* p. 339.

[8] Defoe, *Tour,* ii. 546.   [9] Lincoln MSS., Foss Dyke Tolls.

[10] *Cal. S.P.D., 1655–6,* p. 211.   [11] Defoe, *Tour,* ii. 512.

[12] Houghton, *Collection for the Improvement of Husbandry and Trade,* ed. 1727, ii. 285.

[13] Exch. K.R. Wey Navigation Claims.

[14] Defoe, *Tour,* i. 94.

the growing population of the capital. It was said that, in
1729 to 1730, 2,375 tons of cheese left Abingdon and Newbury for London.[1] In 1715 George Blagrave's mills on the
Kennet ground 90 loads of flour a week for the London
market,[2] and from 1714 to 1730 the Kennet navigation
itself produced £10,000 in tolls.[3] It is clear that the towns
situated on navigable rivers received all the necessities of
life by water,[4] and sent out all their commodities by that
means. From June 1st, 1730, to May 31st, 1731, the
traffic along Beverley Beck comprised 1,465 chaldrons of
coal, 599,400 bricks, 685,000 turfs, 233 packs of wool,
411 quarters of wheat, 623 quarters of oats, 864 quarters
of barley, 2,455½ quarters of malt, besides lesser quantities
of wood, cheese, leather, bark, &c.[5] From Michaelmas
1716 to Michaelmas 1724, 17,595 tons, consisting chiefly
of coal, wood, and miscellaneous goods, passed along the
Foss Dyke, besides 5,471 quarters of corn.[6]

This evidence of considerable trade along the rivers,
especially in the early eighteenth century, is confirmed by
financial statistics. Thus in 1638 a house and wharf near
High Bridge in Reading was leased to Simon Dye for three
lives at a rent of £6 per annum, but the fine was £80.[7] By
1715 Reading wharves produced an income of £150 per
annum,[8] while eight years later the wharf at Newbury was
let to the Kennet Navigation for £106 per annum for 99
years. When this term expired the wharf was worth £400
per annum.[9] The actual incomes of the navigations are still
more decisive proof of their commercial importance. A small
undertaking like Beverley Beck produced, from May 1727
to May 1742, an average annual income from tolls of £99.[10]
During the eleven years 1718 to 1728 the Tone produced
£386 per annum in tolls.[11] Unfortunately the complicated
system of these duties[12] makes it impossible to translate them

---

[1] Maitland, *London*, p. 554.
[2] *J. H. of C.* xviii. 126.   [3] Ibid. xxi. 496.
[4] In 1723 Col. Walter Pallifour got sand and lime by water to build his house
at Sutton on the Yorkshire Derwent, *J. H. of C.* xx. 140.
[5] Beverley MSS., Toll Book, I.
[6] Lincoln MSS., Foss Dyke Tolls.
[7] *Reading Records*, iii. 434.   [8] *J. H. of C.* xviii. 116.
[9] *V.C.H. Berks.* iv. 146.   [10] Beverley MSS., Beck Accounts.
[11] Toulmin, *Taunton*, p. 400.   [12] Under 6 Anne, c. 70, secs. 3 and 5.

into tonnage. The northern rivers were more important still. In 1732 the Yorkshire Ouse was producing £600 per annum in tolls,[1] levied at the rate of 6d. a ton on all goods except wine and groceries, which paid 2s. 6d. a ton.[2] This can hardly have represented the shipment of less than 20,000 tons per annum, for the lower rate appears to have been used for such goods as butter and bacon.[3] The Weaver and Dane, which owed their importance to the salt industry, had an annual income from tolls of £1,674 3s. 5d. between 1733 and 1741.[4] The rate between Frodsham and Winsford Bridge was 1s. a ton,[5] from Winsford Bridge to Nantwich not more than 3s. a ton,[6] and from Northwich to Middlewich not more than 9d. a ton.[7] The average, assuming that the maxima were levied, was 1s. 7d. per ton, which gives an annual tonnage of 21,200. Finally, in 1740, the Don navigation was let for fourteen years at a rent of £1,200 for the first seven and £1,500 for the second seven years.[8] Again it is impossible to estimate with any degree of accuracy the tonnage which these figures represent, but they are illustrative of a form of transport that had become of vital importance.

How this very considerable river trade was organized it is almost impossible to say. Indeed, there is little evidence of any organization at all, and here again is a contrast between England and France. There was nothing in England equivalent to the *communauté des marchands fréquentant la rivière de Loire*, which operated in the fourteenth century and comprised wholesale merchants and the proprietors of boats.[9] Yet this body was by no means unique in France. The Garonne had its *syndicat* in the fifteenth century[10] and the Dordogne and the Saône their *communautés* in the sixteenth century,[11] while even the boatmen were 'organisés en corps de métier'.[12] In England river traffic seems to have

1 *J. H. of C.* xxi. 830.
2 13 Geo. I, c. 33, sec. 7.   3 *J. H. of C.* xxi. 830.
4 Cheshire MSS., River Weaver Commissioners, 1733-41.
5 7 Geo. I, c. 10, sec. 6.   6 7 Geo. II, c. 28, sec. 2.
7 7 Geo. I, c. 17, sec. 6.   8 *J. H. of C.* xxiii. 441.
9 Gabory, *La Marine et le commerce de Nantes*, p. 236; Pigeonneau, *Histoire du commerce de la France*, i. 114.
10 Pigeonneau, *Histoire du commerce de la France*, i. 181.
11 Ibid.; Sée, *Esquisse d'une histoire économique et sociale*, p. 173.
12 Sée, *L'Évolution commerciale et industrielle*, pp. 209-10.

been organized on the lines of barges either carrying cargoes at a fixed freight or being owned and worked by the merchants themselves. It is probable, but by no means certain, that the former system was more prevalent. Thus, on the Severn, trowmen would take in the goods of a traveller like Sir William Brereton,[1] or bargemasters hire out their barges to Gloucester Corporation for work on the quay.[2] About 1717 'a sett of Boats more then usually was imployed on the River Trent', with the result that the rates of carriage fell 2s. a ton 'goeinge downe'.[3] If the evidence of cargoes is any criterion, then the bargemasters of Beverley Beck acted as common carriers. Thus the *Prosperous* of Beverley which paid toll on March 25th, 1731, had on board 5 quarters of malt, 3 bundles of leather, 4 hogsheads, 2 dozen chairs, 4 parcels, ¼ ton of household goods, 10 mets of oatmeal, and 1 ton of wood.[4] More significant is the fact that in June 1747 the *Hopewell* of Beverley included among its cargo of flour, hops, and household goods, '7 Farthing Parshils 1¾d'.[5] On the Great Ouse the coal trade was in the hands of men who bought the coal at King's Lynn and sold it again up the river at St. Ives or Bedford, but they paid freight charges and did not own the lighters themselves.[6] This method was proposed by the promoters of the Chelmer navigation, who suggested that coal from Maldon to Chelmsford would cost 4s. a chaldron, 2s. 6d. being for toll and 1s. 6d. for the use of the barge.[7] Where the undertakers had a monopoly of barges they employed them usually as carriers, but sometimes their connexion with the people supplying the goods was very close. Thus the Douglas undertakers in 1738 entered into a contract with the owner of the colliery at Orrell for the delivery of 800,000 baskets of coal, at 3s. 2d. a score (20 baskets of 72 lb. each), on the banks of the river near Gathurst Bridge. The coal was sold in Fylde and North Lancashire, possibly by the undertakers themselves.[8]

[1] Brereton, *Travels*, p. 178.
[2] Gloucester MSS., Chamberlains' Accounts, 1633–53, f. 395.
[3] 'Derwent Navigation', Stowe MSS. 818, f. 84.
[4] Beverley MSS., Toll Book, I.
[5] Ibid. III.   [6] *J. H. of C.* xiv. 510.
[7] *Intended Navigation of the Chelmer*, pp. 7–8.
[8] Wadsworth and Mann, *Cotton Trade*, p. 216.

On the other hand, the boats were sometimes owned by the people to whom the cargoes belonged. It was not unusual for millers to possess their own boats[1] and an alderman of Norwich bought a small ship in which to bring his coal from Great Yarmouth.[2] In 1605 there was a scheme for sending coal from Nottingham to London by water, in which the undertakers were to do all the shipping themselves. The coal was to cost 6s. a ton at Nottingham Bridge, 6s. 2d. a ton to send down the Trent, and 8s. a ton from Hull to London.[3] Fifty years later Thomas Stringer proposed to send coal from Nottingham down the Trent in five boats which were to belong to the undertakers of the scheme.[4] More interesting is the agreement of 1609 between Sir Percival Willoughby, owner of Wollaton colliery, and Robert Fosbrook, yeoman, of Trent Bridges. Willoughby agreed to stack at Wollaton lane end 3,000 rooks of coal per annum for seven years at the rate of 70 rooks per week and to erect a house for an overseer to see the coal delivered. He also leased to Fosbrook land and 'all those the barges, boates and keeles', now or late in his or Beaumont's possession, 'which they lately bought of John Bate, of London, merchant'. In return for all this and for two houses, one at the Bridges and the other at Newark, Fosbrook was to pay 5s. 6d. a rook for the coals, which he was to sell at Nottingham or send down the Trent, and he was to keep the nine boats in repair. He went weekly with coals to Newark and sometimes as far as Gainsborough, whence he brought back goods from London for Lenton Fair. Finally, Fosbrook, who quotes Horace and Plautus in his letters to Willoughby, met with difficulties, but the whole agreement is an interesting example of an attempt to co-ordinate production and distribution.[5] About a century later yet another Fosbrook was not only carrying goods for merchants in his own boats, but was also acting as a merchant himself and using his power to engross the markets.[6]

Some of the Trent coal went down the Foss Dyke, and

[1] Papers . . . relating to the Navigation on the River Lea, p. 11.
[2] J. H. of C. xiv. 511.   [3] H.M.C. Middleton, 171.
[4] 'Thomas Stringer's Notebook', Add. MSS. 33509, ff. 10–11.
[5] H.M.C. Middleton, pp. 172–6.   [6] Supra, pp. 116–17.

there the merchants appear to have owned the boats. Here there was some concentration of trade in the hands of individuals. From Michaelmas 1714 to Michaelmas 1715 301 quarters of corn and malt, 722 packs (unspecified) and 2,035 tons of goods (chiefly wood and coal) passed along the Foss Dyke and paid £101 5s. 4d. in tolls. Of the merchants responsible for this trade, the three chief, John Durance,[1] Mark Mowbray, and John Hawkshaw, accounted for just over 50 per cent. of the whole. About a quarter of the trade was done by 'The Country People', who carried 492 tons, 20 packs, and 241 quarters, and paid £24 in tolls. The sum of 14s. 1d. was 'Received for the Tunnage of Saxelby Boate'. Among the larger merchants there was some specialization of commodities. Mowbray shipped coal chiefly, which in 1714/15 comprised 76 per cent. of his trade. Captain Rudd shipped coal alone, while James Crooke and Partners sent only wood from Drinsey to the Trent. On the other hand, 'The Country People' shipped miscellaneous and often unspecified goods.[2]

Thus the two different forms which underlie the modern organization of transport, namely, carriage by the merchants themselves and carriage by independent carriers, were present in the river traffic of the seventeenth and eighteenth centuries.

[1] By 1737 Durance owed £108 13s. 9d. in arrears of tolls for five years. Lincoln MSS., Box 29. 650.
[2] Lincoln MSS., Foss Dyke Tolls.

CONCLUSION

IT has been said that 'communications have generally been improved in order to meet the requirements of an existing trade, and not to call one into being'.[1] If this is so, then the improvements in river transport of the seventeenth and early eighteenth centuries were intended to meet the requirements of an existing trade that was also rapidly expanding. The expansion of trade in this period has long been recognized, but the inevitable corollary of such expansion, namely, the improvement of communications, has been largely ignored. It is not the place here to survey the whole field of industrial and commercial activity, but merely to summarize the conclusions derived from a study of river navigation and to relate those conclusions to the general course of English economic history.

Bearing always in mind the close interconnexion between the coasting trade and the river traffic, it is clear that the two together played an important, perhaps a decisive, part in the internal commerce of England. It may be an exaggeration to assume that all places within a day's journey of the coast had commercial access to the sea,[2] but the twenty-one head ports, together with their members, formed a network which brought perhaps the whole coast-line, except that of West Wales, within this condition. According to Yarranton,

Of necessity we must always be Sailing round about the Island, carrying and recarrying such heavy Commodities from Port to Port, to be taken into the more Inward parts of the Kingdom, otherwise the charge of carrying such goods by Land, would rise to a very vast charge, the High-ways of our Island being very uneven, and the ways therein in Winter time very bad.[3]

It was to a great extent the rivers which carried these goods 'into the more Inward parts of the Kingdom'. Not only promoters and pamphleteers, but the people generally realized the importance of river navigation. When the poor

[1] Cunningham, *Growth of English Industry and Commerce, Modern Times*, ed. 1892, p. 190.　　　　　[2] See Maps I–III.
[3] Yarranton, *England's Improvement*, ii. 92.

inhabitants of Guisborough petitioned against ship-money in 1635, they thought it a point in favour of their petition that 'Guisborough is situate divers miles from the sea, and no navigable river can carry any commodity to or from it, to the same'.[1] On July 22nd, 1654, Evelyn visited Stonehenge and remarked of those great stones, 'as to their being brought thither, there being no navigable river neere, is by some admir'd'.[2] Later in the century one of the factors in computing the value of land was given as 'whether near a River running to the Sea, for the exportation of such things as the Land doth produce'.[3] On January 5th, 1704, Edward Repington wrote to Thomas Coke from Amington, 'Poetry and our pockets are at a low ebb in these parts. We have neither wine to raise our fancies, nor navigable rivers, nor passable roads to convey our commodities when they may take a price.'[4] The works which river navigation necessitated were sufficiently well known to be used as similes in describing things with which they had no connexion. In 1708 one Wilson brought forward a proposal for a coal magazine to be paid for by a tax of 1s. per chaldron on coals. This tax, he declared, should not be complained of as a burden 'since all little Taxes of this nature are but like a sluice in a shallow part of a River which by stagnating the waters a little, make it navigable, and afterwards all the water goes into the same River'.[5] He continued by justifying the tax in a sustained simile based on the same comparison.[6] Since the essential quality of comparison is clarity, there must have been many to whom the allusion was intelligible.

When men regretted the absence of navigable rivers in their district, or wondered how the people of the past could have transported huge masses without them, they were perhaps inspired by the example of such rivers in other parts of

[1] *Cal. S.P.D.*, *1635–6*, p. 14.   [2] Evelyn, *Diary*, p. 281.
[3] Primatt, *The City and Country*, p. 9.
[4] *H.M.C. Cowper*, iii. 29. Mr. Lipson gives part of this quotation to show the absence of navigable rivers in England in the early eighteenth century (*Economic History*, ii. 447, 'In 1704 the complaint had been made that England had neither "navigable rivers nor passable roads to convey our merchandise where they may take a price".') It is clear from the context that Repington was writing only of the district round Amington.
[5] 'Scheme for regulating the sale of coals', Add. MSS. 28948, f. 173.
[6] Ibid.

the kingdom. Such examples were indeed never lacking. Between 1600 and 1660 England possessed at least 685 miles of navigable rivers, which included the Thames, the Severn, the Trent, and the Yorkshire and the Great Ouse.[1] The country possessed, in other words, the foundation of its future system of internal water communication. This foundation was largely inherited from a former age, and there were still great tracts of the country which lay more than 15 miles or one day's carriage by land from the sea or from a navigable river.[2] At the end of the next forty years, partly by the actual improvement of rivers and partly, perhaps, because the evidence is more abundant, it is clear that England had at least 960 miles of navigable rivers. The area 'inaccessible' to water transport had suffered a considerable decrease.[3] Finally, when Defoe toured Great Britain, he found in England about 1,160 miles of navigable rivers upon which a considerable part of the commerce of the country passed.[4] The improvement of the Aire and Calder and the Mersey had opened up the industrial regions of the north and broken almost in two the 'backbone' of England, which had hitherto remained inaccessible to water carriage. Now, except for isolated patches, there remained outside the 15 miles radius only the mountainous regions of Cumberland, the Pennines, the Peak, Wales, and Devon and two stretches of lowland west of the Severn, the Warwickshire Avon, and Bristol. Much of this country was never to be opened up by water communications and the remainder, the lowlands, had to wait until the canal era.

It is impossible to assign any single cause for this remarkable development and improvement in the river navigation of England. It was not due to any great advance in technical knowledge, for it only involved the wider application of principles, as that of the pound lock, which were already

[1] See Map I.

[2] The distance of 15 miles is derived from the Ordinance for the sale of Crown lands (1649), which stipulated that naval timber within 15 miles of a navigable river should be excepted from sale (Firth and Rait, *Acts and Ordinances*, ii. 189). An Act of 1559 had forbidden the employment, as fuel for making iron, of oak, beech, and ash within 14 miles of the sea or navigable rivers (Lipson, *Economic History*, ii. 157). According to Albion, 20 miles was the maximum day's haul of naval timber by land (*Forests and Sea Power*, p. 103).

[3] See Map II.   [4] See Map III.

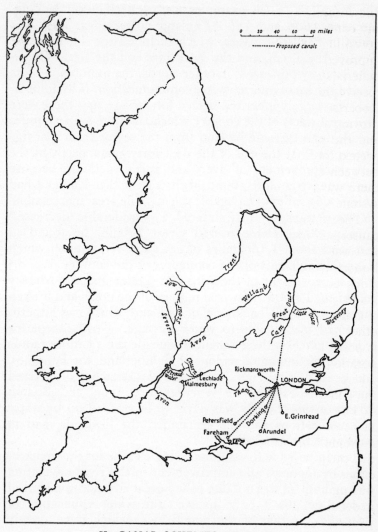

V. CANAL SCHEMES, 1600–1750

known and used. Nor does it seem to have been due to any conscious application of the tenets which underlay the prevailing economic system of mercantilism. In so far as improved communications facilitated the import of raw materials and the export of manufactured goods, they would receive the approval of mercantilists. Pamphleteers such as Roberts might advocate river navigation as a means of improving foreign trade,[1] but the promoters of undertakings and the petitioners for Bills rarely, if ever, made this the pretext for their schemes. There was not the same connexion between English river improvements and mercantilism that there was between continental canal building and the same system.[2]

The improvements were due, in fact, to a number of causes, of which two were of particular importance. The first was financial. The increase of wealth and the accumulation of capital, together with the development of the joint-stock company as the best means of tapping that capital, made possible the financing of undertakings of a local character by a more than local circle of investors. On the other hand, the increasing wealth of the merchant class made it possible for the merchants, either through the town corporations or directly through their appointment as undertakers, to finance these undertakings without an appeal to the general public for capital.

The second cause was largely industrial. The development of industry during this period, and perhaps also its movement 'away from the old urban centres'[3], made necessary the carriage of heavy goods with which water transport, either by sea or river, alone could cope. Of these goods, coal was undoubtedly the most important. 'The more we study in detail the history of communication by water in England', wrote Mantoux, 'the more do we realize how closely it was interwoven with the history of coal.'[4] This is as true of river navigation as of canal. If coal transport were 'the dominant factor in the canal movement',[5] it was also the dominant

---

[1] Roberts, *Treasure of Traffic*, pp. 44–5.
[2] Häpke, *Wirtschaftsgeschichte*, i. 112–13.
[3] Lipson, *Economic History*, iii. 207.
[4] Mantoux, *Industrial Revolution*, p. 126.
[5] Clapham, *Economic History*, i. 78.

factor in the river movement. The tendency to regard the Industrial Revolution as a revolution, as a sudden break with the past, has obscured the importance of this earlier movement. 'During the eighteenth century', wrote Professor Knowles, 'Great Britain began to require coal in increasing quantities, and some better and cheaper method of moving coal than in a cart or in panniers on mules became imperatively necessary.'[1] But long before the eighteenth century England had begun to require coal 'in increasing quantities', and though carts and panniers were indeed used, 'some better and cheaper method' of transport had already been found in the coasting trade and river navigation. It is not too much to say that in the seventeenth century all long distance transport of coal was done by water. It is not suggested that coal monopolized river transport. The Don was improved primarily for the Sheffield steel manufacture, the Aire and Calder for the Yorkshire woollen industry, the Weaver for the Cheshire salt trade, and the Mersey for Manchester cottons, but in most of these industries coal played its part. If agricultural produce came down the Thames, the Great Ouse, and the Warwickshire Avon, it was coal which went up stream. As the inspirer of improved methods of transport, therefore, coal, at the time of the Industrial Revolution, was playing no new role but only a greater part in a greater drama.

Turning from industry to agriculture, it is difficult to say how far the expansion of the market for agricultural produce was a direct cause of river improvements in this period. There is no doubt that the improved rivers carried much corn, butter, and cheese, but this carriage may have been only a result and not a cause of improvement. The growth of towns necessitated an increase in farming for the urban markets, but the supply of those markets could be looked at from two standpoints. The towns themselves, as centres of consumption, were interested in a steady supply at low prices. The farmers, as producers, were interested in maintaining the price of their products, if necessary through a monopoly of the local market based on defective means of communication. These standpoints of consumers and producers are reflected

[1] Knowles, *Industrial and Commercial Revolutions*, p. 240.

in the attitudes of the towns and of the agricultural interest respectively towards river improvements.

It was Defoe's boast that every county in England supplied some product for the London market.[1] The city certainly drew its food supply from a wide area,[2] with the result that its merchants were interested in improved communications almost anywhere in England. Thus the corn merchants of London supported the Don navigation scheme in 1704 on the grounds that they bought great quantities of corn 'and particularly Wheat' around Doncaster.[3] The cheesemongers of London petitioned for the Derwent Bill in 1695 for the cheaper carriage of butter and cheese.[4] The same body favoured the Weaver navigation for similar reasons.[5] When an increase in the number of boats employed brought down the carriage rates on the Trent, it was said that the quantity of cheese sent to London doubled.[6] Other towns besides London were interested in cheap food. In 1702 the inhabitants of Newark and neighbouring towns petitioned in favour of the Derwent Bill on the grounds that corn and grain might be sold in great quantities in Derbyshire at moderate rates if it were not for the dearness of land carriage.[7] The inhabitants of Wisbech and Newton supported the Lark navigation because they got their wheat, rye, and malt from Bury St. Edmunds.[8] Some towns, or the merchants in them, supported improved navigation for the export of grain. Thus Barnsley supported the Don navigation for the cheaper carriage of corn to Hull[9] and St. Neots the navigation of the Great Ouse for the export of malt.[10]

The consumer and merchant might favour improved river navigation, but the farmer seems rarely to have supported it. In 1704 the gentlemen, freeholders, tradesmen, and farmers of the Wapentakes of Strafforth and Tickhill supported the Don navigation because of the export of red wheat, which had

---

[1] Defoe, *Tour*, i. 12, 55.
[2] Cf. F. J. Fisher, 'The Development of the London Food Market, 1540–1640', *Economic History Review*, vol. v, no. 2.
[3] *J. H. of C.* xiv. 467.   [4] Ibid. xi. 416, 435.
[5] Ibid. xix. 252; cf. 'Weaver Navigation, 1699–1720', Add. MSS. 36914, f. 94.
[6] 'Derwent Navigation', Stowe MSS. 818, f. 84.
[7] *J. H. of C.* xiv. 82.   [8] Ibid. xiii. 162.
[9] Ibid. xiv. 462.   [10] Ibid. xix. 245.

a great reputation abroad. Merchants directed their factors to buy the wheat, but as the river was not constantly navigable the seller was forced to carry it or make abatement for land carriage, to the great loss of poor husbandmen.[1] One of the few petitions in favour of navigation from purely agricultural petitioners was that of the farmers and graziers of Long Bennington, Claypole, Doddington, and Westborough in favour of the navigation of the Newark branch of the Trent for the carriage of corn and wool.[2] More often the purely agricultural interest opposed navigation. It was apparently prepared to risk the overstocking of the local market in seasons of plenty in return for the advantage of its monopolistic position in normal times.[3] Its attitude is summed up in a petition against the Derwent Bill presented by the freeholders, copyholders, farmers, and inhabitants of Radford, Bramcote, Sandiacre, Stapleford, Eaton, Long Eaton, and Attenborough. They declared that, with navigation, 'the Price of Corn will fall, whereby the Tenant will be disabled to pay his Rent; and consequently the Rents of Land must abate'.[4] Thus any impulse towards improved navigation which came from farming for the market was due largely to the merchants who traded in agricultural produce and the inhabitants of the towns who ate it. The farmers themselves opposed improvement, partly because they feared competition in their markets and partly, perhaps, because they were land carriers or had 'the Benefit of uttering and vending . . . Produce . . . to the Land-carriers, who pass and repass, in great Numbers'.[5]

The river improvements of the seventeenth and early eighteenth centuries had an importance not only for their own period but also for the future. Just as the Industrial Revolution was 'only the culmination of a long series of industrial experiments',[6] so the improved waterways which helped to make it possible were the natural and inevitable outcome of the river improvements of the previous 150 years. The astonishing outburst of canal building in the late

---

[1] *J. H. of C.* xiv. 468. [2] Ibid. xxiv. 146.
[3] *Supra*, pp. 46–7. [4] *J. H. of C.* xi. 412.
[5] *J. H. of C.* xix. 223. It has been impossible, from the evidence examined, to establish any connexion between the decrease in land carriage and the decline of the yeomanry. [6] Lipson, *Economic History*, ii. 159, and cf. iii. 53.

eighteenth century has been regarded too much as a break with the past, as an isolated and almost providential phenomenon. It has been said that, at the time of the Duke of Bridgwater's canal, 'no one in England could ever have seen a canal barge or a lock'.[1] Even literally this was not true, for many must have seen the foreign canals, their works, and boats. In England itself there was little difference between the river boats and the earlier canal barges. There was no difference of principle between the pound locks on the rivers and those of the canals.

This indeed was the first debt which the canals owed to the past, namely, the inheritance of the engineering skill and practice of at least a hundred years. If that hundred years had produced few real canals in England, it had at least familiarized the use of the pound lock, seen the canalization of rivers, and planned on paper the connexion of the Trent and the Severn by a canal of the modern type. This debt is best symbolized by the activities of the Hore family of Newbury. John Hore was engineer of the Kennet under the Act of 1715. In that capacity he improved the river by canalization and the use of pound locks.[2] In 1730 he suggested similar schemes for the Chelmer and the Stroudwater.[3] Hore's connexion with the Kennet lasted until 1762,[4] and towards the end of the century another of the same family, probably his son, was engineer for the Kennet-Avon Canal.[5] Here there was a continuity not only of technical skill, knowledge, and experience, but also of river navigation. In other words, the Kennet-Avon Canal would have been useless had not the Kennet and the Bristol Avon been already navigable.

That was the second debt that the canals owed to the past. The improved rivers formed the foundation of a system of water communication, which the canals completed by forming that network of waterways of which the pamphleteers had dreamed. It has been said that 'as many of the canals linked up rivers, the rivers also had to be improved'.[6] In a certain sense this is true, for the rivers were further improved

[1] Knowles, *Industrial and Commercial Revolutions*, p. 243.
[2] Thacker, *Kennet Country*, p. 316; Mavor, *Agriculture of Berkshire*, pp. 438-9.
[3] *Supra*, p. 94.   [4] Thacker, *Kennet Country*, p. 318.
[5] *V.C.H. Berks.* i. 377; Money, *Newbury*, p. 367.
[6] Knowles, *Industrial and Commercial Revolutions*, p. 243.

after the building of canals.[1] In France, where the eighteenth
century marked a period of decay in river navigation,[2] too
much attention was paid to connecting rivers by canals without ensuring that the rivers themselves were sufficiently
navigable.[3] But in England it is largely an inversion of the
true order of things to imply that river improvements only
succeeded canal building. It was only after men had appeared
to have exhausted the possibilities of rivers that they turned
to canals. It is true that some canals were designed to overcome the disadvantages of river navigation, but at first more
were planned as a supplement to, rather than a substitute
for, the existing water communications. Thus in the south,
the Kennet-Avon Canal connected the Kennet and so the
Thames with the Bristol Avon; the Thames and Severn
Canal joined Oxford with the Stroudwater Canal and so with
the Severn; the Wiltshire and Berkshire Canal gave Abingdon water communication into the Kennet-Avon Canal near
Semington.[4] In the midlands, the Oxford Canal joined Oxford to the Coventry Canal and so to the Grand Trunk;[5]
the Birmingham and Worcester Canal and the Staffordshire
and Worcestershire, with their branches, connected the
Grand Trunk system to the Severn.[6] In the north, the Trent
and Mersey Canal or the Grand Trunk connected Liverpool
with Wilden Ferry and the Trent navigation;[7] the Leeds and
Liverpool Canal joined the Aire navigation to the west coast;[8]
the Huddersfield Canal gave Huddersfield access to the
Calder navigation at Cooper's Bridge, and the Rochdale
Canal connected the Calder with Manchester.[9] Thus the
canals fitted into that framework of river navigation which
had been created and used during the preceding century and
a half. The improved water communication, which was
essential to the commercial and industrial revolutions, was,
in part, the legacy of the seventeenth and early eighteenth
centuries.

[1] Jackman, *Development of Transportation*, i. 377–89.
[2] Sée, *L'Évolution commerciale et industrielle*, p. 205.
[3] Letaconnoux, *Les Voies de communication en France*, p. 117; cf. Clapham, *Economic Development of France and Germany*, p. 109.
[4] Jackman, *Development of Transportation*, i. 373–5.   [5] Ibid., p. 368.
[6] Ibid., pp. 367, 370.   [7] Ibid., pp. 364–7.
[8] Ibid., p. 370.   [9] Ibid., p. 371.

APPENDIX I

Bibliography of Pamphlets

THE anonymous pamphlets given below are to be found in the Bodleian Library, Oxford, the British Museum, and the Goldsmiths' Library of the University of London. Except for the first three titles, they are grouped under the rivers to which they principally or solely refer.

Reasons Against the Navigable-Scheme. n.p. n.d. (1725?)

An Answer to the Reasons Against the Navigable Scheme. n.p. n.d. (1725?)

Reflections on the General Utility of Inland Navigation. By 'Publicola'. London. n.d.

AIRE AND CALDER.

The Case for Making the Rivers Aire and Calder, in the County of York, Navigable to Leeds and Wakefield. n.p. n.d. (1699?)

Reasons Against the Bill for making the Rivers Ayre and Calder in the West-Riding of the County of York Navigable. n.p. n.d. (1699?)

AVON (BRISTOL).

The Case of making the River Avon in the County of Somerset and Gloucester Navigable. n.p. n.d. (1712?)

CHELMER.

The Intended Navigation of the River Chelmer. London. 1733.

DEE.

Reasons for Recovering the Navigation upon the River Dee to the City of Chester, and for Agreeing with the Committee in the Amendments made to the Bill for that Purpose. n.p. n.d. (1700?) (Dated 1730? in Brit. Mus. Catalogue.)

The Case of the River Dee. n.p. n.d. (1700?)

A Case, Relating to the making Navigable the River Dee in the Counties of Chester and Flint. n.p. n.d. (1700?)

A Bill to Recover and Preserve the Navigation of the River Dee, in the County Palatine of Chester. n.p. 1732.

The Case of the Cheesemongers, In and about the Cities of London and Westminster. n.p. n.d. (1733?)

The Case of the Inhabitants of the County and City of Chester. n.p. n.d. (1733?)

The Case of the Citizens of Chester, in answer to Several Petitions from Liverpool, Parkgate, and the Cheesemongers. n.p. n.d.

(1733?) (Dated 1735 in Jackman, *Development of Transportation*, ii. 799, but printed in the *Chester Weekly Journal*, May 23–30, 1733.)

DERWENT (DERBYSHIRE).

Reasons humbly offered to the Consideration of the Parliament, for the making Navigable the River Derwent, from the Town of Derby to the River Trent. n.p. n.d. (1696?)

The Case of the River Derwent in respect of Navigation, and of the Bill now in Parliament concerning the same. n.p. n.d. (1703?)

DON.

The Methods Proposed for making the River Dunn Navigable. London. 1723.

Reasons for making the River Dunn in the West riding of the County of York navigable. n.p. n.d. (1723.)

DOUGLAS.

Reasons Against the Bill for Making the River Douglas Navigable. n.p. n.d. (1719?)

An Answer to the Reasons for Making the River Douglas Navigable. n.p. n.d. (1719?)

KENNET.

Answers to the (pretended) Reasons Humbly Offer'd for making the River Kennet a Free River. n.p. n.d. (1714?)

The Case of Mr John Hore and Mr John Beale, two of the Proprietors of the Navigation of the River Kennet in the County of Berks. n.p. n.d. (1730?)

NEN.

The Case in Relation to a Clause in the Bill for making more effectual an Act passed . . . in the Twelfth Year . . . of Anne . . . intituled An Act for making the River Nine or Nen . . . Navigable. n.p. n.d. (1725: dated 1714/15 in Brit. Mus. Catalogue.)

GREAT OUSE.

News From the Fens, or, An Answer to a Pamphlet entitled, Navigation prejudiced by the Fen-Drainers. London. 1654.

The Case of the Town and Port of King's-Lynn in Norfolk As to their Navigation. n.p. n.d. (Before 1713.)

The Case of the Corporation of the Great Level of the Fens. n.p. n.d. (Before 1713.)

A Short Demonstration, That Navigation to Bedford, is for the Benefit of Bedfordshire. n.p. n.d. (1720?)

An Answer, Paragraph by Paragraph, to A Report of the present

State of the Great Level of the Fens. n.p. 1724. (The 'Report'
was by Charles Bridgman.)

The Complaints of the Merchants, Mariners, and Watermen of
Lynn about Navigation. n.p. 1724.

The Case of the Land-Owners interested in the Banks on each
Side of the River Ouze, in the County of Norfolk, between
Stowbridge and the Port of Lynn. n.p. n.d. (1749.)

The Case of Augustin Woollaston, Esq; and Reasons humbly offered
To the Honourable House of Commons Against the Bill to prevent the Inning or Imbanking any more Salt-Marshes. n.p. n.d.

STOUR AND SALWARPE.

Reasons for making Navigable the Rivers of Stower and Salwerp.
n.p. n.d. (1703?: dated 1720? in Brit. Mus. Catalogue.)

An Answer, as well to a Paper, intituled Reasons wherefore the
making Navigable of the Rivers of Stower and Salwerp in the
County of Worcester, will be a great advantage to the County of
Salop. . . . As also to another Paper, intituled, An Answer to
some partiall pretences, called, Reasons dispersed by some Shropshire Coal Masters. n.p. n.d. (1703?; dated 1720? in Brit. Mus.
Catalogue.)

THAMES.

News from the Thames; or, The Frozen Thames in Tears.
London. 1685.

The Case of the Barge-Masters and others, Navigating on the
Rivers of Isis and Thames, from Oxford to London. n.p. n.d.
(1730?)

Reasons Against Building a Bridge over the Thames at Westminster.
n.p. n.d. (1740?)

Report from The Committee appointed by the Chamber of London
to consider the Bill for extending the Coventry Canal to Oxford.
n.p. n.d. (1769.)

TRENT.

Reasons humbly offer'd against the Bill for the more speedy and
effectually making Navigable the River Trent in the Counties of
Licester, Derby and Stafford. n.p. n.d. (1714?)

Objections to the Bill for making the Branch of the Trent running
by Newark Navigable. n.p. n.d. (1742.)

TYNE.

The Survey of the River Tyne. n.p. n.d. (1670.)

WEAVER.

A Short Account of a Design for making the River Weaver in the

County of Chester Navigable, from Frodsham-Bridge to Winnington-Bridge, being about 5 or 6 miles only. n.p. n.d. (1669?)

Reasons Humbly Offer'd for making the River Weaver in the County of Chester Navigable, from Northwich to Frodsham-Bridge. n.p. n.d. (1709?)

Reasons against The Bill for making the River Weever Navigable. n.p. n.d. (1719?)

Reasons Against the Bill for making the River Weaver Navigable. n.p. n.d. (1719?)

Reasons Against making the River Weaver Navigable. n.p. n.d. (1719?)

The Case of Charles Cholmondeley Esq. n.p. n.d. (1719?)

Remarks upon the Petitions preferred, and the Cases and Reasons published against the Bill to make the River Weaver Navigable, from Winsford-Bridge to Frodsham-Bridge. With some further Reasons humbly Offer'd for the Committing and Passing the Bill. n.p. n.d. (1719?)

Reasons Humbly Offered For passing the Bill for making the River Weaver Navigable from Frodsham Bridge to Northwich in the County of Chester: With Remarks upon the Proposals from Liverpool. n.p. n.d. (1726?)

Reasons Humbly Offered Against a Bill passed the Honourable House of Commons and now Depending before Your Lordships, Entitled, A Bill for Repealing An Act passed in the Seventh Year of His present Majesty's Reign, for making the River Weaver Navigable, from Frodsham Bridge to Winsford Bridge in the County of Chester, and for the more speedy and effectual carrying on and perfecting the Navigation of the said River, from Frodsham Bridge to Northwych in the said County. n.p. n.d. (1726?)

Reasons Humbly Offered by John Daniel and William Blackburn, Esquires, for themselves, and on behalf of Charles Duckenfield, Thomas Butterworth, and John Reddish, Esquires, and others, Gentlemen and Freeholders of the County of Chester, against a Bill for Repealing an Act made in the Seventh Year of His Majesty's Reign, for making the River Weaver Navigable from Frodsham Bridge to Winsford Bridge in the County of Chester. n.p. n.d. (1726?)

Proposal Humbly Offered For making the River Weever Navigable, from Frodsham-Bridge, to Northwich in the County of Chester. n.p. n.d. (1726?)

Reasons Humbly Offered By the Trustees of Richard Vernon Esq:

deceased, against the Bill for Repealing an Act made in the Seventh Year of his Majesty's Reign, For making the River Weaver Navigable. n.p. n.d. (1726?)

Reasons humbly offered Against allowing the County of Chester any Part of the Tonnage Duty for making the River Weaver Navigable. n.p. n.d. (1726?)

WELLAND.

Mr Halford's Case. n.p. n.d. (1706?)

WEY.

The Case of the Navigation of the River Wye, in the County of Surry. n.p. n.d. (1670?)

A Reply To a Paper Intituled An Answer to the Pretended Case Printed concerning the Navigation of the River Wye, in the County of Surrey, by shewing the true state thereof. n.p. n.d. (1670?)

APPENDIX II

Note on the Maps

MAPS I-III

THE three maps showing the extent of river navigation in England at different periods make no claim to complete accuracy. They show those rivers, or parts of rivers, which contemporaries held to be navigable during part, if not the whole, of the periods in question. The evidence upon which they are based is as follows.

MAP I. *Navigable Rivers,* 1600–60

AVON (WARWICK).

    1641. Navigable to within 4 miles of Warwick. Taylor, *John Taylor's Last Voyage,* pp. 21–2.

    Before 1660. Navigable to Stratford. Habington, *Worcestershire,* ii. 468.

CAM.

    1654. Navigable to Cambridge. *News from the Fens,* p. 22.

DEE.

    1608. Navigable to Chester. Harl. MSS. 2084, f. 31.

    1621.   „   „   Ormerod, *Chester,* i. 170–1.

LEA.

    1621. Navigable to Hertford. *Papers relating to the Navigation on the River Lea,* p. 3.

    1652. 'Navigable.' *Hertford County Records,* i. 97.

MEDWAY.

    1635. Navigable 5 miles above Maidstone. *Cal. S.P.D., 1635–6,* p. 64.

NEN.

    Before 1660. Navigable to Peterborough. Salis, *Chronology of Inland Navigation,* p. 18, quoting Goddard, Recorder of King's Lynn.

GREAT OUSE.

    1638. Navigable to St. Neots. *Cal. S.P.D., 1638–9,* p. 266.

    1655.   „   „   *Cal. S.P.D., 1655–6,* p. 82.

    Before 1660. Navigable to Bedford. Salis, op. cit.

LITTLE OUSE.

Before 1660. Navigable to Thetford. Badeslade, *Ancient and Present State of the Navigation*, p. 54.

YORKSHIRE OUSE.

1634. Navigable to York. Legg, *Relation of a Short Survey*, p. 20.
1654.   „   „   Evelyn, *Diary*, p. 286.

PARRET AND TONE.

1624. Navigable to Bridgwater and Ham Mills. *H.M.C. Wells*, ii. 382.
1635. Navigable to Bridgwater and Ham Mills. Brereton, *Travels*, p. 171.

SEVERN.

1635. Navigable to Shrewsbury. Brereton, op. cit., p. 187.

STOUR (KENT).

1632. Navigable to Fordwich. *Cal. S.P.D.*, *1631–2*, p. 499.

THAMES.

1633. Navigable to Burcot. Thacker, *Thames, General History*, pp. 98–9.
1636. Navigable to within 2 miles of Oxford. Taylor, *The Feareful Summer*, Preface.
1641. Navigable to Oxford. Taylor, *Taylor's Last Voyage*, p. 12.
1649. Navigable to Abingdon. *Cal. S.P.D.*, *1649–50*, p. 556.

TRENT.

1607. Navigable to Nottingham. *Records of Nottingham*, iv. 287.
1609.   „   „   *H.M.C. Middleton*, p. 173.

WEY.

1653. Navigable to Guildford. Scotcher, *River Wey Navigation*, p. 19 (cf. Exch. K.R. Wey Navigation Claims, 1671).

YARE.

1656. Navigable to Norwich. Mathew, *Mediterranean Passage by Water Between . . . Lynn and Yarmouth*, p. 13.

MAP II. *Navigable Rivers*, 1660–1700

AIRE.

1693. Navigable to Allerton. Houghton, *Collection for the Improvement of Husbandry and Trade*, ed. 1727, i. 86.
1697. Navigable to Ferrybridge. Fiennes, *Through England on a Side Saddle*, p. 58.

AVON (WARWICK).

 1677. Navigable to Bidford. *Cal. S.P.D., 1677–8*, p. 136.
 1696. ,,   Stratford. *J. H. of C.* xi. 376.

AVON (WILTSHIRE).

 1687. Navigable to Salisbury. *Cal. of Treas. Books*, viii, pt. iii.
  1250; *J. H. of C.* xiii. 98.

BEVERLEY BECK.

 1689. Navigable to Beverley. *Beverley Records*, p. 179.

CAM.

 1668/9. 'Navigable.' Magalotti, *Travels of Cosmo*, p. 230.
 1672. Navigable to Cambridge. Jorevin [Jouvin], *Description of
  England*, p. 617.

DARENT.

 1673. Navigable to Dartford. Blome, *Britannia*, p. 124.

DEE.

 1697. Navigable to Chester. Fiennes, *Through England on a Side
  Saddle*, p. 148.

DON.

 1693. Navigable to Doncaster. Houghton, *Collection for the Improvement of Husbandry and Trade*, ed. 1727, i. 86.

EXE.

 1668/9. Navigable to Exeter. Magalotti, op. cit., p. 132.

FOSS DYKE.

 1672. Navigable from Lincoln to the Trent. Jorevin, op. cit.

IDLE.

 1670. Navigable to Bawtry. *Cal. S.P.D., 1670*, p. 167; *J. H. of
  C.* xi. 410.

KENNET.

 1673. 'Navigable.' Blome, op. cit., p. 39.

LEA.

 1662. Navigable to Ware. *H.M.C. Portland*, ii. 281.
 1698. ,, ,,   Houghton, op. cit. ii. 285.

MEDWAY.

 1673. 'Navigable.' Blome, op. cit., p. 123.
 1697. Navigable to Maidstone. Fiennes, op. cit., p. 107.

MERSEY.

1697. Navigable to Warrington. *Norris Papers*, p. 38.

GREAT OUSE.

1697. Navigable to St. Ives. Fiennes, op. cit., p. 131.
Ch. II. Navigable to St. Neots. *H.M.C. Portland*, ii. 263.

LITTLE OUSE.

1664. Navigable to Thetford. *Lives of the Norths*, iii. 11.
Ch. II. Navigable to Thetford. *H.M.C. Portland*, ii. 272.

YORKSHIRE OUSE.

Ch. II. Navigable to York. *H.M.C. Portland*, ii. 311.
1693. Navigable to Boroughbridge. Houghton, op. cit., i. 85.
1697. Navigable to York. Fiennes, op. cit., p. 58.

PARRET AND TONE.

1673. Navigable to within 3 miles of Taunton. Blome, op. cit.,
p. 199.
1697. Navigable to Taunton. Fiennes, op. cit., p. 205.

SEVERN.

1672. Navigable to Shrewsbury. Jorevin, op. cit., pp. 581, 584.
1697. Navigable to Worcester. Fiennes, op. cit., p. 196.

THAMES.

1661–6. Navigable to Oxford. Wood, *City of Oxford*, i. 427.
1681. Navigable many miles above Oxford. Delaune, *London*,
p. 195.
Ch. II. Navigable to Lechlade. *H.M.C. Portland*, ii. 299.
1697. Navigable to Oxford. Fiennes, op. cit., p. 29.

TRENT.

1693. Navigable to Wilne Ferry. Houghton, op. cit., i. 108.

WELLAND.

1673. Navigable to Stamford. Blome, op. cit., p. 144.
1696. „ „ *J. H. of C.* xi. 388.

WEY.

1673. Navigable to Guildford. Blome, op. cit., p. 221. (Cf. Exch.
K.R. Wey Navigation Claims, 1671.)

WHARFE.

1693. Navigable to Wetherby. Houghton, op cit. i. 86.

WYE.

1695/6. Navigable to Monmouth. Add. MSS. 21567, f. 3. (Cf. Yarranton, *England's Improvement*, i. 161.)

YARE.

Ch. II. Navigable to Norwich. *H.M.C. Portland*, ii. 270.

MAP III. *Navigable Rivers*, 1724–7

This map differs from the other two in the fact that it is based entirely upon one source, namely Defoe's *Tour*. The references are to the 1927 reprint of the first edition, edited by G. D. H. Cole. The additional references are given merely to substantiate Defoe.

AIRE AND CALDER.

Navigable to Leeds and Wakefield. ii. 603, 614. (*H.M.C. Portland*, vi. 140; Thoresby, *Ducatus Leodiensis*, p. 248.)

AVON (WARWICK).

Navigable to Stratford. ii. 441. (Atkyns, *Glostershire*, p. 24.)

AVON (WILTSHIRE).

Navigable to within two miles of Salisbury. i. 188.

BEVERLEY BECK.

Navigable to Beverley. ii. 647. (Beverley MSS., Toll Book I.)

CAM.

Navigable to Cambridge. i. 83.

COLNE.

Navigable to within 3 miles of Colchester. i. 16. (Colchester MSS., Assembly Book, 1693–1714, f. 403.)

DANE.

Navigable. ii. 667.

DEE.

Navigable. ii. 666. (*H.M.C.* viii. App. pt. i. 394.)

DERWENT.

Navigable to Derby. ii. 546.

DERWENT (CUMBERLAND).

Navigable to Cockermouth. ii. 684.

EXE.

Navigable to Exeter. i. 223.

Foss Dyke.

Navigable. ii. 491. (Lincoln MSS., Account Book of Foss Dyke Tolls.)

Idle.

Navigable to Bawtry. ii. 588.

Kennet.

Navigable. i. 286. (*J. H. of C.* xx. 788; Thacker, *Kennet Country*, p. 313.)

Lark.

Navigable to Bury St. Edmunds. i. 73.

Lea.

Navigable. ii. 618. (*Papers relating to the Navigation on the River Lea*, pp. 10–11; *J. H. of C.* xix. 477–8.)

Medway.

Navigable to Maidstone. i. 113. (Harris, *Kent*, p. 357.)

Mersey.

Navigable to Warrington. i. 261.

Nen.

Navigable to Peterborough. i. 73. (*J. H. of C.* xvii. 49; Morton, *Northampton*, p. 5.)

Orwell.

Navigable to Ipswich. i. 42.

Great Ouse.

Navigable to Bedford. i. 73. (Morton, op. cit., p. 6.)

Little Ouse.

Navigable to Thetford. i. 73.

Yorkshire Ouse.

Navigable to York. ii. 639. (Macky, *Journey through England*, ii. 212.)

Parret and Tone.

Navigable to Taunton. i. 269. (Toulmin, *Taunton*, p. 400.)

Severn.

Navigable to Welshpool. ii. 459. (Cox, *Magna Britannia*, i. 121.)

Stour (Essex).

Navigable to Sudbury. i. 48.

STOUR (KENT).

Navigable to Fordwich. i. 119. (Somner, *Canterbury*, ed. Battely, p. 23.)

THAMES.

Navigable to Lechlade. ii. 432. (Cox, *Magna Britannia*, i. 117.)

TOWY.

Navigable to Carmarthen. ii. 455.

TRENT.

Navigable to Burton-on-Trent. ii. 545. (*Reasons humbly offer'd against the Bill for . . . making Navigable the River Trent.*)

TYNE.

Navigable to Newcastle. ii. 659.

WAVENEY.

Navigable to Beccles. i. 64.

WEAR.

Navigable to Sunderland. ii. 658.

WEAVER.

Navigable. ii. 667.

WELLAND.

Navigable to Stamford. i. 73. (Morton, *Northampton*, p. 3.)

WEY.

Navigable to Guildford. i. 145.

WITHAM.

Navigable to Boston. ii. 494.

WYE AND LUG.

Navigable to Leominster. ii. 447. (Atkyns, *Glostershire*, p. 34.)

YARE.

Navigable to Norwich. i. 63–4.

MAP IV. *River Acts*, 1600–1750

This map shows the rivers, or parts of rivers, for which improvement Acts were passed during this period. It does not include the numerous Acts which were primarily for the improvement of ports, nor does its distinguish between those Acts which were put into execution and those which were not. The Acts were as follows:

AIRE AND CALDER.

1699. 10 Will. III, c. 25. To Leeds and Wakefield.

AVON (BRISTOL).

   1712. 10 Anne, c. 2. Bath to Bristol.

AVON (WILTS.).

   1665. 16/17 Car. II, P.A. To Salisbury.

BEVERLEY BECK.

   1727. 13 Geo. I, c. 4. To Hull River.
   1745. 18 Geo. II, c. 18.

CAM.

   1703. 1 Anne S. 2, c. 11. Cambridge to Clay-Hithe.

COLNE.

   1698. 9 Will. III, c. 19. Colchester to Wivenhoe.
   1719. 5 Geo. I, c. 31. 1740. 13 Geo. II, c. 11. 1750. 23 Geo. II, c. 19.

DANE.

   1721. 7 Geo. I, c. 17. Northwich to Middlewich.

DEE.

   1700. 11 Will. III, c. 24. To Chester.
   1733. 6 Geo. II, c. 30. 1741. 14 Geo. II, c. 8. 1744. 17 Geo. II, c. 28.

DERWENT (DERBYSHIRE).

   1720. 6 Geo. I, c. 27. Derby to the Trent.

DERWENT (YORKSHIRE).

   1702. 1 Anne, c. 14. Scarborough Mills to the Ouse.

DON.

   1726. 12 Geo. I, c. 38. Doncaster to Tinsley.
   1727. 13 Geo. I, c. 30. Holmstile to Wilsick House.
   1733. 6 Geo. II, c. 9. 1740. 13 Geo. II, c. 11.

DOUGLAS.

   1720. 6 Geo. I, c. 28. Wigan to the Ribble.

EDEN.

   1721. 8 Geo. I, c. 14. To Bank End.

FAL.

   1678. 30 Car. II, P.A.

IDLE.

   1720. 6 Geo. I, c. 30. East Retford to Bawtry.

ITCHEN.

1665. 16/17 Car. II, P.A.

KENNET.

1715. 1 Geo. I, P.A. Reading to Newbury.
1721. 7 Geo. I, c. 8. 1730. 3 Geo. II, c. 35.

LARK.

1700. 11 Will. III, c. 22. Mildenhall to Bury St. Edmunds.

LEA.

1739. 12 Geo. II, c. 32.

MEDWAY.

1665. 16/17 Car. II, P.A. 1740. 13 Geo. II, c. 26.

MERSEY.

1721. 7 Geo. I, c. 15. Liverpool to Manchester.

MOLE.

1665. 16/17 Car. II, P.A.

NEN.

1714. 13 Anne, c. 19. Northampton to Peterborough.
1725. 12 Geo. I, c. 19.

GREAT OUSE.

1665. 16/17 Car. II, P.A. 1720. 6 Geo. I, c. 29.

LITTLE OUSE.

1670. 22 Car. II, P.A.

YORKSHIRE OUSE.

1727. 13 Geo. I, c. 33. York to Hull. 1732. 5 Geo. II, c. 15.

RODING.   1657.(*J. H. of C.* vii. 577.)

1737. 10 Geo. II, c. 33. Barking Mill to Ilford Bridge.

SALWARPE.

1662. 14 Car. II, P.A.

STOUR (WORCESTERSHIRE).

1662. 14 Car. II, P.A.

STOUR (ESSEX).

1706. 4/5 Anne, c. 2. Sudbury to Maningtree.

STROUDWATER.

1730. 3 Geo. II, c. 13. Stroud to the Severn.

THAMES.

 1606. 3 Jac. I, c. 20. Burcot to Oxford.
 1624. 21 Jac. I, c. 32. (1694. 6/7 Will. and Mary, c. 16: and
     1730. 3 Geo. II, c. 11. Acts regulating Lock Dues, &c.)

TONE.

 1699. 10 Will. III, c. 8. Bridgwater to Taunton.
 1708. 6 Anne, c. 70.

TRENT.

 1699. 10 Will. III, c. 26. Wilne Ferry to Burton.

WAVENEY.

 1670. 22 Car. II, P.A.

WEAVER.

 1721. 7 Geo. I, c. 10. Frodsham Bridge to Winsford Bridge.
 1734. 7 Geo. II, c. 28. Winsford Bridge to Nantwich.

WELLAND.

 1664/5. 16/17 Car. II, P.A.

WEY.

 1651. To Guildford. (Firth and Rait, *Acts and Ordinances*, ii.
    514–16.)
 1671. 22/23 Car. II, P.A.

WITHAM.

 1671. 22/23 Car. II, P.A. Boston to the Trent.

WORSLEY BROOK.

 1737. 10 Geo. II, c. 11. Worsley to the Irwell.

WYE AND LUG.

 1662. 14 Car. II, P.A. 1696. 7/8 Will. III, c. 14.
 1727. 13 Geo. I, c. 34.

YARE.

 1699. 10 Will. III, c. 5. To Norwich.
 1707. 6 Anne, c. 10. 1723. 9 Geo. I, c. 10.

MAP V. *Canal Schemes*, 1600–1750

For the authorities for these schemes, see Chapter I.

APPENDIX III

Sir Mathew Hale's Opinion on the Wye Navigation

THE following judicial statement is taken from Add. MSS. 11052, ff. 89–90. It sums up the law relating to navigable rivers as it stood about the middle of the seventeenth century.

f. 90 dorso. Sir Mathew Hales opinion concerning the making the river Wye navigable.

f. 89.

1. Although part of a river may bee a comon streame yet it is possible that another part of it may not bee so.

2. If a part of a river bee a comon streame and part not, if, by reason of a nuisance made in that part which is not comon, that part which is comon bee prejudiced, it is a comon nuisance and punishable.

3. If a river bee not passable by boats or vessels of burden, yet if it bee comonly passed by small boats or troughes, it is as to that purpose a comon river as a foote way may be a comon way as well as a Cartway.

4. The question whether a river bee a comon or high streame or river is a question of fact and tryable by jury; and if any have comonly passed there in those small boats, it is an evidence of a comon streame or river.

5. The restraint of any from Landinge upon either side by the owners of lands adjacent or the restraint of fishers or fishinge boats is no evidence to disprove the beinge of a Comon river.

6. If it bee a comon river it may not bee turned, though to the publiqe advantage, without an inquisicon findinge it not to bee a damage and a licence to turne it.

MATH. HALE.

INDEX

Abingdon, 5, 106, 118–19, 125–6, 140.
Aire and Calder, 29, 38, 41, 53, 71, 78, 86, 103, 117, 124, 133, 136, 140.
Alsford, 11.
Ambler, Robert, 33.
Amington, 132.
Antwerp, 122.
Armstrong, John, 82.
Arno, 97.
Arundel, 11.
Ashley, Henry, 48, 57.
Aston, Sir Thomas, 30, 34–6.
Attenborough, 138.
Avon: Bristol, 9–10, 25, 29, 46–8, 50, 56, 74, 78, 81, 86, 101, 105, 111, 114, 122, 139–40; Warwick, 7–10, 24, 26–7, 46, 57–8, 66, 124, 136; Wiltshire, 7, 29, 48, 51, 74, 80, 86, 99, 115.

Bacon, 127.
Badeslade, Thomas, 81–3.
Baily, William, 81, 92.
Baldwin, Charles and Sir Timothy, 66.
Banbury, 10.
Bancroft, John, 52.
Bargemen, see Boatmen.
Barges, see Boats.
Barming, West and East, 16.
Barnsley, 137.
Barren, Sam, 111.
Barrymore, Earl of, 59.
Baskerville, —, 85.
Bate, John, 124.
Bath, 48, 56, 114, 122–3; Mayor and Aldermen of, 25, 48, 74.
Bawtry, 2, 41, 121.
Baxter, Robert, 50.
Bayley, Daniel and James, 61.
Bayly, Lewis, 85.
Bedford, 121, 128; Duke of, 57, 86.
Bennington, Long, 138.
Benthall, 124.
Berkshire, 118.
Beverley, 71–3, 77, 115–16, 124.
Beverley Beck, 5, 31, 50, 71–3, 84, 97, 104, 106, 115–16, 126, 128.
Beverley Fair, 5.
Bevois, Thomas, 103.

Bills, 9–11, 29–30, 33–8, 41, 43–5, 47–8, 117, 137–8.
Birmingham, 1.
Blackwell, Captain, 69.
Blagrave, George, 47.
Blois, 122.
Blythe, 43.
Boatmen, 8, 17, 23, 33, 40, 42, 45, 98, 105–15, 119–20, 128.
Boats, 2, 10, 15, 40, 47, 84, 87–8, 96–106, 108–9, 113–16, 122–3, 129, 139.
Booth, John, 55.
Booth, L., 36.
Boscombe, 38.
Boston, 9, 43.
Bowyer, Robert, 75.
Bradford (Wilts.), 38.
Bramcote, 138.
Brearey, Chris. and Mary, 53.
Brereton, Sir William, 120, 128.
Briare, 13.
Bricks, 2, 126.
Bridgman, Charles, 82.
Bridgwater, 27; Earl of, 10.
Bridlington, 2.
Bristol, 1, 10, 37–8, 46–8, 56, 110, 120, 122–3; Mayor of, 110.
'Bristowe Causey', 11, 29.
Bromfield, William, 111, 115.
Brooke, Sir Thomas, 58.
Brookes, John, 50.
Broseley, 124.
Brown, Jonathan, 112–13.
Bruges, 122.
Brussels, 122.
Bucklow, Hundred of, 34, 47.
Burcot, 63, 91, 118–19.
Burnham, 104
Burton-on-Trent, 44, 65, 116, 120; Manor of, 58.
Bury St. Edmunds, 27–8, 40, 51, 114, 117, 137.
Butter, 5, 46, 127, 136–7.
Butterwick, 103.
Byrom, Joseph and Josiah, 61.

Calais, 13.
Calamy, Edmund, 112–13.
Calder, 12; see also Aire and Calder.

Cam, 11, 48, 79, 97, 123.
Cambridge, 5, 48, 102, 120, 123.
Cambridgeshire, 12.
Campe, Thomas, 110.
Canals, 6, 9–13, 15, 29, 40, 94, 135, 138–40; Belgian, 122; Dutch, 14; Exeter, 81, 89, 91–2; Forth-Clyde, 93; French, 13–14, 140.
Case presented to the Lords the Judges, A, 20.
Castelli, B., 79.
Cardiff, 123.
Carriage, by land, 2–3, 17, 25, 27, 34, 39, 43, 46–7, 114, 119, 120–1, 137–8; by water, rates of, 25, 27, 37–8, 114–21, 128–9.
Cawood, 102–3.
Chalk, 11.
Chandos, Lord, 54–6.
Charity Commissioners, 31.
Cheese, 2, 5, 46, 50, 120, 125–6, 136–7.
Chelmer, 8, 56, 94, 121, 128, 139.
Chelmsford, 42, 121, 128.
Chepstow, 110.
Cherwell, 10.
Cheshire, 5, 18, 31, 58–9.
Chester, 18–20, 49–50, 83; Hugh Lupe, Earl of, 19; Mayor and Aldermen of, 19–20, 74.
Chesterfield, 43; Earl of, 43.
Child, John, 57.
Chippenham, 46.
Cholmondeley, Charles, 35–6, 45, 58.
Cholmondeley, Seymour, 30.
Church, William, 110.
Churn, 9.
Civil War, 25, 28.
Clapham, J. H., 3.
Clay (for pipes), 2.
Claypole, 138.
Clifford, Lord Charles, 59.
Cloth, 19, 38, 124, 136.
Clowes, Samuel, 60–1.
Coal, 2–5, 9–10, 12, 26, 34, 39, 42, 47, 57–8, 74, 103, 117, 119–21, 123–6, 128–30, 135–6.
Coasting trade, 2–5, 131.
Cockman, Richard, 103.
Coke, Thomas, 132.
Colbert, 13.
Colchester, 73–4.
Cole, John, 108.
Collins, John, 112.

Colne, 29, 51–2, 73–4, 93.
Colt, George and John Dutton, 55.
Company of Cutlers of Hallamshire, 48, 75–7.
Company of Weavers of Kendal, 38.
Companies, joint stock, 67, 75–8, 135.
Congreve, Thomas, 12–13.
Coningsby, Sir Thomas, 37, 54–5.
Conwaye, William, 108.
Cooke, Mr., 33.
Corn, 1, 3, 6, 19, 41, 46, 50, 97, 125–6, 130, 136–8.
Corselli, Nicholas, 51.
Cottingham Richmond, manor of, 115.
Cowslade, Richard, 62.
Crau, 14.
Crenbridge, Mr., 69.
Cressy, Thomas, 94.
Crewe, J., 36.
Cricklade, 10, 118.
Crooke, James, 130.
Cully, Nicholas, 112.
Culmstock, 38.
Custis, Edmund, 79.
Cutler, Ellen, 76.
Cuzmin, Andrew, 103.

Dane, 30, 58, 78, 127.
Daniel, John, 49.
Darnelly, Richard, 69.
Dauphiné, 118.
Da Vinci, Leonardo, 14.
Davis, John, 103.
Davis, Joseph, 75.
De Caumartin, Marquis, 122.
De Crapponne, Adam, 14.
Dee, 5, 8, 16, 18–21, 29, 42, 49, 59, 74–5, 77, 83, 94.
Deeping, 66.
Defoe, Daniel, 4, 93, 133, 137.
De Gomme, Sir Bernard, 11.
Della misura dell'acque correnti, 79.
Denbigh, 18.
Deptford, 108–9.
Derby, 42–4, 47, 120.
Derbyshire, 9, 13, 36, 41, 137.
Derwent, 29–30, 36, 38, 40–5, 47, 78, 100, 117, 137–8.
Derwent (Yorks.), 6, 101.
De Saussure, C., 107.
De Vallavon, Marquis, 122.
Dickinson, William, 95.
Dodd, —, 44.

Doddington, 138.
Dodgson, John, 53.
Dodson, W., 82.
Don, 29, 33–4, 41–7, 75–7, 80–1, 93, 127, 136–7.
Doncaster, 33–4, 75–7, 80, 137.
Dordogne, 127.
Dorkin, 11.
Douglas, 30–1, 37, 39–40, 49, 59–60, 70–1, 78, 115, 128.
Doves (of Reading), 108.
Driffield, Mary and Thomas, 53.
Drinsey, 130.
Droitwich, 38, 66.
Dugdale, W., 82.
Dummer, —, 97.
Dunnell, Daniel, 81.
Durance, 14.
Durance, John, 130.
Dutton, John, 50.
Dye, Simon, 126.
Dyson, Thomas, 103.

Eaton, 138.
Eaton, Long, 138.
Eaton, manor of, 57.
Eden, 30, 39, 51.
Egerton, John, 59.
Egerton, Philip, 49.
Elstobb, W., 83.
England's Improvement, 58.
Eratt, Dr., 33–4.
Evans, William, 111.
Evelyn, John, 122, 132.
Exe, 100.
Eyes, John, 121.
Eyre, Thomas, 49.

Farnham, 11.
Finch, —, 47.
Flint (co.), 18.
Flour, 126, 128.
Foley, Hon. Paul, 37, 55.
Foley, Thomas, 36, 54–5.
Forde, Sir Edward, 11, 40, 80.
Forest of Dean, 9–10, 98.
Fortrey, Samuel, 79–80.
Fosbrook, —, 116–17, 129.
Fosbrook, Robert, 124, 129.
Foss Dyke, 9, 78, 80, 99, 124–6, 129–30.
Freese, James, 85.
Frodsham Bridge, 38, 127.
Fulford, 102.
Fylde, 128.

Gainsborough, 120, 129.
Galileo, 79.
Gardner, Thomas, 112.
Garonne, 14, 122, 127.
Gell, Francis, 74.
Geneva, 122.
Gidart, Richard, 60.
Gilbert, John, 85.
Giles, William, 112.
Glass, 2, 120; Bottles, 8.
Gloucester, 103, 123, 128.
Gloucestershire, 21.
Goldwyer, Henry, 111, 115.
Goodman, Eliz. and Mr., 64.
Gorges, Barbara and Ferdinando, 54.
Green, Mr., 44.
Greene, John, 107.
Greytree, Hundred of, 39.
Grinstead, East, 11.
Grosvenor, Sir Richard, 59.
Grundy, John, 81–3.
Guglielmini, 79.
Guildford, 38, 62, 69, 111–12, 121–2.
Guisborough, 132.

Habersham, Mr., 72.
'Halers', see Towers.
Halford, Charles, 66.
Halifax, 121.
'Haling', see Towing.
Hall, John, 107.
Harington, Sir John, 56.
Harley, Edward, 55.
Harley, Robert, 37, 55.
Harley, Sir Edward, 36–7, 55.
Harpham, Mr., 72.
Harris, Alderman, 53.
Harris, J., 85.
Harris, Richard, 108.
Harwich, 104.
Hawkshaw, John, 130.
Hawley, John, 52.
Hawley, Lord, 57.
Hayne, —, 116–17.
Heaton, Robert, 333.
Henley, 107.
Hereford, 21, 33, 37, 54, 99, 122; Bishop of, 54.
Herefordshire, 21, 37, 54, 65.
Hertford, 23, 107.
Hewer, William, 73.
Hill, Mr., 9.
Hill, Simon, 85.

Hitchin, 119.
Holt, Roger, 115.
Hooper, Nicholas and Richard, 112.
Hopewell (of Beverley), 128.
Hore, John, 56, 81, 93–4, 139.
Houghton, John, 30, 46.
Howe, John, 62, 69.
Huddersfield, 140.
Hull, 1–2, 38, 43, 120, 123, 125, 129, 137.
Hull (river), 5.
Hull, J., 100.
Humber, 5.
Hungerford, 38.
Huntingdon, county of, 12.
Huntingdon, Earl of, 26.
Huntspill, 104.

Ibbetson, Joshua and Mary, 53.
Idle, 2, 30, 41, 117, 121.
Iffley, 89, 91.
Impressment, 110–11.
Ipswich, 41.
Ireland, 19, 75.
Iron forges, 16–17, 55.
Irwell, 30, 37–8, 59–61.
Isis, 9–10, 91.
Itchen, 29, 45.
Iveson, Henry, 53.

Jackson, Robert, 50.
James I, 25.
Jemmatt, Samuel, 26, 66.
Jennings, William, 110.
Johnson, Henry and John, 112.

Kempe, Sir Nicholas, 63.
Kennet, 30, 38, 41, 47, 56, 62, 67, 81, 93, 115, 126, 139–40.
Kent, Earl of, 36, 51.
Kenyon, George, 37, 60.
Kinderley, Nathaniel, 74–5, 83.
King, John, 75.
King's Lynn, *see* Lynn.
Kitchingman, Thomas, 53.
Knowles, L. C. A., 3, 136.

Labelye, C., 83.
Lambe, Henry, 27–8, 114.
Lark, 27–9, 40, 48, 51, 57, 137.
Lawley, 'old', 36.
Lawley, 'young', 35.
Lawton, —, 34.
Lazenby, Thomas, 53.
Lea, 23, 28, 88–9, 100, 111, 119.

Leach, John, 50.
Lead, 2, 38.
Leather, 126, 128.
Lechlade, 2, 10, 119.
Leeds, 38, 117; Aldermen of, 53, 71.
Lees, John, 60.
Legh, George, 31.
Leicester, 26, 43.
Leicestershire, 13, 36, 46.
Lelham, Mr., 84.
Leominster, 37, 54.
Letters Patent, 24–8.
Leveson, Sir John, 17–18.
Lightbowne, James, 61.
Lime, 39.
Lincoln, 43, 80, 123–4.
Liverpool, 1, 41–2, 59–60, 140.
Loch Garry, 104.
Locks, 23, 84, 88–9, 91–3, 109–11, 118–19, 133, 139.
Loing, 13.
Loire, 13–14, 122, 127.
London, 1–2, 5, 10–11, 21, 30, 38, 40, 63, 80, 108–10, 113, 118–20, 122–6, 129, 137.
Loughborough, 43; Lord Henry, 11.
Lyme Regis, 2.
Lynn, King's, 1, 6, 82, 102, 120, 125, 128.
Lyon, 122.
Lug, 29, 33, 46, 53, 57, 65.

Macaulay, Lord, 2.
Macclesfield, Lord Chancellor, 24.
Macclesfield, Hundred of, 34.
Machilt, Peter, 50.
Mackworth, Sir Humphrey, 94.
Maghull, Ellen and William, 61.
Magna Carta, 22.
Maidstone, 67.
Maisterson, William, 62.
Maldon, 42, 121, 128.
Malet, John, 27, 56–7, 66.
Malmesbury, 9, 37.
Malt, 98, 125–6, 128, 130, 137.
Malton, New, 117.
Manchester, 59–60, 117, 140.
Maningtree, 117.
Manley, Richard, 59, 75.
Mansfield, 43.
Mantoux, P., 3, 135.
Manure, 11, 39, 50.
Marne, 122.
Mathew, Francis, 8–10, 14.

Meal, 11.

Medway, 16–18, 38, 67, 77, 86, 104, 111, 115.

Mersey, 29–30, 37–8, 41, 59–61, 94, 133, 136.

Mersey and Irwell Navigation Co., 117.

Middleton, Sir Hugh, 80.

Middlewich, 127.

Mildenhall, 27–8, 114, 117.

Mills, 7, 18–19, 23, 26–7, 47, 50–1, 54, 86, 119, 126.

Milner, William, 53.

Misterton, 103.

Mole, 8, 29.

Monmouth, 33, 41.

Monmouthshire, 21.

Montargis, 13.

Moore, Sir Jonas, 11, 79.

Morgan, James, 55.

Mosley, Sir Edward, Sir Oswald, Oswald, 60.

Moth, Hugh and John, 112.

Mowbray, Mark, 130.

Moxon, J., 10.

Mum, 8.

Naburn, 102.

Nantwich, 62, 127.

Nen, 48, 66, 115.

Newark, 43–4, 103, 123–4, 129, 137.

Newbury, 81, 126, 139.

Newcastle, 5, 10, 124.

Newcomen, 100.

New Haven, 92.

New River, Corporation of, 11, 23.

Newton, 137.

Nonconformists, 61–2.

Norfolk, 12.

Norris, Richard, 59, 70.

North, Sir Roger, 27–8.

Northwich, 35, 38, 127.

Norwich, 123, 129.

Nottingham, 40, 42–5, 116–17, 120, 123–4, 129.

Nottinghamshire, 9.

Orleans, 122.

Ormskirk, 49.

Orwell, 30, 41.

Ouse, Great, 9, 26–30, 57, 66, 78, 82–4, 97, 99–100, 102, 105, 107, 110, 120, 125, 128, 133, 136–7; Little, 9; Yorks., 5–6, 9, 37, 41, 80, 83, 94, 99, 102–3, 117, 124, 127, 133.

Oxford, 52, 63–5, 89, 91, 103, 112, 118–19, 140.

Pack-horses, 2.

Paget, Lord William, 58, 65, 116.

Palmer, William, 80, 83.

Papin, D., 100.

Paris, 122.

Parliament, Acts of, 11, 16–17, 20, 22–4, 28–31, 44, 48–9, 52, 56, 59, 62–3, 65–7, 69–71, 73–6, 89, 93, 98, 101–2, 109, 111, 114–19, 121–2, 139.

Parsons, William, 75.

Patten, Thomas, 49.

Pearse, William, 52.

Pemmerton, William, 112.

Pendeford, 12.

Penk, 12.

Penkridge, 12.

Pepys, Samuel, 73, 92, 96, 108–10.

Percival, Sir John, 120.

Perry, Captain, 83–4.

Peter the Great, 83.

Petersfield, 11.

Pett, Peter, 108.

Petty, Sir William, 4, 39, 99–100.

Philpe, Francis, 111.

Pitson, James, 69–70.

Plot, R., 87, 91.

Plymouth, Countess of, 124.

Plymouth, Earl of, see Windsor, Lord.

Poor, employment of, 39–40.

Pope, Robert, 104.

Population, 1.

Port Books, 3.

Potter, Alderman, 53.

Pownoll, Israel, 85.

Prescott, John, 50.

Prestwood, 12.

Privy Council, 18, 20.

Proctor, Thomas, 9–10.

Prosperity (of Beverley), 128.

Radford, 138.

Radnorshire, 37.

Ramsey, David, 99.

Ravald, Oswald and Robert, 60.

Rawcliffe, John, 115.

Read, James, 70.

Reading, 41, 47, 108, 110, 123, 126.

Redforth, Thomas, 81.

Repington, Edward, 132.

Retford, East, 43, 121.

Rhône, 122.

Richelieu, 13.
Rickmansworth, 11.
Rixton, manor of, 38.
Roads, 3, 38–9, 67, 114.
Roberts, L., 135.
Roberts, Sir Walter, 11, 40.
Rochester, 100; Earl of, 57.
Roding, 51.
Rontree, John, 53.
Rooke, William, 53.
Rouen, 122.
Royal Society, 4, 12.
Rudd, Captain, 130.
Russell, Sir William, 24.

St. Ives, 120, 128.
St. Neots, 137.
St. Omer, 13.
Salisbury, 46, 51, 74.
'Salsamenta, pairs of', 119.
Salt, 38, 58, 60, 66, 97, 120, 127, 136.
Saltpetre, 119.
Salwarpe, 28, 66, 115.
Sandford, 89, 91.
Sandiacre, 138.
Sandys, Henry, 53, 57, 65, 77.
Sandys, Sir Myles, 57.
Sandys, Thomas, 57.
Sandys, Sir William, 57.
Sandys, William (later Sir William, son of above), 24, 26–7, 53, 57, 65–6, 77, 92, 124.
Sandys, Windsor, 53, 57, 65, 77.
Saône, 14, 122, 127.
Savery, T., 100.
Scarsdale, Earl of, 44.
Schipiloff, Ivan, 103.
Schirisoff, Juan, 103.
Scotcher, Richard, 69–70.
Scott, Sir John, 17–18.
Scott, Thomas, 108.
Scudamore, Lord, 54.
Seine, 122.
Selby, 102.
Semington, 140.
Severn, 6–7, 9–13, 98–9, 105, 110, 119–20, 123–4, 128, 133, 136–40.
Sewers, Commissions of, 16–23, 63.
Sewers, The Law of, 22.
Shakerley, Peter, 34–7.
Sheffield, 76–7, 80; steel, 136.
Shipston, 10.
Shirehampton, 98.
Shotbolte, John, 85.

Shower, Sir Bartholomew, 66.
Shrewsbury, 100, 120.
Simpson, Mr., 33.
Skarvill, John, 115.
Skipwith, Thomas, 26.
Slates, 2.
Smith, Mr. Alderman, 44.
Smith, Alderman, 53.
Soap, 120.
Soar, 26.
Somerset, 46.
Southampton, 11, 75.
South Sea speculation, 30, 70.
Southwell, Sir Robert, 4, 12, 40, 119, 123.
Sow, 12.
Spain, 19.
Spencer, Arnold, 25–6, 66.
Spinola, Marquis of, 122.
Squire, William, 59, 70.
Staffordshire, 13.
Stamford, 66; Earl of, 26.
Stapleford, 138.
Steers, Thomas, 59–60, 70.
Stevens, Gregory, 107.
Steward, Thomas, 27–8.
Stillingfleet, 102.
Stockwith, East and West, 47, 103.
Stour, Essex, 26; Worcester, 10, 13, 28, 58.
Stourbridge, 12, 55.
Stourbridge Fair, 97, 123.
Stowmarket, 41.
Strafforth, Wapentake of, 137.
Stratford-on-Avon, 8.
Stringer, Thomas, 129.
Stroudwater, 9, 29, 37, 51, 56, 93–4, 139.
Subsidy Book, 17.
Sudbury, 117.
Sully, 13.
Sunderland, 123.
Sutton, manor of, 69.
Swale, 6.
Swift Ditch, 89, 109.

Taff, 123.
Tain, 122.
Taney, Edward and Nicholas, 112.
Taunton, 56.
Taylor, John, 7–9, 86–7, 89.
Teme, 57.
Terante, Edward, 108–9.
Teston, 16.
Tettenhall Regis, 12.
Tewkesbury, 103.

Thames, 2, 6–12, 23, 40, 58, 63–5, 78–9, 85, 87–9, 91, 96–101, 103, 110, 118–19, 123, 125, 133, 136, 140.
Thames Ditton, 103.
Thompson, Edward, 27.
Tickhill, Wapentake of, 137.
Timber, 17–18, 38, 98, 125–6, 128, 130.
Tinsley, 75.
Toll Dish, The, 106.
Tolls, 23, 26, 38, 42, 50, 66, 71–2, 74, 91, 111, 114–19, 122, 126–8, 130.
Tolson, John, 52.
Tonbridge, 18, 67.
Tone, 2, 27, 29, 31, 38, 48, 52, 56, 66, 77, 126.
Towers, 45, 105–7, 115.
Towing, 101–2; in France, 100.
'Trayford' (Trafford ?), Henry, 60.
Trent, 2, 5, 9, 12, 26, 29, 33, 41–5, 47, 58, 65, 93, 108, 116–17, 119–20, 124–5, 128–30, 133, 137–40.
Trevor, Sir Richard, 19–20.
Trew, John, 89.
Trowbridge, 38.
Trows, *see* Boats.
True Briton, The, 106.
Turfs, 126.
Twyne, —, 91.
Tyndall, Thomas, 94.
Tyne, 123.

Ure, 6.

Van Berg, Sir John Christopher, 85.
Vernon, Richard, 31.
Vienne, 122.

Waitte, Mr., 86.
Wakefield, 117, 121; Aldermen of, 53, 71.
Wales, 46, 94.
Wallingford, 119.
Wallop, Sir Henry, 108.
Waltham, John, 69.
Warburton, Sir Charles, 36.
Warburton, John, 84.
Ware, 113, 120, 125.
Warsop, 43.
Warton, Sir Ralph, 72.
Warwickshire, 46.
Wateringbury, 16.
Watermen, *see* Boatmen.
Watts, Thomas, 75.
Waveney, 9.
Weaver, 29–31, 34–6, 45, 47, 49, 59, 62, 67, 106, 127, 136–7.
Weeland, 117.

Weirs, 7, 16–17, 20–1, 25, 45, 47, 54–5, 86–8.
Welland, 9, 29, 66, 102, 125.
Wellington, 38.
Wells, Dean and Chapter of, 104.
Westborough, 138.
Weston, Sir Richard, 69, 80, 89.
Wey, 29, 38, 57, 62, 69–70, 78, 92, 94–5, 101, 111, 114–15, 121–2, 125.
Weybridge, 121.
Wharfe, 6.
Whitaker, Mr., 34.
Wigan, 37, 49.
Wigmore, Daniel, 66.
Wilbraham, Roger, 49, 58.
Wilden Ferry, 44, 65, 116, 140.
Wildman, Major, 54.
William and Jane (of Milford), 111.
Williams, John, 111.
Williams, Thomas, 62.
Williams, William, 33.
Willoughby, Sir Percival, 124, 129.
Willoughby, Sir Thomas, 43.
Wilne, 43, 120.
Wilson, —, 132.
Wilson, Robert, 80.
Wilton, 56.
Winchester, 11.
Windsor, Lord, 58.
Winsford Bridge, 127.
Wirksworth, 33.
Wisbech, 137.
Wistow, 102.
Witham, 9.
Woodden, Daniel, 103.
Wool, 1, 121, 124, 126, 138.
Woolwich, 108–9.
Worcester, 38, 100, 103, 110, 120, 123.
Worcester, Marquis of, 100.
Worlington, 27.
Wormelow, Hundred of, 39.
Worsley, 61.
Wright, Alderman, 53.
Wright, Henry, 49.
Wye, 7, 16, 21, 28, 33, 36–7, 41, 45–6, 53–4, 57, 65, 84, 86, 88, 92, 99, 115, 122.
Yalding, 17.
Yare, 23, 29, 85, 125.
Yarmouth, Great, 1, 9, 75, 85, 123, 125, 129.
Yarranton, Andrew, 7–8, 10, 15, 46, 58, 92, 131.
Yates, Joseph, 61.
York, 6, 9, 37–8, 41, 99, 103, 124.
Yorkshire, 5.